BREAD FOR THE DAY

DAILY BIBLE READINGS AND PRAYERS

2011

AUGSBURG FORTRESS

Minneapolis

BREAD FOR THE DAY 2011
Daily Bible Readings and Prayers

Editors: Dennis Bushkofsky, Suzanne Burke
Cover design: Laurie Ingram
Interior design: Jessica Hillstrom
Cover art: Nicholas Wilton
Interior art: Joel Nickel, Margaret Adams Parker, Robyn Sand Anderson, Margaret Bussey, M. Paula Wiggins

Contributors to the weekday prayers: Joshua Elliott-McGuffie, Los Angeles, California (January); Jim Drury, Price, Utah (February); Thomas L. Weitzel, Largo, Florida (March); Audrey Novak Riley, River Forest, Illinois (April); Melissa Bergstrom, Maple Grove, Minnesota (May); Tom Lyberg, Findlay, Ohio (June); Richard Bruxvoort Colligan, Strawberry Point, Iowa (July); Luke Smetters, Wiota, Wisconsin (August); Joel Nau, Winterset, Iowa (September); Kent A. Mechler, Sheffield, Iowa (October); Julie Eileen Ryan, Woodridge, Illinois (November); Bradley Hales, Culpeper, Virginia (December)

ACKNOWLEDGMENTS
Scripture quotations are from the New Revised Standard Version Bible © 1989 Division of Christian Education of the National Council of the Churches of Christ in the United States of America. Used by permission.

Hymn suggestions and prayers of the day for Sundays and festivals are from *Evangelical Lutheran Worship*, copyright © 2006 Evangelical Lutheran Church in America.

Materials prepared by the Consultation on Common Texts (CCT), published in *Revised Common Lectionary* © 1992 and *Revised Common Lectionary Daily Readings* © 2005. Used by permission.

Materials prepared by the English Language Liturgical Consultation (ELLC), published in *Praying Together* © 1988: "Blessed are you, Lord" and "My soul proclaims the greatness of the Lord." Used by permission.

ISBN 978-0-8066-9527-3

Contents

FOREWORD

Beloved of God,

For generations, the living word has sustained God's people. In times of prosperity and turmoil, joy and sorrow, the church has found hope and consolation in scripture.

The Evangelical Lutheran Church in America has embraced the initiative called Book of Faith. In it we have committed ourselves to deepening our fluency in the first language of faith, holy scripture. *Bread for the Day* is a wonderful resource for your daily encounter with the word. You will be nourished, encouraged, and sustained, as have the saints before you.

As the Conference of Bishops, we invite you to join us, and this whole church in persistent attentiveness to the word. Your faith will be deepened, your witness empowered, and your church enriched. God bless your journey in faith.

Conference of Bishops
Evangelical Lutheran Church in America

For more about Book of Faith, visit www.bookoffaith.org.

Introduction

Daily prayer is an essential practice for those who seek to hear God's voice and cultivate an inner life. Whether you pray alone or with others, with brevity or sustained meditation, the rhythm of daily prayer reveals the life-sustaining communion to which God invites all human beings. Such prayer is a serene power silently at work, drawing us into the ancient yet vital sources of faith, hope, and love.

The guiding principle of the selection of daily readings in *Bread for the Day* is their relationship to the Sunday readings as presented in the Revised Common Lectionary (a system of readings in widespread use across denominations). The readings are chosen so that the days leading up to Sunday (Thursday through Saturday) prepare for the Sunday readings. The days flowing out from Sunday (Monday through Wednesday) reflect upon the Sunday readings.

How this book is organized

- Each day's page is dated and named in relationship to the church's year. Lesser festivals are listed along with the date as part of the day heading. Commemorations are listed just below in smaller type. Notes on those commemorated can be found on pages 415–423.
- Several verses of one of the appointed scripture texts are printed. The full text citation is provided for those who would like to reflect on the entire text. In addition, two or three additional reading citations with short descriptions are provided.
- Two psalms are appointed for each week; one psalm for Monday through Wednesday and a second psalm for Thursday through Saturday. In this way the days leading up to Sunday or flowing out from Sunday have a distinct

relationship with one another, in addition to their relationship with the Sunday readings.

- Following the printed scripture text is a hymn suggestion from *Evangelical Lutheran Worship* and a prayer that incorporates a theme present in one or more of the readings.
- Household prayers and blessings appropriate to the changing seasons are placed throughout the book. Simplified forms of morning and evening prayer, waking prayers, and bedtime prayers, including prayers with children, can be found on pages 424–432.

How to use this book

- Use the weekday readings to prepare for and reflect on the Sunday readings.
- Use the questions printed on the inside back cover to guide your reflection on the scripture texts.
- Use the resources for household prayer placed throughout the book. See the Contents on pages 3–4 for a complete list.
- Use the page at the beginning of each month to record prayer requests.
- In addition to being used to guide individual prayer, this book may also be used to guide family prayer, prayer in congregational or other settings during the week, prayer with those who are sick or homebound, or with other groups.

Even though Christians gather on the Lord's day, Sunday, for public worship, much of our time is spent in the home. We first learn the words, gestures, and songs of faith in the home. We discover our essential identity as a community of faith and mark significant transitions of life in the home. To surround and infuse the daily rhythm of sleeping and waking, working, resting, and eating with the words and gestures of Christian prayer is to discover the ancient truth of the gospel: the ordinary and the human can reveal the mystery of God and divine grace.

Like planets around the sun, our daily prayer draws us to the Sunday assembly where we gather for the word and the breaking of the bread in the changing seasons of the year. From the Sunday assembly, our daily prayer flows into the week.

_____

_____

_____

_____

_____

_____

_____

_____

_____

_____

_____

Blessing for the New Year

O God,
you have been our help in ages past,
our hope for years to come.
As we welcome this new year,
bless us with peace.
Fill our days with the light of Christ
and lead us on the path of life
until we see you in our heavenly home.
You live and reign forever and ever.
Amen.

Saturday, January 1, 2011

Name of Jesus

Philippians 2:5-11
God takes on human form

Therefore God also highly exalted him
  and gave him the name
  that is above every name,
so that at the name of Jesus
  every knee should bend,
  in heaven and on earth and under the earth,
and every tongue should confess
  that Jesus Christ is Lord,
  to the glory of God the Father. (Phil. 2:9-11)

Psalm	Additional Readings	
Psalm 8	**Numbers 6:22-27**	**Luke 2:15-21**
How exalted is your name	*The Aaronic blessing*	*The child is named Jesus*

Hymn: All Hail the Power of Jesus' Name! ELW 634

Eternal Father, you gave your incarnate Son the holy name of Jesus to be a sign of our salvation. Plant in every heart the love of the Savior of the world, Jesus Christ our Lord, who lives and reigns with you and the Holy Spirit, one God, now and forever.

Sunday, January 2, 2011

Second Sunday of Christmas

Johann Konrad Wilhelm Loehe, renewer of the church, 1872

John 1:[1-9] 10-18

God with us

And the Word became flesh and lived among us, and we have seen his glory, the glory as of a father's only son, full of grace and truth. (John testified to him and cried out, "This was he of whom I said, 'He who comes after me ranks ahead of me because he was before me.'") From his fullness we have all received, grace upon grace. The law indeed was given through Moses; grace and truth came through Jesus Christ. No one has ever seen God. It is God the only Son, who is close to the Father's heart, who has made him known. (John 1:14-18)

Psalm

Psalm 147:12-20

Praising God in Zion

Additional Readings

Jeremiah 31:7-14

Joy as God's scattered flock gathers

Ephesians 1:3-14

The will of God made known in Christ

Hymn: Hark! The Herald Angels Sing, ELW 270

Almighty God, you have filled all the earth with the light of your incarnate Word. By your grace empower us to reflect your light in all that we do, through Jesus Christ, our Savior and Lord, who lives and reigns with you and the Holy Spirit, one God, now and forever.

Monday, January 3, 2011

Week of Christmas 2

Psalm 72
Prayers for the king

Give the king your justice, O God,
and your righteousness to a king's son.
May he judge your people with righteousness,
and your poor with justice.
May the mountains yield prosperity for the people,
and the hills, in righteousness.
May he defend the cause of the poor of the people,
give deliverance to the needy,
and crush the oppressor. (Ps. 72:1-4)

Additional Readings
Genesis 28:10-22   **Hebrews 11:13-22**
Jacob's ladder   *Abraham, Isaac, and Jacob act on faith*

Hymn: The First Noel, ELW 300

*Lord God, in your compassion grant new beginnings to all who are in
need. Convict those who fail to love their neighbors and bring peace and
justice into the world. Finally, help us to make your church a welcoming
and loving community.*

Tuesday, January 4, 2011

Week of Christmas 2

Exodus 3:1-5
The burning bush

Moses was keeping the flock of his father-in-law Jethro, the priest of Midian; he led his flock beyond the wilderness, and came to Horeb, the mountain of God. There the angel of the LORD appeared to him in a flame of fire out of a bush; he looked, and the bush was blazing, yet it was not consumed. Then Moses said, "I must turn aside and look at this great sight, and see why the bush is not burned up." When the LORD saw that he had turned aside to see, God called to him out of the bush, "Moses, Moses!" And he said, "Here I am." Then he said, "Come no closer! Remove the sandals from your feet, for the place on which you are standing is holy ground." (Exod. 3:1-5)

Psalm
Psalm 72
Prayers for the king

Additional Reading
Hebrews 11:23-31
Moses acts on faith

Hymn: Your Little Ones, Dear Lord, ELW 286

Loving Father, you have shown us your Son in the miracle of the incarnation. May we live every day seeing our Lord's face in our sisters and brothers.

Wednesday, January 5, 2011

Week of Christmas 2

Hebrews 11:32—12:2

Surrounded by a cloud of witnesses

Therefore, since we are surrounded by so great a cloud of witnesses, let us also lay aside every weight and the sin that clings so closely, and let us run with perseverance the race that is set before us, looking to Jesus the pioneer and perfecter of our faith, who for the sake of the joy that was set before him endured the cross, disregarding its shame, and has taken his seat at the right hand of the throne of God. (Heb. 12:1-2)

Psalm

Psalm 72
Prayers for the king

Additional Reading

Joshua 1:1-9
Be strong

Hymn: It Came Upon the Midnight Clear, ELW 282

God, from upon your throne you glory in the worship of the saints and holy angels. Through Jesus' birth, life, death, and resurrection, gather us together in paradise with the blessed ones who have gone before us.

Blessing of the Home at Epiphany

Matthew writes that when the magi saw the shining star stop overhead, they were filled with joy. "On entering the house, they saw the child with Mary his mother" (Matt. 2:10-11). In the home, Christ is met in family and friends, in visitors and strangers. In the home, faith is shared, nurtured, and put into action. In the home, Christ is welcome.

Twelfth Night (January 5) or another day during the twelve days of Christmas or the time after Epiphany offers an occasion for gathering with friends and family members for a blessing of the home, using the following as a model. Someone may lead the greeting and blessing, while another person may read the scripture passage. Following an eastern European tradition, a visual blessing may be inscribed with white chalk above the main door; for example, 20 + CMB + 11. The numbers change with each new year. The three letters stand for either the ancient Latin blessing *Christe mansionem benedica*, which means, "Christ, bless this house," or the legendary names of the magi (Caspar, Melchior, and Balthasar).

Gathering

Peace to this *house/dwelling/room* and to all who enter here.
A reading from Proverbs: By wisdom a house is built,
and through understanding it is established;
through knowledge its rooms are filled
with rare and beautiful treasures. *(Prov. 24:3-4)*

Reading

As we prepare to ask God's blessing on this household,
let us listen to the words of scripture.
A reading from John: In the beginning was the Word,
and the Word was with God, and the Word was God.
He was in the beginning with God.

All things came into being through him,
and without him not one thing came into being.
What has come into being in him was life,
and the life was the light of all people.
The Word became flesh and lived among us, and we have seen his glory,
the glory as of a father's only son, full of grace and truth.
From his fullness we have all received, grace upon grace.
(John 1:1-4, 14, 16)

Inscription

This inscription may be made with chalk above the entrance:

20 + C M B + 11

The magi of old, known as

C   Caspar,

M   Melchior, and

B   Balthasar

followed the star of God's Son who came to dwell among us

20   two thousand

11   and eleven years ago.

+   Christ, bless this house,

+   and remain with us throughout the new year.

Prayer of Blessing

O God,
you revealed your Son to all people by the shining light of a star.
We pray that you bless this home and all who live here
with your gracious presence.
May your love be our inspiration, your wisdom our guide,
your truth our light and your peace our benediction;
through Christ our Lord. **Amen.**

*Then everyone may walk from room to room, blessing the house with incense or by
sprinkling with water, perhaps using a branch from the Christmas tree.*

Thursday, January 6, 2011

Epiphany of Our Lord

Matthew 2:1-12
Christ revealed to the nations

Then Herod secretly called for the wise men and learned from them the exact time when the star had appeared. Then he sent them to Bethlehem, saying, "Go and search diligently for the child; and when you have found him, bring me word so that I may also go and pay him homage." When they had heard the king, they set out; and there, ahead of them, went the star that they had seen at its rising, until it stopped over the place where the child was. When they saw that the star had stopped, they were overwhelmed with joy. On entering the house, they saw the child with Mary his mother; and they knelt down and paid him homage. Then, opening their treasure chests, they offered him gifts of gold, frankincense, and myrrh. (Matt. 2:7-11)

Psalm
Psalm 72:1-7, 10-14
All shall bow down

Additional Readings
Isaiah 60:1-6
Nations come to the light

Ephesians 3:1-12
The gospel's promise for all

Hymn: Bright and Glorious Is the Sky, ELW 301

O God, on this day you revealed your Son to the nations by the leading of a star. Lead us now by faith to know your presence in our lives, and bring us at last to the full vision of your glory, through your Son, Jesus Christ our Lord, who lives and reigns with you and the Holy Spirit, one God, now and forever.

TIME AFTER EPIPHANY

On the Epiphany of Our Lord (January 6), the household joins the church throughout the world in celebrating the manifestation, the "epiphany," of Christ to the world. The festival of Christmas is thus set within the context of outreach to the larger community; it possesses an outward movement. The festival of the Epiphany asks the Christian household: How might our faith in Christ the Light be shared with friends and family, with our neighbors, with the poor and needy in our land, with those who live in other nations?

Table Prayer for Epiphany and the Time after Epiphany (January 6–March 8)

Generous God,
you have made yourself known in Jesus, the light of the world.
As this food and drink give us refreshment,
so strengthen us by your Spirit,
that as your baptized sons and daughters
we may share your light with all the world.
Grant this through Christ our Lord.
Amen.

Friday, January 7, 2011

Time after Epiphany

1 Kings 10:1-13
Gifts to Solomon from Sheba

When the queen of Sheba heard of the fame of Solomon, (fame due to the name of the LORD), she came to test him with hard questions. She came to Jerusalem with a very great retinue, with camels bearing spices, and very much gold, and precious stones; and when she came to Solomon, she told him all that was on her mind. Solomon answered all her questions; there was nothing hidden from the king that he could not explain to her. When the queen of Sheba had observed all the wisdom of Solomon, the house that he had built, the food of his table, the seating of his officials, and the attendance of his servants, their clothing, his valets, and his burnt offerings that he offered at the house of the LORD, there was no more spirit in her. (1 Kings 10:1-5)

Psalm
Psalm 72
Prayers for the king

Additional Reading
Ephesians 3:14-21
Knowing the love of Christ

Hymn: Brightest and Best of the Stars, ELW 303

Giver of wisdom, may we use our intellects to glorify you and may we use our possessions to do your will. May our knowledge give way to your wisdom, that we might share the good news of your Son.

Saturday, January 8, 2011

Time after Epiphany

Ephesians 4:7, 11-16

Gifts according to Christ

The gifts he gave were that some would be apostles, some prophets, some evangelists, some pastors and teachers, to equip the saints for the work of ministry, for building up the body of Christ, until all of us come to the unity of the faith and of the knowledge of the Son of God, to maturity, to the measure of the full stature of Christ. (Eph. 4:11-13)

Psalm

Psalm 72

Prayers for the king

Additional Reading

1 Kings 10:14-25

Solomon's splendor

Hymn: As with Gladness Men of Old, ELW 302

Father, give us eyes to see the gifts that your Holy Spirit has given to our sisters and brothers. Help us remember that you bless all humankind and that you favor everyone equally.

Sunday, January 9, 2011

Baptism of Our Lord

Matthew 3:13-17
Christ revealed as God's servant

Then Jesus came from Galilee to John at the Jordan, to be baptized by him. John would have prevented him, saying, "I need to be baptized by you, and do you come to me?" But Jesus answered him, "Let it be so now; for it is proper for us in this way to fulfill all righteousness." Then he consented. And when Jesus had been baptized, just as he came up from the water, suddenly the heavens were opened to him and he saw the Spirit of God descending like a dove and alighting on him. And a voice from heaven said, "This is my Son, the Beloved, with whom I am well pleased." (Matt. 3:13-17)

Psalm
Psalm 29
The voice of God upon the waters

Additional Readings
Isaiah 42:1-9
The servant of God brings justice

Acts 10:34-43
Jesus' ministry after his baptism

Hymn: When Jesus Came to Jordan, ELW 305

O God our Father, at the baptism of Jesus you proclaimed him your beloved Son and anointed him with the Holy Spirit. Make all who are baptized into Christ faithful to their calling to be your daughters and sons, and empower us all with your Spirit, through Jesus Christ, our Savior and Lord, who lives and reigns with you and the Holy Spirit, one God, now and forever.

Monday, January 10, 2011

Time after Epiphany

Psalm 89:5-37
God anoints David to be a son

Then you spoke in a vision to your faithful one, and said:
   "I have set the crown on one who is mighty,
   I have exalted one chosen from the people.
I have found my servant David;
   with my holy oil I have anointed him;
my hand shall always remain with him;
   my arm also shall strengthen him.
The enemy shall not outwit him,
   the wicked shall not humble him.
I will crush his foes before him
   and strike down those who hate him." (Ps. 89:19-23)

Additional Readings

Genesis 35:1-15
God calls and blesses Jacob

Acts 10:44-48
Through Peter, God calls Gentiles to be baptized

Hymn: Blessed Be the God of Israel, ELW 250

Father of our Lord Jesus Christ, may we see your goodness always, even as David received your blessing. When sin and the trials of this world close in on us, give us eyes to see your love and care.

Tuesday, January 11, 2011

Time after Epiphany

Jeremiah 1:4-10
God calls Jeremiah

Now the word of the LORD came to me saying,
 "Before I formed you in the womb I knew you,
 and before you were born I consecrated you;
 I appointed you a prophet to the nations."
Then I said, "Ah, Lord GOD! Truly I do not know how to speak,
for I am only a boy." But the LORD said to me,
 "Do not say, 'I am only a boy';
 for you shall go to all to whom I send you,
 and you shall speak whatever I command you,
 Do not be afraid of them,
 for I am with you to deliver you, says the LORD." (Jer. 1:4-8)

Psalm
Psalm 89:5-37
God anoints David to be a son

Additional Reading
Acts 8:4-13
Philip preaches and baptizes

Hymn: Lord, Speak to Us, That We May Speak, ELW 676

We thank you, God, that you have chosen us freely for the sake of your Son. As we live out our lives, point us always to his cross and to the empty tomb, so that we will be strengthened by his grace.

Wednesday, January 12, 2011

Time after Epiphany

Isaiah 51:1-16
Through water God's people cross over

Awake, awake, put on strength,
   O arm of the LORD!
Awake, as in days of old,
   the generations of long ago!
Was it not you who cut Rahab in pieces,
   who pierced the dragon?
Was it not you who dried up the sea,
   the waters of the great deep;
who made the depths of the sea a way
   for the redeemed to cross over?
So the ransomed of the LORD shall return,
   and come to Zion with singing;
everlasting joy shall be upon their heads;
   they shall obtain joy and gladness,
   and sorrow and sighing shall flee away. (Isa. 51:9-11)

Psalm
Psalm 89:5-37
God anoints David to be a son

Additional Reading
Matthew 12:15-21
The words of Isaiah applied to Jesus

Hymn: Come, We That Love the Lord, ELW 625

Powerful Lord, cast away suffering and sorrow so that joy and gladness may grace our lives. Give us ears to hear your word so that evil may be crushed underfoot.

Thursday, January 13, 2011

Time after Epiphany

Psalm 40:1-11
Doing the will of God

I waited patiently for the LORD;
   he inclined to me and heard my cry.
He drew me up from the desolate pit,
   out of the miry bog,
and set my feet upon a rock,
   making my steps secure.
He put a new song in my mouth,
   a song of praise to our God.
Many will see and fear,
   and put their trust in the LORD.
Happy are those who make
   the LORD their trust,
who do not turn to the proud,
   to those who go astray after false gods.
You have multiplied, O LORD my God,
   your wondrous deeds and your thoughts toward us;
   none can compare with you.
Were I to proclaim and tell of them,
   they would be more than can be counted. (Ps. 40:1-5)

Additional Readings

Isaiah 22:15-25
God replaces disobedient leaders

Galatians 1:6-12
Paul's calling through a revelation of Christ

Hymn: Out of the Depths I Cry to You, ELW 600

Caring creator, help us to see your compassion as we wade through the trials of this life. When we are stricken, may the mercy of your Son turn our mourning into a new and joyful song.

Friday, January 14, 2011

Time after Epiphany

Acts 1:1-5

The promise of the Holy Spirit

In the first book, Theophilus, I wrote about all that Jesus did and taught from the beginning until the day when he was taken up to heaven, after giving instructions through the Holy Spirit to the apostles whom he had chosen. After his suffering he presented himself alive to them by many convincing proofs, appearing to them during forty days and speaking about the kingdom of God. While staying with them, he ordered them not to leave Jerusalem, but to wait there for the promise of the Father. "This," he said, "is what you have heard from me; for John baptized with water, but you will be baptized with the Holy Spirit not many days from now." (Acts 1:1-5)

Psalm	**Additional Reading**
Psalm 40:1-11	Genesis 27:30-38
Doing the will of God	*Isaac and Esau discover Jacob's deceit*

Hymn: This Is the Spirit's Entry Now, ELW 448

Eternal God, you sent your Son into the world that we might know you intimately. Help us to die daily to sin and be born daily to righteousness, trusting in your Spirit's baptismal promise.

Saturday, January 15, 2011

Time after Epiphany

Martin Luther King Jr., renewer of society, martyr, 1968

1 Kings 19:19-21

Elijah calls Elisha to follow him

So he set out from there, and found Elisha son of Shaphat, who was plowing. There were twelve yoke of oxen ahead of him, and he was with the twelfth. Elijah passed by him and threw his mantle over him. He left the oxen, ran after Elijah, and said, "Let me kiss my father and my mother, and then I will follow you." Then Elijah said to him, "Go back again; for what have I done to you?" He returned from following him, took the yoke of oxen, and slaughtered them; using the equipment from the oxen, he boiled their flesh, and gave it to the people, and they ate. Then he set out and followed Elijah, and became his servant. (1 Kings 19:19-21)

Psalm	Additional Reading
Psalm 40:1-11	Luke 5:1-11
Doing the will of God	*Jesus calls the first disciples*

Hymn: How Clear Is Our Vocation, Lord, ELW 580

God, we thank you for the prophets who followed your call and proclaimed your word. May we faithfully follow their teaching and see the grace of your Son in their words.

Sunday, January 16, 2011

Second Sunday after Epiphany

John 1:29-42
Christ revealed as the Lamb of God

The next day he saw Jesus coming toward him and declared, "Here is the Lamb of God who takes away the sin of the world! This is he of whom I said, 'After me comes a man who ranks ahead of me because he was before me.' I myself did not know him; but I came baptizing with water for this reason, that he might be revealed to Israel." And John testified, "I saw the Spirit descending from heaven like a dove, and it remained on him. I myself did not know him, but the one who sent me to baptize with water said to me, 'He on whom you see the Spirit descend and remain is the one who baptizes with the Holy Spirit.' And I myself have seen and have testified that this is the Son of God." (John 1:29-34)

Psalm
Psalm 40:1-11
Doing the will of God

Additional Readings
Isaiah 49:1-7
The servant brings light to the nations

I Corinthians 1:1-9
Paul's greeting to the church at Corinth

Hymn: Lamb of God, ELW 336

Holy God, our strength and our redeemer, by your Spirit hold us forever, that through your grace we may worship you and faithfully serve you, follow you and joyfully find you, through Jesus Christ, our Savior and Lord.

Monday, January 17, 2011

Time after Epiphany

Antony of Egypt, renewer of the church, c. 356
Pachomius, renewer of the church, 346

Psalm 40:6-17
Not sacrifice, but divine mercy

Sacrifice and offering you do not desire,
  but you have given me an open ear.
Burnt offering and sin offering
  you have not required.
Then I said, "Here I am;
  in the scroll of the book it is written of me.
I delight to do your will, O my God;
  your law is within my heart." (Ps. 40:6-8)

Additional Readings
Exodus 12:1-13, 21-28
The passover lamb

Acts 8:26-40
Philip teaches about the lamb

Hymn: Lord of Glory, You Have Bought Us, ELW 707

Send your Holy Spirit to write your law upon our hearts, creator and lover of humankind. May we rejoice in your teaching and strive always to live according to your will.

Tuesday, January 18, 2011

Confession of Peter

Week of Prayer for Christian Unity begins

Matthew 16:13-19

Peter confesses, You are the Messiah

He said to them, "But who do you say that I am?" Simon Peter answered, "You are the Messiah, the Son of the living God." And Jesus answered him, "Blessed are you, Simon son of Jonah! For flesh and blood has not revealed this to you, but my Father in heaven. And I tell you, you are Peter, and on this rock I will build my church, and the gates of Hades will not prevail against it. I will give you the keys of the kingdom of heaven, and whatever you bind on earth will be bound in heaven, and whatever you loose on earth will be loosed in heaven." (Matt. 16:15-19)

Psalm	Additional Readings	
Psalm 18:1-6, 16-19	Acts 4:8-13	1 Corinthians 10:1-5
My God, my rock, worthy of praise	*Salvation is in no one other than Jesus*	*Drinking from the spiritual rock of Christ*

Hymn: Built on a Rock, ELW 652

Almighty God, you inspired Simon Peter to confess Jesus as the Messiah and Son of the living God. Keep your church firm on the rock of this faith, so that in unity and peace it may proclaim one truth and follow one Lord, your Son, Jesus Christ, our Savior, who lives and reigns with you and the Holy Spirit, one God, now and forever.

Wednesday, January 19, 2011

Time after Epiphany

Henry, Bishop of Uppsala, martyr, 1156

Isaiah 48:12-21
God saves the people through water

Thus says the LORD,
  your Redeemer, the Holy One of Israel:
I am the LORD your God,
  who teaches you for your own good,
  who leads you in the way you should go.
O that you had paid attention to my commandments!
  Then your prosperity would have been like a river,
  and your success like the waves of the sea;
your offspring would have been like the sand,
  and your descendants like its grains;
their name would never be cut off
  or destroyed from before me.
Go out from Babylon, flee from Chaldea,
  declare this with a shout of joy, proclaim it,
send it forth to the end of the earth;
  say, "The LORD has redeemed his servant Jacob!" (Isa. 48:17-20)

Psalm
Psalm 40:6-17
Not sacrifice, but divine mercy

Additional Reading
Matthew 9:14-17
Christ, the bridegroom, the new wine

Hymn: When Peace like a River, ELW 785

Strong God, you liberate your people from captivity to sin, death, and the false gods of this world. Help us always to proclaim and trust the name of your Son, our eternal Lord, Jesus Christ.

Thursday, January 20, 2011

Time after Epiphany

Psalm 27:1-6
God is light and salvation

The LORD is my light and my salvation;
    whom shall I fear?
The LORD is the stronghold of my life;
    of whom shall I be afraid?
When evildoers assail me
    to devour my flesh—
my adversaries and foes—
    they shall stumble and fall.
Though an army encamp against me,
    my heart shall not fear;
though war rise up against me,
    yet I will be confident. (Ps. 27:1-3)

Additional Readings
1 Samuel 1:1-20
The birth of Samuel

Galatians 1:11-24
The divine origin of Paul's gospel

Hymn: If God My Lord Be for Me, ELW 788

No force of evil can overpower you, O God. You send the Lord of hosts to die for us, to defeat the legions of demons, and to free us from sin. Give us trust to call upon your Son in times of need.

Friday, January 21, 2011

Time after Epiphany

Agnes, martyr, c. 304

Galatians 2:1-10
Paul's authority in the growing church

Then after fourteen years I went up again to Jerusalem with Barnabas, taking Titus along with me. I went up in response to a revelation. Then I laid before them (though only in a private meeting with the acknowledged leaders) the gospel that I proclaim among the Gentiles, in order to make sure that I was not running, or had not run, in vain. But even Titus, who was with me, was not compelled to be circumcised, though he was a Greek. But because of false believers secretly brought in, who slipped in to spy on the freedom we have in Christ Jesus, so that they might enslave us— we did not submit to them even for a moment, so that the truth of the gospel might always remain with you. (Gal. 2:1-5)

Psalm
Psalm 27:1-6
God is light and salvation

Additional Reading
1 Samuel 9:27—10:8
Saul anointed by Samuel as king

Hymn: God, Whose Almighty Word, ELW 673

God, bring your whole church together by the goodness of your grace. Humble us so that we do not create barriers to those who would believe, but let your Word and Spirit have free reign.

Saturday, January 22, 2011

Time after Epiphany

1 Samuel 15:34—16:13
David anointed as king to replace King Saul

Samuel said to Jesse, "Are all your sons here?" And he said, "There remains yet the youngest, but he is keeping the sheep." And Samuel said to Jesse, "Send and bring him; for we will not sit down until he comes here." He sent and brought him in. Now he was ruddy, and had beautiful eyes, and was handsome. The LORD said, "Rise and anoint him; for this is the one." Then Samuel took the horn of oil, and anointed him in the presence of his brothers; and the spirit of the LORD came mightily upon David from that day forward. Samuel then set out and went to Ramah. (1 Sam. 16:11-13)

Psalm
Psalm 27:1-6
God is light and salvation

Additional Reading
Luke 5:27-32
The call of Levi

Hymn: In Christ Called to Baptize, ELW 575

Father in heaven, you show us strength in weakness and you fulfill us in ways we do not expect. When we search for our own glory and righteousness, point us to your Son on the cross.

Sunday, January 23, 2011

Third Sunday after Epiphany

Matthew 4:12-23

Christ revealed as a prophet

Now when Jesus heard that John had been arrested, he withdrew to Galilee. He left Nazareth and made his home in Capernaum by the sea, in the territory of Zebulun and Naphtali, so that what had been spoken through the prophet Isaiah might be fulfilled:

"Land of Zebulun, land of Naphtali,
   on the road by the sea, across the Jordan, Galilee of the Gentiles—
the people who sat in darkness
   have seen a great light,
and for those who sat in the region and shadow of death
   light has dawned." (Matt. 4:12-16)

Psalm

Psalm 27:1, 4-9
God is light and salvation

Additional Readings

Isaiah 9:1-4
Light shines for those in darkness

1 Corinthians 1:10-18
An appeal for unity in the gospel

Hymn: Light Shone in Darkness, ELW 307

Lord God, your lovingkindness always goes before us and follows after us. Summon us into your light, and direct our steps in the ways of goodness that come through the cross of your Son, Jesus Christ, our Savior and Lord.

Monday, January 24, 2011

Time after Epiphany

Psalm 27:7-14
Take courage in God

Teach me your way, O LORD,
  and lead me on a level path
  because of my enemies.
Do not give me up to the will of my adversaries,
  for false witnesses have risen against me,
  and they are breathing out violence.
I believe that I shall see the goodness of the LORD
  in the land of the living.
Wait for the LORD;
  be strong, and let your heart take courage;
  wait for the LORD! (Ps. 27:11-14)

Additional Readings

Judges 6:11-24
God calls Gideon to lead the people

Ephesians 5:6-14
Live as children of the light

Hymn: Lead Me, Guide Me, ELW 768

Father, give us trust so that we too can proclaim that we will see your goodness in the land of the living. Guide us along the path of discipleship so that we strive always for the joys of your Son.

Tuesday, January 25, 2011

Conversion of Paul

Week of Prayer for Christian Unity ends

Galatians 1:11-24
Paul receives a revelation of Christ

You have heard, no doubt, of my earlier life in Judaism. I was
violently persecuting the church of God and was trying to destroy it.
I advanced in Judaism beyond many among my people of the same
age, for I was far more zealous for the traditions of my ancestors. But
when God, who had set me apart before I was born and called me
through his grace, was pleased to reveal his Son to me, so that I might
proclaim him among the Gentiles, I did not confer with any human
being, nor did I go up to Jerusalem to those who were already apostles
before me, but I went away at once into Arabia, and afterwards I
returned to Damascus. (Gal. 1:13-17)

Psalm
Psalm 67
Let all the peoples praise you, O God

Additional Readings
Acts 9:1-22
Saul is converted to Christ

Luke 21:10-19
The end times will require endurance

Hymn: By All Your Saints, ELW 420 (stanza 8)

*O God, by the preaching of your apostle Paul you have caused the light
of the gospel to shine throughout the world. Grant that we may follow
his example and be witnesses to the truth of your Son, Jesus Christ, our
Savior and Lord, who lives and reigns with you and the Holy Spirit, one
God, now and forever.*

Wednesday, January 26, 2011

Time after Epiphany

Timothy, Titus, and Silas, missionaries

Luke 1:67-79

Christ, the light dawning

Then his father Zechariah was filled with the Holy Spirit and spoke this prophecy:

"And you, child, will be called the prophet of the Most High;
for you will go before the Lord to prepare his ways,
to give knowledge of salvation to his people
by the forgiveness of their sins.
By the tender mercy of our God,
the dawn from on high will break upon us,
to give light to those who sit in darkness and in the shadow of death,
to guide our feet into the way of peace." (Luke 1:67, 76-79)

Psalm	Additional Reading
Psalm 27:7-14	Genesis 49:1-2, 8-13, 21-26
Take courage in God	*Judah, Zebulun, Naphtali, and Joseph blessed*

Hymn: Blessed Be the God of Israel, ELW 552

Merciful creator, we long for the day when your dawn breaks upon us and your Son returns in glory. Keep us steadfast as we await your kingdom and the redemption of all that you have made.

Thursday, January 27, 2011

Time after Epiphany

Lydia, Dorcas, and Phoebe, witnesses to the faith

Psalm 15

Abiding on God's holy hill

O LORD, who may abide in your tent?
   Who may dwell on your holy hill?
Those who walk blamelessly, and do what is right,
   and speak the truth from their heart;
who do not slander with their tongue,
   and do no evil to their friends,
      nor take up a reproach against their neighbors;
in whose eyes the wicked are despised,
   but who honor those who fear the LORD;
who stand by their oath even to their hurt;
who do not lend money at interest,
   and do not take a bribe against the innocent.

Those who do these things shall never be moved. (Ps. 15:1-5)

Additional Readings
Deuteronomy 16:18-20
Pursue only justice

1 Peter 3:8-12
Repay evil with a blessing

Hymn: God of Grace and God of Glory, ELW 705

God, we give you thanks that you have sent your Son to be our living temple. Help us turn to him in the midst of our sins and trust that he redeems us for our lack of love, hope, and trust.

Friday, January 28, 2011

Time after Epiphany

Thomas Aquinas, teacher, 1274

1 Timothy 5:17-24
Good works are conspicuous

In the presence of God and of Christ Jesus and of the elect angels, I warn you to keep these instructions without prejudice, doing nothing on the basis of partiality. Do not ordain anyone hastily, and do not participate in the sins of others; keep yourself pure.

No longer drink only water, but take a little wine for the sake of your stomach and your frequent ailments.

The sins of some people are conspicuous and precede them to judgment, while the sins of others follow them there. (1 Tim. 5:21-24)

Psalm
Psalm 15
Abiding on God's holy hill

Additional Reading
Deuteronomy 24:17—25:4
Do not deprive others of justice

Hymn: To Be Your Presence, ELW 546

Lord God, we thank you for the joys of this world which support us as we await your Son's return. May your holy angels continually have charge over us and keep us from danger.

Saturday, January 29, 2011

Time after Epiphany

Micah 3:1-4
Should you not know justice?

And I said:
Listen, you heads of Jacob
    and rulers of the house of Israel!
Should you not know justice?—
    you who hate the good and love the evil,
who tear the skin off my people,
    and the flesh off their bones;
who eat the flesh of my people,
    flay their skin off them,
break their bones in pieces,
    and chop them up like meat in a kettle,
    like flesh in a caldron.
Then they will cry to the LORD,
    but he will not answer them;
he will hide his face from them at that time,
    because they have acted wickedly. (Micah 3:1-4)

Psalm
Psalm 15
Abiding on God's holy hill

Additional Reading
John 13:31-35
The new commandment

Hymn: There's a Wideness in God's Mercy, ELW 587/588

Forgive us, loving God, for the times we have acted wickedly. Change our hearts and give us faith to trust in Jesus' death and resurrection. Hear us when we cry out to you.

Sunday, January 30, 2011

Fourth Sunday after Epiphany

Matthew 5:1-12

The teaching of Christ: Beatitudes

When Jesus saw the crowds, he went up the mountain; and after he sat down, his disciples came to him. Then he began to speak, and taught them, saying:

"Blessed are those who are persecuted for righteousness' sake, for theirs is the kingdom of heaven.

"Blessed are you when people revile you and persecute you and utter all kinds of evil against you falsely on my account. Rejoice and be glad, for your reward is great in heaven, for in the same way they persecuted the prophets who were before you." (Matt. 5:1-2, 10-12)

Psalm
Psalm 15
Abiding on God's holy hill

Additional Readings
Micah 6:1-8
The offering of justice, kindness, humility

1 Corinthians 1:18-31
Christ crucified, the wisdom and power of God

Hymn: When the Poor Ones, ELW 725

Holy God, you confound the world's wisdom in giving your kingdom to the lowly and the pure in heart. Give us such a hunger and thirst for justice, and perseverance in striving for peace, that in our words and deeds the world may see the life of your Son, Jesus Christ, our Savior and Lord.

Monday, January 31, 2011

Time after Epiphany

Psalm 37:1-17
God will bless the righteous

The wicked draw the sword and bend their bows
    to bring down the poor and needy,
    to kill those who walk uprightly;
their sword shall enter their own heart,
    and their bows shall be broken.
Better is a little that the righteous person has
    than the abundance of many wicked.
For the arms of the wicked shall be broken,
    but the LORD upholds the righteous. (Ps. 37:14-17)

Additional Readings
Ruth 1:1-18
Ruth, one of the poor

Philemon 1-25
Concerning the slave Onesimus

Hymn: The People Walk, ELW 706

For all the times we have used words and actions to pierce the hearts of our neighbors, forgive us, O God. May we rest secure in the compassionate arms of our Savior.

_____

_____

_____

_____

_____

_____

_____

_____

_____

_____

_____

_____

Tuesday, February 1, 2011

Time after Epiphany

James 5:1-6
A warning to the ungenerous

Come now, you rich people, weep and wail for the miseries that
are coming to you. Your riches have rotted, and your clothes are
moth-eaten. Your gold and silver have rusted, and their rust will be
evidence against you, and it will eat your flesh like fire. You have laid
up treasure for the last days. Listen! The wages of the laborers who
mowed your fields, which you kept back by fraud, cry out, and the
cries of the harvesters have reached the ears of the Lord of hosts. You
have lived on the earth in luxury and in pleasure; you have fattened
your hearts in a day of slaughter. You have condemned and murdered
the righteous one, who does not resist you. (James 5:1-6)

Psalm
Psalm 37:1-17
God will bless the righteous

Additional Reading
Ruth 2:1-16
Ruth, one of the hungry

Hymn: Where Charity and Love Prevail, ELW 359

*Almighty God, you give us the riches of your grace and call us to share
your constant love. Help us live with generosity and thanksgiving for
the sake of our neighbors and our world, through Christ our Lord.*

Wednesday, February 2, 2011

Presentation of Our Lord

Luke 2:22-40

The child is brought to the temple

Simeon took him in his arms and praised God, saying,
  "Master, now you are dismissing your servant in peace,
    according to your word;
  for my eyes have seen your salvation,
    which you have prepared in the presence of all peoples,
    a light for revelation to the Gentiles
    and for glory to your people Israel." (Luke 2:28-32)

Psalm

Psalm 84

How dear to me is your dwelling, O LORD

Additional Readings

Malachi 3:1-4

My messenger, a refiner and purifier

Hebrews 2:14-18

Jesus shares human flesh and sufferings

Hymn: In Peace and Joy I Now Depart, ELW 440

Almighty and ever-living God, your only-begotten Son was presented this day in the temple. May we be presented to you with clean and pure hearts by the same Jesus Christ our great high priest, who lives and reigns with you and the Holy Spirit, one God, now and forever.

Thursday, February 3, 2011

Time after Epiphany

Ansgar, Bishop of Hamburg, missionary to Denmark and Sweden, 865

Psalm 112:1-9 [10]
Light shines in the darkness

Praise the LORD!
  Happy are those who fear the LORD,
    who greatly delight in his commandments.
Their descendants will be mighty in the land;
    the generation of the upright will be blessed.
Wealth and riches are in their houses,
    and their righteousness endures forever.
They rise in the darkness as a light for the upright;
    they are gracious, merciful, and righteous. (Ps. 112:1-4)

Additional Readings
Deuteronomy 4:1-14   1 John 5:1-5
The discipline of faith   *God's children obey God's commandments*

Hymn: My Lord of Light, ELW 832

*Almighty God, we rejoice that all our gifts come from your hands.
Guide us to live in your holy light and send us into this world's darkness
to bring the brightness of your grace and mercy to all people in need.*

Friday, February 4, 2011

Time after Epiphany

James 3:13-18

A gentle life born of wisdom

Who is wise and understanding among you? Show by your good life that your works are done with gentleness born of wisdom. But if you have bitter envy and selfish ambition in your hearts, do not be boastful and false to the truth. Such wisdom does not come down from above, but is earthly, unspiritual, devilish. For where there is envy and selfish ambition, there will also be disorder and wickedness of every kind. But the wisdom from above is first pure, then peaceable, gentle, willing to yield, full of mercy and good fruits, without a trace of partiality or hypocrisy. And a harvest of righteousness is sown in peace for those who make peace. (James 3:13-18)

Psalm
Psalm 112:1-9 [10]
Light shines in the darkness

Additional Reading
Isaiah 29:1-12
Hunger that goes unsatisfied

Hymn: Salvation unto Us Has Come, ELW 590

Holy Lord, you filled creation and our lives with goodness from the beginning. Guide us to be wise thinkers, intelligent workers, and merciful stewards of your bounty that all people may feast at the harvest of your righteousness.

Saturday, February 5, 2011

Time after Epiphany

The Martyrs of Japan, 1597

Isaiah 29:13-16

Hearts far from God

The Lord said:
Because these people draw near with their mouths
    and honor me with their lips,
    while their hearts are far from me,
and their worship of me is a human commandment learned by rote;
so I will again do
    amazing things with this people,
    shocking and amazing.
The wisdom of their wise shall perish,
    and the discernment of the discerning shall be hidden.
(Isa. 29:13-14)

Psalm
Psalm 112:1-9 [10]
Light shines in the darkness

Additional Reading
Mark 7:1-8
The hypocrisy of lip service

Hymn: Glorious Things of You Are Spoken, ELW 647

Almighty God, you created us in love and for your love's sake. When our hearts are cold, send us faithful witnesses and wise disciples who will bring us out of our ignorance into understanding.

Sunday, February 6, 2011

Fifth Sunday after Epiphany

Matthew 5:13-20

The teaching of Christ: salt and light

"You are the salt of the earth; but if salt has lost its taste, how can its saltiness be restored? It is no longer good for anything, but is thrown out and trampled under foot.

"You are the light of the world. A city built on a hill cannot be hid. No one after lighting a lamp puts it under the bushel basket, but on the lampstand, and it gives light to all in the house. In the same way, let your light shine before others, so that they may see your good works and give glory to your Father in heaven." (Matt. 5:13-16)

Psalm
Psalm 112:1-9 [10]
Light shines in the darkness

Additional Readings
Isaiah 58:1-9a [9b-12]
The fast that God chooses

1 Cor. 2:1-12 [13-16]
God's wisdom revealed through the Spirit

Hymn: Gather Us In, ELW 532

Lord God, with endless mercy you receive the prayers of all who call upon you. By your Spirit show us the things we ought to do, and give us the grace and power to do them, through Jesus Christ, our Savior and Lord.

Monday, February 7, 2011

Time after Epiphany

Psalm 119:105-112
The law is light

Accept my offerings of praise, O LORD,
    and teach me your ordinances.
I hold my life in my hand continually,
    but I do not forget your law.
The wicked have laid a snare for me,
    but I do not stray from your precepts.
Your decrees are my heritage forever;
    they are the joy of my heart.
I incline my heart to perform your statutes
    forever, to the end. (Ps. 119:108-112)

Additional Readings
2 Kings 22:3-20
Huldah urges Josiah to keep the law

Romans 11:2-10
A remnant remains faithful

Hymn: Oh, That the Lord Would Guide My Ways, ELW 772

Lord of all creation, you continually offer us abundant life through your Son, Jesus Christ. Protect us from our frailties and from this world's dangers, and enable us to live as you commanded us, loving our neighbors as ourselves.

Tuesday, February 8, 2011

Time after Epiphany

2 Corinthians 4:1-12

Christ, the light

Therefore, since it is by God's mercy that we are engaged in this ministry, we do not lose heart. We have renounced the shameful things that one hides; we refuse to practice cunning or to falsify God's word; but by the open statement of the truth we commend ourselves to the conscience of everyone in the sight of God. And even if our gospel is veiled, it is veiled to those who are perishing. In their case the god of this world has blinded the minds of the unbelievers, to keep them from seeing the light of the gospel of the glory of Christ, who is the image of God. For we do not proclaim ourselves; we proclaim Jesus Christ as Lord and ourselves as your slaves for Jesus' sake. For it is the God who said, "Let light shine out of darkness," who has shone in our hearts to give the light of the knowledge of the glory of God in the face of Jesus Christ. (2 Cor. 4:1-6)

Psalm
Psalm 119:105-112
The law is light

Additional Reading
2 Kings 23:1-8, 21-25
King Josiah keeps the law

Hymn: Christ, Be Our Light, ELW 715

Almighty God, you constantly surprise us with your word and your presence. Help us not to veil that presence or to proclaim our own ideas as gospel. Guide us to live in the powerful light we see shining in the face of our Lord Jesus Christ.

Wednesday, February 9, 2011

Time after Epiphany

John 8:12-30
Christ the light of the world

Again Jesus spoke to them, saying, "I am the light of the world. Whoever follows me will never walk in darkness but will have the light of life." Then the Pharisees said to him, "You are testifying on your own behalf; your testimony is not valid." Jesus answered, "Even if I testify on my own behalf, my testimony is valid because I know where I have come from and where I am going, but you do not know where I come from or where I am going." (John 8:12-14)

Psalm
Psalm 119:105-112
The law is light

Additional Reading
Proverbs 6:6-23
The law is a lamp

Hymn: Drawn to the Light, ELW 593

Lord of eternity, you gave us Jesus to put away the darkness of sin and death. Keep us always in this light and help us see that we will be wherever the Light of the world brings love.

Thursday, February 10, 2011

Time after Epiphany

Psalm 119:1-8
Happy are those who walk in the law

Happy are those whose way is blameless,
    who walk in the law of the LORD.
Happy are those who keep his decrees,
    who seek him with their whole heart,
who also do no wrong,
    but walk in his ways. (Ps. 119:1-3)

Additional Readings
Genesis 26:1-5   **James 1:12-16**
God blesses Isaac   *God tempts no one*

Hymn: O God beyond All Praising, ELW 880

*Almighty God, you give us yourself in word and sacrament, in prayer
and praise, in fellowship and celebration. Guide us to live in your word
and walk in your ways, through Christ our Lord.*

Friday, February 11, 2011

Time after Epiphany

1 John 2:7-17
Old and new commandments

Beloved, I am writing you no new commandment, but an old commandment that you have had from the beginning; the old commandment is the word that you have heard. Yet I am writing you a new commandment that is true in him and in you, because the darkness is passing away and the true light is already shining. Whoever says, "I am in the light," while hating a brother or sister, is still in the darkness. Whoever loves a brother or sister lives in the light, and in such a person there is no cause for stumbling. But whoever hates another believer is in the darkness, walks in the darkness, and does not know the way to go, because the darkness has brought on blindness. (1 John 2:7-11)

Psalm
Psalm 119:1-8
Happy are those who walk in the law

Additional Reading
Leviticus 26:34-46
God's covenant remembered

Hymn: The Right Hand of God, ELW 889

Almighty God, you created us to live in relationship with you and with one another. In our families, communities of faith, and the neighborhoods we inhabit, teach us to bring forgiveness and love to all.

Saturday, February 12, 2011

Time after Epiphany

Deuteronomy 30:1-9a

God's fidelity assured

When all these things have happened to you, the blessings and the curses that I have set before you, if you call them to mind among all the nations where the LORD your God has driven you, and return to the LORD your God, and you and your children obey him with all your heart and with all your soul, just as I am commanding you today, then the LORD your God will restore your fortunes and have compassion on you, gathering you again from all the peoples among whom the LORD your God has scattered you. Even if you are exiled to the ends of the world, from there the LORD your God will gather you, and from there he will bring you back. The LORD your God will bring you into the land that your ancestors possessed, and you will possess it; he will make you more prosperous and numerous than your ancestors. (Deut. 30:1-5)

Psalm
Psalm 119:1-8
Happy are those who walk in the law

Additional Reading
Matthew 15:1-9
God's commandments and religious tradition

Hymn: Day by Day, ELW 790

Holy Lord, day by day you offer us nourishment that we grow in grace and favor with you. Remind us that you keep your promises and will use us to bless all those around us.

Sunday, February 13, 2011

Sixth Sunday after Epiphany

Matthew 5:21-37

The teaching of Christ: forgiveness

"You have heard that it was said to those of ancient times, 'You shall not murder'; and 'whoever murders shall be liable to judgment.' But I say to you that if you are angry with a brother or sister, you will be liable to judgment; and if you insult a brother or sister, you will be liable to the council; and if you say, 'You fool,' you will be liable to the hell of fire. So when you are offering your gift at the altar, if you remember that your brother or sister has something against you, leave your gift there before the altar and go; first be reconciled to your brother or sister, and then come and offer your gift. Come to terms quickly with your accuser while you are on the way to court with him, or your accuser may hand you over to the judge, and the judge to the guard, and you will be thrown into prison. Truly I tell you, you will never get out until you have paid the last penny." (Matt. 5:21-26)

Psalm

Psalm 119:1-8

Happy are those who walk in the law

Additional Readings

Deuteronomy 30:15-20   1 Corinthians 3:1-9

Choose life   *God gives the growth*

Hymn: God, When Human Bonds Are Broken, ELW 603

O God, the strength of all who hope in you, because we are weak mortals we accomplish nothing good without you. Help us to see and understand the things we ought to do, and give us grace and power to do them; through Jesus Christ, our Savior and Lord.

Monday, February 14, 2011

Time after Epiphany

Cyril, monk, 869; Methodius, bishop, 885; missionaries to the Slavs

Psalm 119:9-16
I delight in the law

Blessed are you, O LORD;
   teach me your statutes.
With my lips I declare
   all the ordinances of your mouth.
I delight in the way of your decrees
   as much as in all riches.
I will meditate on your precepts,
   and fix my eyes on your ways.
I will delight in your statutes;
   I will not forget your word. (Ps. 119:12-16)

Additional Readings
Exodus 20:1-21
The ten commandments

James 1:2-8
Facing trials

Hymn: All Depends on Our Possessing, ELW 589

Holy Lord, in all times and places you send us disciples and witnesses to your love. As we remember all who delighted in loving and serving your word, lead us to keep your word and follow your ways for the sake of the world.

Tuesday, February 15, 2011

Time after Epiphany

James 2:1-13
The law, judgment, and mercy

You do well if you really fulfill the royal law according to the scripture, "You shall love your neighbor as yourself." But if you show partiality, you commit sin and are convicted by the law as transgressors. For whoever keeps the whole law but fails in one point has become accountable for all of it. For the one who said, "You shall not commit adultery," also said, "You shall not murder." Now if you do not commit adultery but if you murder, you have become a transgressor of the law. So speak and so act as those who are to be judged by the law of liberty. For judgment will be without mercy to anyone who has shown no mercy; mercy triumphs over judgment. (James 2:8-13)

Psalm
Psalm 119:9-16
I delight in the law

Additional Reading
Deuteronomy 23:21—24:4, 10-15
Israel's communal laws

Hymn: Our Father, God in Heaven Above, ELW 747

Almighty God, you come into our lives not to judge us and find us wanting but always to give us mercy, forgiveness, and joy. Help us be merciful, offer forgiveness, and seek to bring others into your joy.

Wednesday, February 16, 2011

Time after Epiphany

Proverbs 2:1-15
The way of wisdom

My child, if you accept my words
 and treasure up my commandments within you,
making your ear attentive to wisdom
 and inclining your heart to understanding;
if you indeed cry out for insight,
 and raise your voice for understanding;
if you seek it like silver,
 and search for it as for hidden treasures—
then you will understand the fear of the LORD
and find the knowledge of God. (Prov. 2:1-5)

Psalm
Psalm 119:9-16
I delight in the law

Additional Reading
Matthew 19:1-12
Jesus teaches about divorce

Hymn: Be Thou My Vision, ELW 793

*Holy Lord, you listen to our prayers as we seek to know your will in our
lives. Guide us to seek the treasure that is your love and to proclaim the
abundance of life in your name.*

Thursday, February 17, 2011

Time after Epiphany

Psalm 119:33-40
Walking in the path of the law

Teach me, O LORD, the way of your statutes,
   and I will observe it to the end.
Give me understanding, that I may keep your law
   and observe it with my whole heart.
Lead me in the path of your commandments,
   for I delight in it.
Turn my heart to your decrees,
   and not to selfish gain. (Ps. 119:33-36)

Additional Readings
Exodus 22:21-27   1 Corinthians 10:23—11:1
Compassion for neighbors   *Do not seek your own advantage*

Hymn: If You But Trust in God to Guide You, ELW 769

Almighty God, you show compassion for us when we fail to follow your call to serve. In your forgiveness, lead us to show compassion for those around us and remind us of the joy that comes when we delight in serving others.

Friday, February 18, 2011

Time after Epiphany

Martin Luther, renewer of the church, 1546

Galatians 5:2-6
Faith working through love

Listen! I, Paul, am telling you that if you let yourselves be circumcised, Christ will be of no benefit to you. Once again I testify to every man who lets himself be circumcised that he is obliged to obey the entire law. You who want to be justified by the law have cut yourselves off from Christ; you have fallen away from grace. For through the Spirit, by faith, we eagerly wait for the hope of righteousness. For in Christ Jesus neither circumcision nor uncircumcision counts for anything; the only thing that counts is faith working through love. (Gal. 5:2-6)

Psalm
Psalm 119:33-40
Walking in the path of the law

Additional Reading
Leviticus 6:1-7
Sin against a neighbor

Hymn: O Christ, Your Heart, Compassionate, ELW 722

Lord of all goodness, when we fall away you seek us out and bring us back into your loving embrace. In the power of Christ's love, send us to put our faith into action for all in need.

Saturday, February 19, 2011

Time after Epiphany

Matthew 7:1-12
The golden rule

"Ask, and it will be given you; search, and you will find; knock, and the door will be opened for you. For everyone who asks receives, and everyone who searches finds, and for everyone who knocks, the door will be opened. Is there anyone among you who, if your child asks for bread, will give a stone? Or if the child asks for a fish, will give a snake? If you then, who are evil, know how to give good gifts to your children, how much more will your Father in heaven give good things to those who ask him!

"In everything do to others as you would have them do to you; for this is the law and the prophets." (Matt. 7:7-12)

Psalm
Psalm 119:33-40
Walking in the path of the law

Additional Reading
Leviticus 24:10-23
An eye for an eye

Hymn: O Master, Let Me Walk with You, ELW 818

Lord of all creation, in your self-giving life you showed us a way to live, taught us how to pray, and offered us hope. Help us continue to learn and practice this way of living beyond ourselves and enable us to reach out to others freely.

Sunday, February 20, 2011

Seventh Sunday after Epiphany

Matthew 5:38-48

The teaching of Christ: love

"You have heard that it was said, 'You shall love your neighbor and hate your enemy.' But I say to you, Love your enemies and pray for those who persecute you, so that you may be children of your Father in heaven; for he makes his sun rise on the evil and on the good, and sends rain on the righteous and on the unrighteous. For if you love those who love you, what reward do you have? Do not even the tax collectors do the same? And if you greet only your brothers and sisters, what more are you doing than others? Do not even the Gentiles do the same? Be perfect, therefore, as your heavenly Father is perfect." (Matt. 5:43-48)

Psalm
Psalm 119:33-40
Walking in the path of the law

Additional Readings
Leviticus 19:1-2, 9-18
Acts of mercy and justice

1 Cor. 3:10-11, 16-23
Allegiance to Christ, not human leaders

Hymn: Lord of All Nations, Grant Me Grace, ELW 716

Holy God of compassion, you invite us into your way of forgiveness and peace. Lead us to love our enemies, and transform our words and deeds to be like his through whom we pray, Jesus Christ, our Savior and Lord.

Monday, February 21, 2011

Time after Epiphany

Psalm 119:57-64
Keeping the law in spite of the wicked

When I think of your ways,
   I turn my feet to your decrees;
I hurry and do not delay
   to keep your commandments.
Though the cords of the wicked ensnare me,
   I do not forget your law.
At midnight I rise to praise you,
   because of your righteous ordinances.
I am a companion of all who fear you,
   of those who keep your precepts.
The earth, O LORD, is full of your steadfast love;
   teach me your statutes. (Ps. 119:59-64)

Additional Readings

Proverbs 25:11-22
Caring for the enemy

Romans 12:9-21
Caring for the enemy

Hymn: Let the Whole Creation Cry, ELW 876

Almighty God, you showed mercy to all when your Son forgave those who crucified or abandoned him. Give us this same mercy to help us forgive our enemies and minister to their hearts.

Tuesday, February 22, 2011

Time after Epiphany

Hebrews 12:14-16

Pursue peace with everyone

Pursue peace with everyone, and the holiness without which no one will see the Lord. See to it that no one fails to obtain the grace of God; that no root of bitterness springs up and causes trouble, and through it many become defiled. See to it that no one becomes like Esau, an immoral and godless person, who sold his birthright for a single meal. (Heb. 12:14-16)

Psalm

Psalm 119:57-64

Keeping the law in spite of the wicked

Additional Reading

Genesis 31:1-3, 17-50

Laban and Jacob reconcile

Hymn: Oh, Praise the Gracious Power, ELW 651

God of hope, you reconciled the world to yourself through your Son's life, death, and resurrection. Use our actions in daily life to bring reconciliation into broken relationships and to create opportunities for peace to flourish.

Wednesday, February 23, 2011

Time after Epiphany

Polycarp, Bishop of Smyrna, martyr, 156

Luke 18:18-30
The rich young ruler

A certain ruler asked him, "Good Teacher, what must I do to inherit eternal life?" Jesus said to him, "Why do you call me good? No one is good but God alone. You know the commandments: 'You shall not commit adultery; You shall not murder; You shall not steal; You shall not bear false witness; Honor your father and mother.'" He replied, "I have kept all these since my youth." When Jesus heard this, he said to him, "There is still one thing lacking. Sell all that you own and distribute the money to the poor, and you will have treasure in heaven; then come, follow me." (Luke 18:18-22)

Psalm
Psalm 119:57-64
Keeping the law in spite of the wicked

Additional Reading
Proverbs 3:27-35
Regard for neighbors

Hymn: Let Streams of Living Justice, ELW 710

Almighty God, you offer us a heavenly treasure: your very heart in your Son, Jesus. Teach us to keep your grace at the center of our lives, and help us learn that when we give this treasure away there is always more.

Thursday, February 24, 2011

Time after Epiphany

Psalm 131

A child upon its mother's breast

O LORD, my heart is not lifted up,
   my eyes are not raised too high;
I do not occupy myself with things
   too great and too marvelous for me.
But I have calmed and quieted my soul,
   like a weaned child with its mother;
     my soul is like the weaned child that is with me.
O Israel, hope in the LORD
   from this time on and forevermore. (Ps. 131)

Additional Readings

Proverbs 12:22-28
Anxiety burdens the heart

Philippians 2:19-24
Timothy's worth

Hymn: Mothering God, You Gave Me Birth, ELW 735

Lord of all creation, you humbled yourself to become our flesh. When our lives get noisy and we become anxious and frightened, send us your Spirit to calm our fears. Break through the noise and speak peace to our hearts.

Friday, February 25, 2011

Time after Epiphany

Elizabeth Fedde, deaconess, 1921

Philippians 2:25-30
Paul overcomes anxiety

Still, I think it necessary to send to you Epaphroditus—my brother and co-worker and fellow soldier, your messenger and minister to my need; for he has been longing for all of you, and has been distressed because you heard that he was ill. He was indeed so ill that he nearly died. But God had mercy on him, and not only on him but on me also, so that I would not have one sorrow after another. I am the more eager to send him, therefore, in order that you may rejoice at seeing him again, and that I may be less anxious. Welcome him then in the Lord with all joy, and honor such people, because he came close to death for the work of Christ, risking his life to make up for those services that you could not give me. (Phil. 2:25-30)

Psalm
Psalm 131
A child upon its mother's breast

Additional Reading
Isaiah 26:1-6
Trust in God

Hymn: Remember and Rejoice, ELW 454

Almighty God, at all times and in all places you send messengers to carry your word to us. Guide us to trust the good news they bring, so that in all things we do not get anxious but rejoice in your presence.

Saturday, February 26, 2011

Time after Epiphany

Isaiah 31:1-9

Misplaced trust

Alas for those who go down to Egypt for help
   and who rely on horses,
who trust in chariots because they are many
   and in horsemen because they are very strong,
but do not look to the Holy One of Israel
   or consult the LORD!
Yet he too is wise and brings disaster;
   he does not call back his words,
but will rise against the house of the evildoers,
   and against the helpers of those who work iniquity.
The Egyptians are human, and not God;
   their horses are flesh, and not spirit.
When the LORD stretches out his hand,
   the helper will stumble, and the one helped will fall,
and they will all perish together. (Isa. 31:1-3)

Psalm	**Additional Reading**
Psalm 131	Luke 11:14-23
A child upon its mother's breast	*A house divided falls*

Hymn: Jesus, Priceless Treasure, ELW 775

Lord of creation, you came to create life and unity. In our stubborn insistence on getting our own way, we often cause division and disharmony. Fill us with hope instead of fear that we will reach across the barriers of our own making to create blessings for all.

Sunday, February 27, 2011

Eighth Sunday after Epiphany

Matthew 6:24-34
The teaching of Christ: trust in God

"Therefore do not worry, saying, 'What will we eat?' or 'What will we drink?' or 'What will we wear?' For it is the Gentiles who strive for all these things; and indeed your heavenly Father knows that you need all these things. But strive first for the kingdom of God and his righteousness, and all these things will be given to you as well.

"So do not worry about tomorrow, for tomorrow will bring worries of its own. Today's trouble is enough for today." (Matt. 6:31-34)

Psalm
Psalm 131
A child upon its mother's breast

Additional Readings
Isaiah 49:8-16a
God's motherly compassion

1 Corinthians 4:1-5
Servants accountable to God

Hymn: Praise to the Lord, the Almighty, ELW 858

God of tender care, like a mother, like a father, you never forget your children, and you know already what we need. In all our anxiety give us trusting and faithful hearts, that in confidence we may embody the peace and justice of your Son, Jesus Christ, our Savior and Lord.

Monday, February 28, 2011

Time after Epiphany

Psalm 104
God cares for all the earth

O LORD, how manifold are your works!
  In wisdom you have made them all;
  the earth is full of your creatures.
Yonder is the sea, great and wide,
  creeping things innumerable are there,
  living things both small and great.
There go the ships,
  and Leviathan that you formed to sport in it.
These all look to you
  to give them their food in due season;
when you give to them, they gather it up;
  when you open your hand, they are filled with good things.
  (Ps. 104:24-28)

Additional Readings
Deuteronomy 32:1-14   Hebrews 10:32-39
God's care for the chosen people   *Confidence that rewards*

Hymn: All Creatures, Worship God Most High! ELW 835

Lord of all creation, everything you have made praises you in earth, sea, and sky. In your boundless joy and love for us, we sing with all the earth and rejoice in the goodness you bring into our lives.

_____

_____

_____

_____

_____

_____

_____

_____

_____

_____

Tuesday, March 1, 2011

Time after Epiphany

George Herbert, hymnwriter, 1633

1 Kings 17:1-16

God feeds the widow

Elijah said to the widow, "Do not be afraid; go and do as you have said; but first make me a little cake of it and bring it to me, and afterwards make something for yourself and your son. For thus says the LORD the God of Israel: The jar of meal will not be emptied and the jug of oil will not fail until the day that the LORD sends rain on the earth." She went and did as Elijah said, so that she as well as he and her household ate for many days. The jar of meal was not emptied, neither did the jug of oil fail, according to the word of the LORD that he spoke by Elijah. (1 Kings 17:13-16)

Psalm
Psalm 104
God cares for all the earth

Additional Reading
1 Corinthians 4:6-21
The life of an apostle

Hymn: Guide Me Ever, Great Redeemer, ELW 618

God of hope and salvation, your powerful word comes to us still today in promises that are trustworthy and true. Keep us ever close to your word and help us to trust in your promises always.

Wednesday, March 2, 2011

Time after Epiphany

John Wesley, 1791; Charles Wesley, 1788; renewers of the church

Luke 12:22-31

Do not worry

[Jesus] said to his disciples, "Therefore I tell you, do not worry about your life, what you will eat, or about your body, what you will wear. For life is more than food, and the body more than clothing. Consider the ravens: they neither sow nor reap, they have neither storehouse nor barn, and yet God feeds them. Of how much more value are you than the birds! And can any of you by worrying add a single hour to your span of life? If then you are not able to do so small a thing as that, why do you worry about the rest?" (Luke 12:22-26)

Psalm
Psalm 104
God cares for all the earth

Additional Reading
Isaiah 66:7-13
God as a nursing mother

Hymn: Love Divine, All Loves Excelling, ELW 631

O God, worry sometimes consumes us and weighs us down, even as we pray for direction. Make your presence known in our lives and help us to hand our worries over to you, who alone can bring what is needed.

Thursday, March 3, 2011

Time after Epiphany

Psalm 2

The one begotten of God

I will tell of the decree of the LORD:
  He said to me, "You are my son;
    today I have begotten you.
  Ask of me, and I will make the nations your heritage,
    and the ends of the earth your possession.
  You shall break them with a rod of iron,
    and dash them in pieces like a potter's vessel."
  Now therefore, O kings, be wise;
    be warned, O rulers of the earth.
  Serve the LORD with fear,
    with trembling kiss his feet,
  or he will be angry, and you will perish in the way;
    for his wrath is quickly kindled. (Ps. 2:7-12)

Additional Readings

Exodus 6:2-9   Hebrews 8:1-7
God promises deliverance through Moses   *Christ, the mediator*

Hymn: O God of Love, O King of Peace, ELW 749

God of all creation, all power and majesty belong to you, and yet you bow down to show your love for each one of us. For this we thank you, and pray that you would keep us ever close to you.

Friday, March 4, 2011

Time after Epiphany

Hebrews 11:23-28
The faith of Moses

By faith Moses was hidden by his parents for three months after his birth, because they saw that the child was beautiful; and they were not afraid of the king's edict. By faith Moses, when he was grown up, refused to be called a son of Pharaoh's daughter, choosing rather to share ill-treatment with the people of God than to enjoy the fleeting pleasures of sin. He considered abuse suffered for the Christ to be greater wealth than the treasures of Egypt, for he was looking ahead to the reward. By faith he left Egypt, unafraid of the king's anger; for he persevered as though he saw him who is invisible. By faith he kept the Passover and the sprinkling of blood, so that the destroyer of the firstborn would not touch the firstborn of Israel. (Heb. 11:23-28)

Psalm
Psalm 2
The one begotten of God

Additional Reading
Exodus 19:9b-25
Israel consecrated at Sinai

Hymn: We've Come This Far by Faith, ELW 633

Spirit of God, deepen our faith through your holy word, so that our lives may be enriched, our spirits lifted, our paths enlightened, and our love for others filled with the love and presence of God.

Saturday, March 5, 2011

Time after Epiphany

Mark 9:9-13

The coming of Elijah

As they were coming down the mountain, he ordered them to tell no one about what they had seen, until after the Son of Man had risen from the dead. So they kept the matter to themselves, questioning what this rising from the dead could mean. Then they asked him, "Why do the scribes say that Elijah must come first?" He said to them, "Elijah is indeed coming first to restore all things. How then is it written about the Son of Man, that he is to go through many sufferings and be treated with contempt? But I tell you that Elijah has come, and they did to him whatever they pleased, as it is written about him." (Mark 9:9-13)

Psalm

Psalm 2

The one begotten of God

Additional Reading

1 Kings 21:20-29

Elijah pronounces God's sentence

Hymn: How Good, Lord, to Be Here! ELW 315

All knowing God, we are frequently confounded by life, and even your ways sometimes seem inscrutable, leaving us with many questions. Help us to find answers to our questions and refuge in your Son, Jesus Christ our Lord.

Sunday, March 6, 2011

Transfiguration of Our Lord

Matthew 17:1-9
Christ revealed as God's beloved Son

Six days later, Jesus took with him Peter and James and his brother John and led them up a high mountain, by themselves. And he was transfigured before them, and his face shone like the sun, and his clothes became dazzling white. Suddenly there appeared to them Moses and Elijah, talking with him. Then Peter said to Jesus, "Lord, it is good for us to be here; if you wish, I will make three dwellings here, one for you, one for Moses, and one for Elijah." While he was still speaking, suddenly a bright cloud overshadowed them, and from the cloud a voice said, "This is my Son, the Beloved; with him I am well pleased; listen to him!" (Matt. 17:1-5)

Psalm
Psalm 2
The one begotten of God

Additional Readings
Exodus 24:12-18
Moses enters the cloud of God's glory

2 Peter 1:16-21
Shining with the glory of God

Hymn: Jesus on the Mountain Peak, ELW 317

O God, in the transfiguration of your Son you confirmed the mysteries of the faith by the witness of Moses and Elijah, and in the voice from the bright cloud declaring Jesus your beloved Son, you foreshadowed our adoption as your children. Make us heirs with Christ of your glory, and bring us to enjoy its fullness, through Jesus Christ, our Savior and Lord, who lives and reigns with you and the Holy Spirit, one God, now and forever.

Monday, March 7, 2011

Time after Epiphany

Perpetua and Felicity and companions, martyrs at Carthage, 202

Psalm 78:17-20, 52-55
Israel led to God's holy mountain

Then he led out his people like sheep,
  and guided them in the wilderness like a flock.
He led them in safety, so that they were not afraid;
  but the sea overwhelmed their enemies.
And he brought them to his holy hill,
  to the mountain that his right hand had won.
He drove out nations before them;
  he apportioned them for a possession
  and settled the tribes of Israel in their tents. (Ps. 78:52-55)

Additional Readings
Exodus 33:7-23
Moses asks to see God's glory

Acts 7:30-34
Moses on holy ground

Hymn: All People That on Earth Do Dwell, ELW 883

Only in you, O God, do we find safety and direction for our lives. Guide us as you guided your people Israel in the wilderness and bring us also into the land of your promise.

Tuesday, March 8, 2011

Time after Epiphany

Romans 11:1-6
A remnant chosen by grace

I ask, then, has God rejected his people? By no means! I myself am an Israelite, a descendant of Abraham, a member of the tribe of Benjamin. God has not rejected his people whom he foreknew. Do you not know what the scripture says of Elijah, how he pleads with God against Israel? "Lord, they have killed your prophets, they have demolished your altars; I alone am left, and they are seeking my life." But what is the divine reply to him? "I have kept for myself seven thousand who have not bowed the knee to Baal." So too at the present time there is a remnant, chosen by grace. (Rom. 11:1-5)

Psalm
Psalm 78:17-20, 52-55
Israel led to God's holy mountain

Additional Readings
1 Kings 19:9-18
Elijah hears God

Hymn: Through the Night of Doubt and Sorrow, ELW 327

God of power and providence, there is nothing on earth that can confound or thwart your plan for the world and our lives. In times that may bewilder us, keep us faithful by your grace through Jesus Christ.

LENT

Lent is a forty-day journey to Easter. Christians keep company with Noah and his family, who were in the ark for forty days; with the Hebrews, who journeyed through the desert for forty years; and with Moses, Elijah, and Jesus, who fasted for forty days before they embarked on the tasks God had prepared for them.

During Lent Christians journey with those who are making final preparations for baptism at Easter. Together, Christians struggle with the meaning of their baptismal promises: Do you reject evil? Do you believe in God the Father, the Son, and the Holy Spirit? Do you believe in the church, the forgiveness of sins, the resurrection of the dead?

The disciples of the Lord Jesus are called to contend against everything that leads them away from love of God and neighbor. Fasting, prayer, and works of love—the disciplines of Lent—help the household rejoice in the gifts of baptism: God's forgiveness and mercy.

Blessing for the Lenten Season

Use this blessing to begin your prayer time during the season of Lent.

God of mercy,
as we move through the journey of this season
incite us to truthful reflection, faithful action,
and quiet release of all that is false and fleeting.
Deliver us from every evil and protect us from all anxiety
as we wait in joyful hope for the great feast of Easter,
the passover of the Lord Jesus from death to life with you.
Amen.

Table Prayer for the Season of Lent

Blessed are you, O Lord our God, maker of all things.
Through your goodness you have blessed us
with the gifts of this table.
Turn our hearts toward you,
and toward all those in need.
May our Lenten journey bring us to the rebirth of Easter,
through Christ our Lord.
Amen.

Table Prayer for Ash Wednesday (March 9)

Now, O Lord, is the day of salvation;
now, O Lord, you have given us life.
On this day of dust hear our praise
for all the life you grant us,
and hear our plea for all the world,
that you may have pity on the people
and gather them all into life,
through Christ our Lord.
Amen.

Wednesday, March 9, 2011

Ash Wednesday

Matthew 6:1-6, 16-21

The practice of faith

"Do not store up for yourselves treasures on earth, where moth and rust consume and where thieves break in and steal; but store up for yourselves treasures in heaven, where neither moth nor rust consumes and where thieves do not break in and steal. For where your treasure is, there your heart will be also." (Matt. 6:19-21)

Psalm
Psalm 51:1-17
Plea for mercy

Additional Readings
Joel 2:1-2, 12-17
Return to God

2 Cor. 5:20b—6:10
Now is the day of salvation

Hymn: The Glory of These Forty Days, ELW 320

Almighty and ever-living God, you hate nothing you have made, and you forgive the sins of all who are penitent. Create in us new and honest hearts, so that, truly repenting of our sins, we may receive from you, the God of all mercy, full pardon and forgiveness through your Son, Jesus Christ, our Savior and Lord, who lives and reigns with you and the Holy Spirit, one God, now and forever.

Thursday, March 10, 2011

Week before Lent 1

Harriet Tubman, 1913; Sojourner Truth, 1883; renewers of society

Psalm 51
Create in me a clean heart

Have mercy on me, O God,
   according to your steadfast love;
according to your abundant mercy
   blot out my transgressions.
Wash me thoroughly from my iniquity,
   and cleanse me from my sin.
For I know my transgressions,
   and my sin is ever before me.
Against you, you alone, have I sinned,
   and done what is evil in your sight,
so that you are justified in your sentence
   and blameless when you pass judgment.
Indeed, I was born guilty,
   a sinner when my mother conceived me. (Ps. 51:1-5)

Additional Readings

Jonah 3:1-10
Nineveh hears Jonah's preaching and repents

Romans 1:1-7
Appointed to preach the good news of Christ

Hymn: Lord, Teach Us How to Pray Aright, ELW 745

Have mercy on us, O God, as we enter into these holy days of Lent. Turn our hearts and our actions to you in repentance, faith, and renewal, that we may know the joy of your saving love through Jesus Christ.

Friday, March 11, 2011

Week before Lent 1

Jonah 4:1-11

God mercifully reproves Jonah

But this was very displeasing to Jonah, and he became angry. He prayed to the LORD and said, "O LORD! Is not this what I said while I was still in my own country? That is why I fled to Tarshish at the beginning; for I knew that you are a gracious God and merciful, slow to anger, and abounding in steadfast love, and ready to relent from punishing. And now, O LORD, please take my life from me, for it is better for me to die than to live." And the LORD said, "Is it right for you to be angry?" Then Jonah went out of the city and sat down east of the city, and made a booth for himself there. He sat under it in the shade, waiting to see what would become of the city. (Jonah 4:1-5)

Psalm
Psalm 51
Create in me a clean heart

Additional Reading
Romans 1:8-17
Live by faith

Hymn: God, Whose Giving Knows No Ending, ELW 678

Soften our hard hearts, O God, and fill us with forgiveness and compassion for those who so desperately need your love and guidance. Keep us from judging others and make us instruments of your peace and love.

Saturday, March 12, 2011

Week before Lent 1

Gregory the Great, Bishop of Rome, 604

Isaiah 58:1-12
The fast that God chooses

Is not this the fast that I choose:
    to loose the bonds of injustice,
    to undo the thongs of the yoke,
to let the oppressed go free,
    and to break every yoke?
Is it not to share your bread with the hungry,
    and bring the homeless poor into your house;
when you see the naked, to cover them,
    and not to hide yourself from your own kin?
Then your light shall break forth like the dawn,
    and your healing shall spring up quickly;
your vindicator shall go before you,
    the glory of the LORD shall be your rear guard.
Then you shall call, and the LORD will answer;
    you shall cry for help, and he will say, Here I am. (Isa. 58:6-9a)

Psalm
Psalm 51
Create in me a clean heart

Additional Reading
Matthew 18:1-7
The humble one is the greatest

Hymn: To Be Your Presence, ELW 546

O God, our help and our blessing, open our eyes to see and respond to injustice, oppression, hunger, and homelessness. Use our time, talents, and resources as blessings for the poor and make us beacons of your light.

Sunday, March 13, 2011

First Sunday in Lent

Matthew 4:1-11

The temptation of Jesus

Then Jesus was led up by the Spirit into the wilderness to be tempted by the devil. He fasted forty days and forty nights, and afterwards he was famished. The tempter came and said to him, "If you are the Son of God, command these stones to become loaves of bread." But he answered, "It is written,

'One does not live by bread alone,
but by every word that comes from the mouth of God.'"
(Matt. 4:1-4)

Psalm

Psalm 32
Mercy embraces us

Additional Readings

Genesis 2:15-17; 3:1-7   Romans 5:12-19

Eating of the tree of knowledge   *Death came, life comes*

Hymn: O Lord, throughout These Forty Days, ELW 319

Lord God, our strength, the struggle between good and evil rages within and around us, and the devil and all the forces that defy you tempt us with empty promises. Keep us steadfast in your word, and when we fall, raise us again and restore us through your Son, Jesus Christ, our Savior and Lord, who lives and reigns with you and the Holy Spirit, one God, now and forever.

Monday, March 14, 2011

Week of Lent 1

Psalm 32

Mercy embraces us

Happy are those whose transgression is forgiven,
    whose sin is covered.
Happy are those to whom the LORD imputes no iniquity,
    and in whose spirit there is no deceit.
While I kept silence, my body wasted away
    through my groaning all day long.
For day and night your hand was heavy upon me;
    my strength was dried up as by the heat of summer.
Then I acknowledged my sin to you,
    and I did not hide my iniquity;
I said, "I will confess my transgressions to the LORD,"
    and you forgave the guilt of my sin. (Ps. 32:1-5)

Additional Readings

1 Kings 19:1-8
An angel feeds Elijah in the wilderness

Hebrews 2:10-18
Christ goes before us in suffering

Hymn: God, My Lord, My Strength, ELW 795

O God, your Son Jesus Christ carried our sins to the cross so that they might be remembered no more. Help us always to confess our sins through him and receive the joy of your forgiveness and salvation.

Tuesday, March 15, 2011

Week of Lent 1

Hebrews 4:14—5:10
Christ was tempted as we are

Since, then, we have a great high priest who has passed through the heavens, Jesus, the Son of God, let us hold fast to our confession. For we do not have a high priest who is unable to sympathize with our weaknesses, but we have one who in every respect has been tested as we are, yet without sin. Let us therefore approach the throne of grace with boldness, so that we may receive mercy and find grace to help in time of need. (Heb. 4:14-16)

Psalm
Psalm 32
Mercy embraces us

Additional Reading
Genesis 4:1-16
God protects Cain

Hymn: Lord Jesus, Think on Me, ELW 599

Heavenly Father, you sent Jesus to be one of us so that he might bring our needs and struggles to you. Make us bold in prayer and constant in faith, that we might receive daily mercy and grace.

Wednesday, March 16, 2011

Week of Lent 1

Matthew 18:10-14
Not one of these little ones should be lost

"Take care that you do not despise one of these little ones; for, I tell you, in heaven their angels continually see the face of my Father in heaven. What do you think? If a shepherd has a hundred sheep, and one of them has gone astray, does he not leave the ninety-nine on the mountains and go in search of the one that went astray? And if he finds it, truly I tell you, he rejoices over it more than over the ninety-nine that never went astray. So it is not the will of your Father in heaven that one of these little ones should be lost." (Matt. 18:10-14)

Psalm
Psalm 32
Mercy embraces us

Additional Reading
Exodus 34:1-9, 27-28
God's revelation of mercy

Hymn: Have No Fear, Little Flock, ELW 764

Too often, O God, we feel like the lost sheep that has gone astray and we are frightened. Come to us when we are lost, great Shepherd, and surround us with your forgiving love.

Thursday, March 17, 2011

Week of Lent 1

Patrick, bishop, missionary to Ireland, 461

Psalm 121
The Lord watches over you

The LORD is your keeper;
  the LORD is your shade at your right hand.
The sun shall not strike you by day,
  nor the moon by night.
The LORD will keep you from all evil;
  he will keep your life.
The LORD will keep
  your going out and your coming in
  from this time on and forevermore. (Ps. 121:5-8)

Additional Readings
Isaiah 51:1-3   2 Timothy 1:3-7
Look to Abraham and Sarah   *Faith handed down from faithful mothers*

Hymn: Sing Praise to God, the Highest Good, ELW 871

We do not take a step in this life, O God, without your knowledge and care. Watch over our going out and our coming in, keep us safe from all evil, and guide us safely to your heavenly home.

Friday, March 18, 2011

Week of Lent 1

Micah 7:18-20
God's faithfulness

Who is a God like you, pardoning iniquity
   and passing over the transgression
   of the remnant of your possession?
He does not retain his anger forever,
   because he delights in showing clemency.
He will again have compassion upon us;
   he will tread our iniquities under foot.
You will cast all our sins
   into the depths of the sea.
You will show faithfulness to Jacob
   and unswerving loyalty to Abraham,
as you have sworn to our ancestors
   from the days of old. (Micah 7:18-20)

Psalm
Psalm 121
The Lord watches over you

Additional Reading
Romans 3:21-31
Paul relates law and faith

Hymn: Abide, O Dearest Jesus, ELW 539

God of faithfulness, your word speaks again and again of your steadfast love, even when your chosen people turn from you. Call us back to you as you called them back, that we too may know your grace and forgiveness.

Saturday, March 19, 2011

Joseph, Guardian of Jesus

Matthew 1:16, 18-21, 24a

The Lord appears to Joseph in a dream

Now the birth of Jesus the Messiah took place in this way. When his mother Mary had been engaged to Joseph, but before they lived together, she was found to be with child from the Holy Spirit. Her husband Joseph, being a righteous man and unwilling to expose her to public disgrace, planned to dismiss her quietly. But just when he had resolved to do this, an angel of the Lord appeared to him in a dream and said, "Joseph, son of David, do not be afraid to take Mary as your wife, for the child conceived in her is from the Holy Spirit. She will bear a son, and you are to name him Jesus, for he will save his people from their sins." (Matt. 1:18-21)

Psalm

Psalm 89:1-29

The Lord's steadfast love is established forever

Additional Readings

2 Samuel 7:4, 8-16

God makes a covenant with David

Romans 4:13-18

The promise to those who share Abraham's faith

Hymn: By All Your Saints, ELW 420 (stanza 9)

O God, from the family of your servant David you raised up Joseph to be the guardian of your incarnate Son and the husband of his blessed mother. Give us grace to imitate his uprightness of life and his obedience to your commands, through Jesus Christ, our Savior and Lord, who lives and reigns with you and the Holy Spirit, one God, now and forever.

Sunday, March 20, 2011

Second Sunday in Lent

John 3:1-17
The mission of Christ: saving the world

"And just as Moses lifted up the serpent in the wilderness, so must the Son of Man be lifted up, that whoever believes in him may have eternal life.

"For God so loved the world that he gave his only Son, so that everyone who believes in him may not perish but may have eternal life.

"Indeed, God did not send the Son into the world to condemn the world, but in order that the world might be saved through him." (John 3:14-17)

Psalm	**Additional Readings**	
Psalm 121	Genesis 12:1-4a	Romans 4:1-5, 13-17
The Lord watches over you	*The blessing of God upon Abram*	*The promise to those of Abraham's faith*

Hymn: God Loved the World, ELW 323

O God, our leader and guide, in the waters of baptism you bring us to new birth to live as your children. Strengthen our faith in your promises, that by your Spirit we may lift up your life to all the world through your Son, Jesus Christ, our Savior and Lord, who lives and reigns with you and the Holy Spirit, one God, now and forever.

Monday, March 21, 2011

Week of Lent 2

Thomas Cranmer, Bishop of Canterbury, martyr, 1556

Psalm 128
God promises life

Happy is everyone who fears the LORD,
  who walks in his ways.
You shall eat the fruit of the labor of your hands;
  you shall be happy, and it shall go well with you.
Your wife will be like a fruitful vine
  within your house;
your children will be like olive shoots
  around your table.
Thus shall the man be blessed
  who fears the LORD. (Ps. 128:1-4)

Additional Readings
Numbers 21:4-9
Moses lifts up the serpent

Hebrews 3:1-6
Moses the servant, Christ the son

Hymn: What a Fellowship, What a Joy Divine, ELW 774

You bless those who are faithful to you, O God. Keep us close to you through daily prayer, regular worship, study of the scriptures, and following your commands. Help us always to put you first in our lives.

Tuesday, March 22, 2011

Week of Lent 2

Jonathan Edwards, teacher, missionary to American Indians, 1758

Isaiah 65:17-25
God promises a new creation

For I am about to create new heavens
    and a new earth;
the former things shall not be remembered
    or come to mind.
But be glad and rejoice forever
    in what I am creating;
for I am about to create Jerusalem as a joy,
    and its people as a delight.
I will rejoice in Jerusalem,
    and delight in my people;
no more shall the sound of weeping be heard in it,
    or the cry of distress. (Isa. 65:17-19)

Psalm
Psalm 128
God promises life

Additional Reading
Romans 4:6-13
Abraham saved through faith

Hymn: Jerusalem, My Happy Home, ELW 628

O God, you are the hope of all who know despair and longing in this life. You are the creator of new things and new possibilities. Open our eyes to see the hope that you send us through Jesus Christ.

Wednesday, March 23, 2011

Week of Lent 2

John 7:53—8:11

Jesus does not condemn the sinner

The scribes and the Pharisees brought a woman who had been caught in adultery; and making her stand before all of them, they said to him, "Teacher, this woman was caught in the very act of committing adultery. Now in the law Moses commanded us to stone such women. Now what do you say?" They said this to test him, so that they might have some charge to bring against him. Jesus bent down and wrote with his finger on the ground. When they kept on questioning him, he straightened up and said to them, "Let anyone among you who is without sin be the first to throw a stone at her." (John 8:3-7)

Psalm

Psalm 128

God promises life

Additional Reading

Ezekiel 36:22-32

God will renew the people

Hymn: Softly and Tenderly Jesus Is Calling, ELW 608

Without your love and grace, O God, no one on this earth would survive your judgment, for we are all equally sinners in your sight. Thank you for sending your Son Jesus Christ, that we might be saved.

Thursday, March 24, 2011

Week of Lent 2

Oscar Arnulfo Romero, Bishop of El Salvador, martyr, 1980

Psalm 95
The rock of our salvation

O come, let us sing to the LORD;
　　let us make a joyful noise to the rock of our salvation!
Let us come into his presence with thanksgiving;
　　let us make a joyful noise to him with songs of praise!
For the LORD is a great God,
　　and a great King above all gods.
In his hand are the depths of the earth;
　　the heights of the mountains are his also.
The sea is his, for he made it,
　　and the dry land, which his hands have formed. (Ps. 95:1-5)

Additional Readings

Exodus 16:1-8
Israel complains of hunger in the wilderness

Colossians 1:15-23
Christ, the reconciliation of all things

Hymn: Let All Things Now Living, ELW 881

Creator God, the universe holds such wonders that we cannot behold them all, and yet you fashioned each intricate part. Make us good stewards of what you have made and help us to share that wonder with our children.

Friday, March 25, 2011

Annunciation of Our Lord

Luke 1:26-38

The angel greets Mary

In the sixth month the angel Gabriel was sent by God to a town in Galilee called Nazareth, to a virgin engaged to a man whose name was Joseph, of the house of David. The virgin's name was Mary. And he came to her and said, "Greetings, favored one! The Lord is with you." But she was much perplexed by his words and pondered what sort of greeting this might be. The angel said to her, "Do not be afraid, Mary, for you have found favor with God. And now, you will conceive in your womb and bear a son, and you will name him Jesus." (Luke 1:26-31)

Psalm
Psalm 45
Your name will be remembered

Additional Readings
Isaiah 7:10-14
A young woman will bear a son

Hebrews 10:4-10
The offering of Jesus' body sanctifies us

Hymn: The Only Son from Heaven, ELW 309

Pour your grace into our hearts, O God, that we who have known the incarnation of your Son, Jesus Christ, announced by an angel, may by his cross and passion be brought to the glory of his resurrection; for he lives and reigns with you, in the unity of the Holy Spirit, one God, now and forever.

Saturday, March 26, 2011

Week of Lent 2

Exodus 16:27-35
Manna and the sabbath

On the seventh day some of the people went out to gather [manna], and they found none. The LORD said to Moses, "How long will you refuse to keep my commandments and instructions? See! The LORD has given you the sabbath, therefore on the sixth day he gives you food for two days; each of you stay where you are; do not leave your place on the seventh day." So the people rested on the seventh day. (Exod. 16:27-30)

Psalm
Psalm 95
The rock of our salvation

Additional Reading
John 4:1-6
Jesus travels to Jacob's well in Samaria

Hymn: O Day of Rest and Gladness, ELW 521

O God, you created the sabbath as a day of rest and holiness for our lives. Keep us faithful to your sabbath commandment so that our bodies might be refreshed and our lives be kept holy in you.

Sunday, March 27, 2011

Third Sunday in Lent

John 4:5-42

The woman at the well

Jesus said to [the Samaritan woman], "Everyone who drinks of this water will be thirsty again, but those who drink of the water that I will give them will never be thirsty. The water that I will give will become in them a spring of water gushing up to eternal life." The woman said to him, "Sir, give me this water, so that I may never be thirsty or have to keep coming here to draw water." (John 4:13-15)

Psalm

Psalm 95

The rock of our salvation

Additional Readings

Exodus 17:1-7

Water from the rock

Romans 5:1-11

Reconciled to God by Christ's death

Hymn: Come to Me, All Pilgrims Thirsty, ELW 777

Merciful God, the fountain of living water, you quench our thirst and wash away our sin. Give us this water always. Bring us to drink from the well that flows with the beauty of your truth through Jesus Christ, our Savior and Lord, who lives and reigns with you and the Holy Spirit, one God, now and forever.

Monday, March 28, 2011

Week of Lent 3

Psalm 81
We drink from the rock

"But my people did not listen to my voice;
    Israel would not submit to me.
So I gave them over to their stubborn hearts,
    to follow their own counsels.
O that my people would listen to me,
    that Israel would walk in my ways!
Then I would quickly subdue their enemies,
    and turn my hand against their foes.
Those who hate the LORD would cringe before him,
    and their doom would last forever.
I would feed you with the finest of the wheat,
    and with honey from the rock I would satisfy you." (Ps. 81:11-16)

Additional Readings
Genesis 24:1-27
Rebekah at the well

2 John 1-13
A woman reminded to abide in Christ

Hymn: You Satisfy the Hungry Heart, ELW 484

Stubbornness plagues us, O God! In sorrow, we confess it. Yet we hear your promise of blessing and forgiveness for those who return to you. By your Holy Spirit, dispel our stubbornness and turn us lovingly to you.

Tuesday, March 29, 2011

Week of Lent 3

Hans Nielsen Hauge, renewer of the church, 1824

1 Corinthians 10:1-4

Drinking from Christ, the spiritual rock

I do not want you to be unaware, brothers and sisters, that our ancestors were all under the cloud, and all passed through the sea, and all were baptized into Moses in the cloud and in the sea, and all ate the same spiritual food, and all drank the same spiritual drink. For they drank from the spiritual rock that followed them, and the rock was Christ. (1 Cor. 10:1-4)

Psalm
Psalm 81
We drink from the rock

Additional Reading
Genesis 29:1-14
Rachel at the well

Hymn: O Jesus, Joy of Loving Hearts, ELW 658

O God, during these days of Lent we long for spiritual refreshment as one in the wilderness longs for food and water. Bring us faithfully to the feasting of Easter and the joys of the resurrection in Christ.

Wednesday, March 30, 2011

Week of Lent 3

John 7:14-31, 37-39

Drink of Jesus, the Messiah

On the last day of the festival, the great day, while Jesus was standing there, he cried out, "Let anyone who is thirsty come to me, and let the one who believes in me drink. As the scripture has said, 'Out of the believer's heart shall flow rivers of living water.'" Now he said this about the Spirit, which believers in him were to receive; for as yet there was no Spirit, because Jesus was not yet glorified. (John 7:37-39)

Psalm
Psalm 81
We drink from the rock

Additional Reading
Jeremiah 2:4-13
God, the living water

Hymn: Shall We Gather at the River, ELW 423

God our Father, you have washed us of our sins and adopted us as your children through the waters of baptism. Through every confession in Christ's name, return us to those baptismal waters for forgiveness, refreshment, and renewal.

Thursday, March 31, 2011

Week of Lent 3

John Donne, poet, 1631

Psalm 23

My head anointed with oil

Even though I walk through the darkest valley,
  I fear no evil;
for you are with me;
  your rod and your staff—
  they comfort me.
You prepare a table before me
  in the presence of my enemies;
you anoint my head with oil;
  my cup overflows.
Surely goodness and mercy shall follow me
  all the days of my life,
and I shall dwell in the house of the LORD
  my whole life long. (Ps. 23:4-6)

Additional Readings

1 Samuel 15:10-21
The prophet Samuel confronts the king

Ephesians 4:25-32
Called to honesty and forbearance

Hymn: My Shepherd, You Supply My Need, ELW 782

Loving God, dark valleys of loss and despair cannot be avoided in this life. Thank you for walking with us through these dark times and lending your rod and your staff to guide and comfort us.

_____

_____

_____

_____

_____

_____

_____

_____

_____

_____

_____

Friday, April 1, 2011

Week of Lent 3

Ephesians 5:1-9
Now in the Lord you are light

Let no one deceive you with empty words, for because of these things the wrath of God comes on those who are disobedient. Therefore do not be associated with them. For once you were darkness, but now in the Lord you are light. Live as children of light—for the fruit of the light is found in all that is good and right and true. (Eph. 5:6-9)

Psalm
Psalm 23
My head anointed with oil

Additional Reading
1 Samuel 15:22-31
The king confesses his sinful disobedience

Hymn: I Want to Walk as a Child of the Light, ELW 815

Creator God, in the holy season of Lent we call to mind our own empty words and deceptions. In your mercy, grant us grace to amend our sinful ways, through our Lord Jesus Christ.

Saturday, April 2, 2011

Week of Lent 3

1 Samuel 15:32-34
Samuel grieves over Saul

Then Samuel said, "Bring Agag king of the Amalekites here to me." And Agag came to him haltingly. Agag said, "Surely this is the bitterness of death." But Samuel said,

"As your sword has made women childless,
    so your mother shall be childless among women."

And Samuel hewed Agag in pieces before the LORD in Gilgal. Then Samuel went to Ramah; and Saul went up to his house in Gibeah of Saul. (1 Sam. 15:32-34)

Psalm
Psalm 23
My head anointed with oil

Additional Reading
John 1:1-9
Christ comes with light and life

Hymn: In All Our Grief, ELW 615

All-powerful God, your thoughts are not our thoughts and your ways are not our ways. In your mercy, grant us grace and humility to seek your will and act on it, trusting your wisdom above our own. This we ask through Christ our Lord.

Sunday, April 3, 2011

Fourth Sunday in Lent

John 9:1-41
The man born blind

Jesus heard that they had driven [out the man who had been blind], and when he found him, he said, "Do you believe in the Son of Man?" He answered, "And who is he, sir? Tell me, so that I may believe in him." Jesus said to him, "You have seen him, and the one speaking with you is he." He said, "Lord, I believe." And he worshiped him. Jesus said, "I came into this world for judgment so that those who do not see may see, and those who do see may become blind." (John 9:35-39)

Psalm
Psalm 23
My head anointed with oil

Additional Readings
1 Samuel 16:1-13
David is chosen and anointed

Ephesians 5:8-14
Live as children of light

Hymn: O Christ, Our Light, O Radiance True, ELW 675

Bend your ear to our prayers, Lord Christ, and come among us. By your gracious life and death for us, bring light into the darkness of our hearts, and anoint us with your Spirit, for you live and reign with the Father and the Holy Spirit, one God, now and forever.

Monday, April 4, 2011

Week of Lent 4

Benedict the African, confessor, 1589

Psalm 146
God opens the eyes of the blind

The LORD sets the prisoners free;
    the LORD opens the eyes of the blind.
The LORD lifts up those who are bowed down;
    the LORD loves the righteous.
The LORD watches over the strangers;
    he upholds the orphan and the widow,
    but the way of the wicked he brings to ruin.
The LORD will reign forever,
    your God, O Zion, for all generations.
Praise the LORD! (Ps. 146:7c-10)

Additional Readings
Isaiah 59:9-19
The blindness of injustice

Acts 9:1-20
Saul is baptized, his sight restored

Hymn: Praise the One Who Breaks the Darkness, ELW 843

Merciful One, your kindness is never-ending. Grant us grace to recognize our own blindnesses, our own prisons, and our own wickednesses, and then, help us to be freed from them as well. We pray through your Son, our Lord Jesus Christ.

Tuesday, April 5, 2011

Week of Lent 4

Isaiah 42:14-21

God will heal the blind

For a long time I have held my peace,
　I have kept still and restrained myself;
now I will cry out like a woman in labor,
　I will gasp and pant.
I will lay waste mountains and hills,
　and dry up all their herbage;
I will turn the rivers into islands,
　and dry up the pools.
I will lead the blind
　by a road they do not know,
by paths they have not known
　I will guide them.
I will turn the darkness before them into light,
　the rough places into level ground.
These are the things I will do,
　and I will not forsake them. (Isa. 42:14-16)

Psalm

Psalm 146
God opens the eyes of the blind

Additional Reading

Colossians 1:9-14
The inheritance of the saints in light

Hymn: In Deepest Night, ELW 699

*Holy One, you guide us along roads we do not know, smoothing our
paths and lighting our ways. Grant us grace to trust in you, O Lord, for
you will not forsake us. We pray through Jesus Christ our Lord.*

Wednesday, April 6, 2011

Week of Lent 4

Albrecht Dürer, 1528; Matthias Grünewald, 1529;
Lucas Cranach, 1553; artists

Matthew 9:27-34
Jesus heals the blind

As Jesus went on from there, two blind men followed him, crying loudly, "Have mercy on us, Son of David!" When he entered the house, the blind men came to him; and Jesus said to them, "Do you believe that I am able to do this?" They said to him, "Yes, Lord." Then he touched their eyes and said, "According to your faith let it be done to you." And their eyes were opened. Then Jesus sternly ordered them, "See that no one knows of this." But they went away and spread the news about him throughout that district. (Matt. 9:27-31)

Psalm
Psalm 146
God opens the eyes of the blind

Additional Reading
Isaiah 60:17-22
God our light

Hymn: You Are Mine, ELW 581

Lord our God, you heal the sick and give sight to the blind. Grant us grace to believe and help us to spread the good news to all we meet. This we ask through Jesus Christ our Lord.

Thursday, April 7, 2011

Week of Lent 4

Psalm 130
Mercy and redemption

Out of the depths I cry to you, O Lord.
  Lord, hear my voice!
Let your ears be attentive
  to the voice of my supplications!
If you, O Lord, should mark iniquities,
  Lord, who could stand?
But there is forgiveness with you,
  so that you may be revered. (Ps. 130:1-4)

Additional Readings

Ezekiel 1:1-3; 2:8—3:3
The word of God: lamentation and sweetness

Revelation 10:1-11
The word of God: bitter and sweet

Hymn: Out of the Depths I Cry to You, ELW 600

Merciful and loving God, with you we find mercy and fullness of redemption. Hear our voices as we cry to you and grant us grace ever to trust in you. We make our prayer through our Lord Jesus Christ.

Friday, April 8, 2011

Week of Lent 4

Revelation 11:15-19

The word of God: thanksgiving and singing

Then the twenty-four elders who sit on their thrones before God fell
on their faces and worshiped God, singing,
> "We give you thanks, Lord God Almighty,
>> who are and who were,
> for you have taken your great power
>> and begun to reign.
> The nations raged,
>> but your wrath has come,
>> and the time for judging the dead,
> for rewarding your servants, the prophets
>> and saints and all who fear your name,
>> both small and great,
> and for destroying those who destroy the earth."

Then God's temple in heaven was opened, and the ark of his
covenant was seen within his temple; and there were flashes of
lightning, rumblings, peals of thunder, an earthquake, and heavy
hail. (Rev. 11:16-19)

Psalm	Additional Reading
Psalm 130	Ezekiel 33:10-16
Mercy and redemption	*The word of God: repent and live*

Hymn: Blessing and Honor, ELW 854

*O Lord God Almighty, in the fullness of time your justice will reign.
Grant that we who fear your name will be judged worthy of reward
when that day shall come. We pray through our Lord Jesus Christ.*

Saturday, April 9, 2011

Week of Lent 4

Dietrich Bonhoeffer, theologian, 1945

Ezekiel 36:8-15
Blessings upon Israel

But you, O mountains of Israel, shall shoot out your branches, and yield your fruit to my people Israel; for they shall soon come home. See now, I am for you; I will turn to you, and you shall be tilled and sown; and I will multiply your population, the whole house of Israel, all of it; the towns shall be inhabited and the waste places rebuilt; and I will multiply human beings and animals upon you. They shall increase and be fruitful; and I will cause you to be inhabited as in your former times, and will do more good to you than ever before. Then you shall know that I am the LORD. I will lead people upon you—my people Israel—and they shall possess you, and you shall be their inheritance. No longer shall you bereave them of children. (Ezek. 36:8-12)

Psalm	Additional Reading
Psalm 130	Luke 24:44-53
Mercy and redemption	*Jesus blesses the disciples*

Hymn: Open Now Thy Gates of Beauty, ELW 533

O God of Israel, you promise good to us in more ways than we can imagine. Grant us grace to recognize the fulfillment of your timeless promise, through Jesus Christ, our Lord and Savior.

Sunday, April 10, 2011

Fifth Sunday in Lent

Michael Agricola, Bishop of Turku, 1557

John 11:1-45
The raising of Lazarus

And Jesus looked upward and said, "Father, I thank you for having heard me. I knew that you always hear me, but I have said this for the sake of the crowd standing here, so that they may believe that you sent me." When he had said this, he cried with a loud voice, "Lazarus, come out!" The dead man came out, his hands and feet bound with strips of cloth, and his face wrapped in a cloth. Jesus said to them, "Unbind him, and let him go."

Many of the Jews therefore, who had come with Mary and had seen what Jesus did, believed in him. (John 11:41b-45)

Psalm
Psalm 130
Mercy and redemption

Additional Readings
Ezekiel 37:1-14
The dry bones of Israel

Romans 8:6-11
Life in the Spirit

Hymn: When We Are Living, ELW 639

Almighty God, your Son came into the world to free us all from sin and death. Breathe upon us the power of your Spirit, that we may be raised to new life in Christ and serve you in righteousness all our days, through Jesus Christ, our Savior and Lord, who lives and reigns with you and the Holy Spirit, one God, now and forever.

Monday, April 11, 2011

Week of Lent 5

Psalm 143

Save me from death

Save me, O LORD, from my enemies;
   I have fled to you for refuge.
Teach me to do your will,
   for you are my God.
Let your good spirit lead me
   on a level path.
For your name's sake, O LORD, preserve my life.
   In your righteousness bring me out of trouble.
In your steadfast love cut off my enemies,
   and destroy all my adversaries,
     for I am your servant. (Ps. 143:9-12)

Additional Readings

1 Kings 17:17-24

Elijah raises the widow's son

Acts 20:7-12

Paul raises a young man

Hymn: Lord of Our Life, ELW 766

Saving Lord, we flee to you for refuge from our enemies, those that are both outside and within ourselves. Trusting in your steadfast love, we pray for salvation, through Jesus Christ our Lord.

Tuesday, April 12, 2011

Week of Lent 5

2 Kings 4:18-37

Elisha raises a child from death

When Elisha came into the house, he saw the child lying dead on his bed. So he went in and closed the door on the two of them, and prayed to the LORD. Then he got up on the bed and lay upon the child, putting his mouth upon his mouth, his eyes upon his eyes, and his hands upon his hands; and while he lay bent over him, the flesh of the child became warm. He got down, walked once to and fro in the room, then got up again and bent over him; the child sneezed seven times, and the child opened his eyes. Elisha summoned Gehazi and said, "Call the Shunammite woman." So he called her. When she came to him, he said, "Take your son." She came and fell at his feet, bowing to the ground; then she took her son and left. (2 Kings 4:32-37)

Psalm

Psalm 143

Save me from death

Additional Reading

Ephesians 2:1-10

Alive in Christ

Hymn: O God beyond All Praising, ELW 880

Live-giving Lord, we are awed by your mercy and power. Grant that we who have passed through the waters of the font may walk in newness of life filled with thanks and praise. This we pray through Jesus Christ our Lord.

Wednesday, April 13, 2011

Week of Lent 5

Jeremiah 32:1-9, 36-41
Jeremiah buys a field

Jeremiah said, The word of the LORD came to me: Hanamel son of your uncle Shallum is going to come to you and say, "Buy my field that is at Anathoth, for the right of redemption by purchase is yours." Then my cousin Hanamel came to me in the court of the guard, in accordance with the word of the LORD, and said to me, "Buy my field that is at Anathoth in the land of Benjamin, for the right of possession and redemption is yours; buy it for yourself." Then I knew that this was the word of the LORD. (Jer. 32:6-8)

Psalm
Psalm 143
Save me from death

Additional Reading
Matthew 22:23-33
God of the living

Hymn: Jesus, Priceless Treasure, ELW 775

Holy God, you have sent messengers and prophets to your people throughout the ages. Grant us the gift of discernment, that we may recognize your word when it comes to us. This we ask through our Lord Jesus Christ.

Thursday, April 14, 2011

Week of Lent 5

Psalm 31:9-16
I commend my spirit

Be gracious to me, O LORD, for I am in distress;
   my eye wastes away from grief,
   my soul and body also.
For my life is spent with sorrow,
   and my years with sighing;
my strength fails because of my misery,
   and my bones waste away.
But I trust in you, O LORD;
   I say, "You are my God."
My times are in your hand;
   deliver me from the hand of my enemies and persecutors.
Let your face shine upon your servant;
   save me in your steadfast love. (Ps. 31:9-10, 14-16)

Additional Readings
I Samuel 16:11-13
Samuel anoints David

Philippians 1:1-11
Encouraged to follow Christ's righteousness

Hymn: Jesus, Still Lead On, ELW 624

Gracious Lord, when we are in distress and wasting away from grief we are still in your hand. Grant us grace to trust in you and call upon you in our need. We pray through your Son, our Savior Jesus Christ.

Friday, April 15, 2011

Week of Lent 5

Philippians 1:21-30

Seeing Christ in this life

Only, live your life in a manner worthy of the gospel of Christ, so
that, whether I come and see you or am absent and hear about you,
I will know that you are standing firm in one spirit, striving side
by side with one mind for the faith of the gospel, and are in no way
intimidated by your opponents. For them this is evidence of their
destruction, but of your salvation. And this is God's doing. For he
has graciously granted you the privilege not only of believing in
Christ, but of suffering for him as well—since you are having the
same struggle that you saw I had and now hear that I still have.
(Phil. 1:27-30)

Psalm
Psalm 31:9-16
I commend my spirit

Additional Reading
Job 13:13-19
A servant keeps silence

Hymn: Give Thanks for Saints, ELW 428

*Lord our God, even when we are divided your mercy never ends. Grant
us courage to stand firm in one Spirit, living in a manner worthy of the
gospel. This we ask this through Jesus Christ our Lord.*

Saturday, April 16, 2011

Week of Lent 5

Mark 10:32-34

Going up to Jerusalem

They were on the road, going up to Jerusalem, and Jesus was walking ahead of them; they were amazed, and those who followed were afraid. He took the twelve aside again and began to tell them what was to happen to him, saying, "See, we are going up to Jerusalem, and the Son of Man will be handed over to the chief priests and the scribes, and they will condemn him to death; then they will hand him over to the Gentiles; they will mock him, and spit upon him, and flog him, and kill him; and after three days he will rise again." (Mark 10:32-34)

Psalm
Psalm 31:9-16
I commend my spirit

Additional Reading
Lamentations 3:55-66
A cry for help

Hymn: Tree of Life and Awesome Mystery, ELW 334

Lord our God, the road can seem dark at times. Grant us grace to follow close behind your Son when we are afraid and never lose faith in him. This we ask through our Lord Jesus Christ.

Holy Week

On the Sunday of the Passion, Christians enter into Holy Week. This day opens before the Christian community the final period of preparation before the celebration of the Three Days of the Lord's passion, death, and resurrection.

In many churches, palm branches will be given to worshipers for the procession into the worship space. Following an ancient custom, many Christians bring their palms home and place them in the household prayer center, behind a cross or sacred image, or above the indoor lintel of the entryway.

At sunset on Maundy Thursday, Lent comes to an end as the church begins the celebration of the events through which Christ has become the life and the resurrection for all who believe.

Prayer for Placing Palms in the Home
Use this blessing when placing palms in the home after the Palm Sunday liturgy.

Blessed is the One who comes in the name of the Lord!
May we who place these palms receive Christ into our midst
with the joy that marked the entrance to Jerusalem.
May be hold no betrayal in our hearts,
but peacefully welcome Christ
who lives and reigns with you and the Holy Spirit,
one God, now and forever. Amen.

Sunday, April 17, 2011

Sunday of the Passion
Palm Sunday

Matthew 26:14—27:66
The passion and death of Jesus

Then Jesus cried again with a loud voice and breathed his last. At that moment the curtain of the temple was torn in two, from top to bottom. The earth shook, and the rocks were split. The tombs also were opened, and many bodies of the saints who had fallen asleep were raised. After his resurrection they came out of the tombs and entered the holy city and appeared to many. Now when the centurion and those with him, who were keeping watch over Jesus, saw the earthquake and what took place, they were terrified and said, "Truly this man was God's Son!" (Matt. 27:50-54)

Psalm
Psalm 31:9-16
I commend my spirit

Additional Readings
Isaiah 50:4-9a
The servant submits to suffering

Philippians 2:5-11
Death on a cross

Hymn: Sing, My Tongue, ELW 355/356

Everlasting God, in your endless love for the human race you sent our Lord Jesus Christ to take on our nature and to suffer death on the cross. In your mercy enable us to share in his obedience to your will and in the glorious victory of his resurrection, who lives and reigns with you and the Holy Spirit, one God, now and forever.

Monday, April 18, 2011

Monday in Holy Week

Psalm 36:5-11
Refuge under the shadow of your wings

Your steadfast love, O Lord, extends to the heavens,
    your faithfulness to the clouds.
Your righteousness is like the mighty mountains,
    your judgments are like the great deep;
    you save humans and animals alike, O Lord.
How precious is your steadfast love, O God!
    All people may take refuge in the shadow of your wings.
They feast on the abundance of your house,
    and you give them drink from the river of your delights.
For with you is the fountain of life;
    in your light we see light. (Ps. 36:5-9)

Additional Readings

Isaiah 42:1-9
The servant brings forth justice

Hebrews 9:11-15
The blood of Christ redeems for eternal life

John 12:1-11
Mary of Bethany anoints Jesus

Hymn: My Song Is Love Unknown, ELW 343

O God, your Son chose the path that led to pain before joy and the cross before glory. Plant his cross in our hearts, so that in its power and love we may come at last to joy and glory, through Jesus Christ, our Savior and Lord, who lives and reigns with you and the Holy Spirit, one God, now and forever.

Tuesday, April 19, 2011

Tuesday in Holy Week

Olavus Petri, priest, 1552; Laurentius Petri, Bishop of Uppsala, 1573;
renewers of the church

1 Corinthians 1:18-31

The cross of Christ reveals God's power and wisdom

Where is the one who is wise? Where is the scribe? Where is the
debater of this age? Has not God made foolish the wisdom of the
world? For since, in the wisdom of God, the world did not know
God through wisdom, God decided, through the foolishness of our
proclamation, to save those who believe. For Jews demand signs and
Greeks desire wisdom, but we proclaim Christ crucified, a stumbling
block to Jews and foolishness to Gentiles, but to those who are the
called, both Jews and Greeks, Christ the power of God and the
wisdom of God. For God's foolishness is wiser than human wisdom,
and God's weakness is stronger than human strength. (1 Cor. 1:20-25)

Psalm	Additional Readings	
Psalm 71:1-14	Isaiah 49:1-7	John 12:20-36
From my mother's womb you have been my strength	*The servant brings salvation to earth's ends*	*Jesus speaks of his death*

Hymn: Jesus, Keep Me Near the Cross, ELW 335

*Lord Jesus, you have called us to follow you. Grant that our love may
not grow cold in your service, and that we may not fail or deny you in
the time of trial, for you live and reign with the Father and the Holy
Spirit, one God, now and forever.*

Wednesday, April 20, 2011

Wednesday in Holy Week

Isaiah 50:4-9a
The servant is vindicated by God

The Lord GOD has opened my ear,
 and I was not rebellious, I did not turn backward.
I gave my back to those who struck me,
 and my cheeks to those who pulled out the beard;
I did not hide my face from insult and spitting.
The Lord GOD helps me;
 therefore I have not been disgraced;
therefore I have set my face like flint,
 and I know that I shall not be put to shame;
 he who vindicates me is near.
Who will contend with me?
 Let us stand up together.
Who are my adversaries?
 Let them confront me.
It is the Lord GOD who helps me; who will declare me guilty? (Isa. 50:5-9a)

Psalm
Psalm 70
Be pleased, O God, to deliver me

Additional Readings
Hebrews 12:1-3
Look to Jesus, who endured the cross

John 13:21-32
Jesus foretells his betrayal

Hymn: Ah, Holy Jesus, ELW 349

Almighty God, your Son our Savior suffered at human hands and endured the shame of the cross. Grant that we may walk in the way of his cross and find it the way of life and peace, through Jesus Christ, our Savior and Lord, who lives and reigns with you and the Holy Spirit, one God, now and forever.

THE THREE DAYS

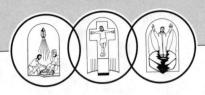

As the sun sets on Maundy Thursday, so Lent ends and the Three Days begin, ending with sunset on Easter Day. During these central days, Christians prepare to celebrate God's gift of new life given in baptism. Indeed, the readings of the Three Days move toward the baptismal font where new brothers and sisters are born of water and the Spirit, and where the baptized renew their baptismal promises.

In the home and in the church community, special attention is given to these days through prayer and keeping greater silence until the great Vigil of Easter is celebrated. Many Christians keep a fast from food, work, and entertainment on Good Friday and Holy Saturday. In the home, preparations can be made for the celebration of Easter: cleaning, coloring eggs, baking Easter breads, gathering greens or flowers to adorn crosses and sacred images. In those communities where baptisms will be celebrated, prayers may be offered for those to be received into the church.

Table Prayer for the Three Days

Blessed are you, O Lord our God.
With this food strengthen us on our journey from death to life.
We glory in the cross of Christ.
Raise us, with him, to the joy of the resurrection,
through Jesus Christ our Lord. Amen.

Blessing for Maundy Thursday

O God of love,
as your Son washed the feet of his disciples,
he revealed his undying love that would lead him to the cross.
May this simple act be a sign of our love for one another,
and our call to serve our neighbors and all those in need,
through Jesus Christ, our Savior and Lord. Amen.

Thursday, April 21, 2011

Maundy Thursday

Anselm, Bishop of Canterbury, 1109

John 13:1-17, 31b-35
The service of Christ: footwashing and meal

After [Jesus] had washed their feet, had put on his robe, and had returned to the table, he said to them, "Do you know what I have done to you? You call me Teacher and Lord—and you are right, for that is what I am. So if I, your Lord and Teacher, have washed your feet, you also ought to wash one another's feet. For I have set you an example, that you also should do as I have done to you." (John 13:12-15)

Psalm
Psalm 116:1-2, 12-19
The cup of salvation

Additional Readings
Exod. 12:1-4 [5-10] 11-14
The passover of the Lord

1 Corinthians 11:23-26
Proclaim the Lord's death

Hymn: Great God, Your Love Has Called Us, ELW 358

Holy God, source of all love, on the night of his betrayal, Jesus gave us a new commandment, to love one another as he loves us. Write this commandment in our hearts, and give us the will to serve others as he was the servant of all, your Son, Jesus Christ, our Savior and Lord, who lives and reigns with you and the Holy Spirit, one God, now and forever.

Blessing for Good Friday

O Christ, Lamb of God,
on this day we offer you the adoration of our hearts,
for on the cross you reveal your suffering love.
May we who celebrate the triumph of the cross,
receive the assurance of your victory over death
and the hope of resurrection,
for you live and reign forever and ever. Amen.

Friday, April 22, 2011

Good Friday

John 18:1—19:42
The passion and death of Jesus

When Jesus saw his mother and the disciple whom he loved standing beside her, he said to his mother, "Woman, here is your son." Then he said to the disciple, "Here is your mother." And from that hour the disciple took her into his own home.

After this, when Jesus knew that all was now finished, he said (in order to fulfill the scripture), "I am thirsty." A jar full of sour wine was standing there. So they put a sponge full of the wine on a branch of hyssop and held it to his mouth. When Jesus had received the wine, he said, "It is finished." Then he bowed his head and gave up his spirit. (John 19:26-30)

Psalm
Psalm 22
Why have you forsaken me?

Additional Readings
Isaiah 52:13—53:12
The suffering servant

Hebrews 10:16-25
The way to God is opened

Hymn: There in God's Garden, ELW 342

Almighty God, look with loving mercy on your family, for whom our Lord Jesus Christ was willing to be betrayed, to be given over to the hands of sinners, and to suffer death on the cross; who now lives and reigns with you and the Holy Spirit, one God, now and forever.

Blessing for Easter Eve

God of new life,
through our baptism into Christ you have raised us with him
to the joy of the resurrection.
You have brought us through the Red Sea
and fed us with the food and drink of the promised land.
May the fire of your love renew our faith
and deepen our commitment to you,
that we might faithfully live in the covenant of our baptism,
through Christ our Lord. Amen.

Prayer for Those Preparing for Baptism

Merciful and most high God, creator and giver of life,
you have called all people from darkness into light,
from error into truth, from death into life.
Grant grace to *name/s* and bless *them*.
Raise *them* by your Spirit.
Revive *them* by your word.
Form *them* by your hand.
Bring *them* to the water of life and to the bread and cup of blessing,
that with all you people *they* may bear witness to your grace
and praise you forever through Jesus Christ our Lord. Amen.

Saturday, April 23, 2011

Resurrection of Our Lord
Vigil of Easter

Toyohiko Kagawa, renewer of society, 1960

Romans 6:3-11
Dying and rising with Christ

Do you not know that all of us who have been baptized into Christ Jesus were baptized into his death? Therefore we have been buried with him by baptism into death, so that, just as Christ was raised from the dead by the glory of the Father, so we too might walk in newness of life.

For if we have been united with him in a death like his, we will certainly be united with him in a resurrection like his. (Rom. 6:3-5)

Psalm
Isaiah 12:2-6
With joy you will draw water from the wells of salvation

Additional Readings
Isaiah 55:1-11
Salvation freely offered to all

John 20:1-18
Seeing the risen Christ

Hymn: Come, You Faithful, Raise the Strain, ELW 363

Eternal giver of life and light, this holy night shines with the radiance of the risen Christ. Renew your church with the Spirit given us in baptism, that we may worship you in sincerity and truth and may shine as a light in the world, through your Son, Jesus Christ our Lord, who lives and reigns with you and the Holy Spirit, one God, now and forever.

Sunday, April 24, 2011

Resurrection of Our Lord
Easter Day

Matthew 28:1-10
Proclaim the resurrection

But the angel said to the women, "Do not be afraid; I know that you are looking for Jesus who was crucified. He is not here; for he has been raised, as he said. Come, see the place where he lay. Then go quickly and tell his disciples, 'He has been raised from the dead, and indeed he is going ahead of you to Galilee; there you will see him.' This is my message for you." So they left the tomb quickly with fear and great joy, and ran to tell his disciples. (Matt. 28:5-8)

Psalm
Psalm 118:1-2, 14-24
On this day God has acted

Additional Readings
Acts 10:34-43
God raised Jesus on the third day

Colossians 3:1-4
Raised with Christ

Hymn: Christ Has Arisen, Alleluia, ELW 364

O God, you gave your only Son to suffer death on the cross for our redemption, and by his glorious resurrection you delivered us from the power of death. Make us die every day to sin, that we may live with him forever in the joy of the resurrection, through your Son, Jesus Christ our Lord, who lives and reigns with you and the Holy Spirit, one God, now and forever.

EASTER

The Three Days flow into the rejoicing of the fifty days of Easter. During this "week of weeks," Christians explore the meaning of the central actions of baptism for daily life: the renouncing of evil and the professing of faith, washing in water, being marked with the cross, clothing in the white robe, receiving the light of the paschal/Easter candle, and eating and drinking the bread of life and the cup of salvation.

The fifty days were once called *Pentecost*, Greek for "fifty." On the fiftieth day of Easter, Christians celebrate the pentecostal mystery of the risen Christ breathing on the church the breath, the wind, and the fire of the Holy Spirit.

Blessing of the Easter Meal

Use this reading and prayer before your first meal on Easter

On this mountain the LORD of hosts
will make for all peoples
a feast of rich food, a feast of well-aged wines,
of rich food filled with marrow, or well-aged wines strained clear.
And he will destroy on this mountain
the shroud that is cast over all peoples,
the sheet that is spread over all nations;
he will swallow up death forever. (Isa. 26:6-7)

O Lord our God, creator of the universe,
we praise you with greater joy than ever on this day
as we celebrate your triumph over the power of death.
You prepare a rich feast and invite the hungry to your table.
Bless us and this food of our first Easter meal
which we have received from your goodness.
Strengthen us in faith and lead us to the heavenly banquet,
through Christ our Lord. Amen.

Table Prayer for the Season of Easter

O God of our risen Lord, we praise you, we bless you,
we worship you for the gifts of life you give us.
Always you offer us life, and for this we bless your holy name.
And we ask you,
give your life also to all who know only hunger and the pangs of death.
So may the whole world be raised to life,
through Jesus Christ, our Savior and Lord. Amen.

Monday, April 25, 2011

Mark, Evangelist

Mark 1:1-15
The beginning of the gospel of Jesus Christ

The beginning of the good news of Jesus Christ, the Son of God.
   As it is written in the prophet Isaiah,
   "See, I am sending my messenger ahead of you,
      who will prepare your way;
   the voice of one crying out in the wilderness:
      'Prepare the way of the Lord,
      make his paths straight,'"
John the baptizer appeared in the wilderness, proclaiming a baptism of repentance for the forgiveness of sins. And people from the whole Judean countryside and all the people of Jerusalem were going out to him, and were baptized by him in the river Jordan, confessing their sins. (Mark 1:1-5)

Psalm
Psalm 57
Be merciful to me, O God

Additional Readings
Isaiah 52:7-10
The messenger announces salvation

2 Timothy 4:6-11, 18
The good fight of faith

Hymn: Open Your Ears, O Faithful People, ELW 519

Almighty God, you have enriched your church with Mark's proclamation of the gospel. Give us grace to believe firmly in the good news of salvation and to walk daily in accord with it, through Jesus Christ, our Savior and Lord, who lives and reigns with you and the Holy Spirit, one God, now and forever.

Tuesday, April 26, 2011

Week of Easter I

Psalm 118:1-2, 14-24

On this day God has acted

The stone that the builders rejected
   has become the chief cornerstone.
This is the LORD's doing;
   it is marvelous in our eyes.
This is the day that the LORD has made;
   let us rejoice and be glad in it. (Ps. 118:22-24)

Additional Readings

Exodus 15:1-18   Colossians 3:12-17
Song at the sea   *The new life in Christ*

Hymn: Christ Is Risen! Shout Hosanna! ELW 383

Blessed are you, O God, for you do marvelous things! Let all your creation give you thanks and praise together. This we pray through our risen Lord Jesus Christ, who lives and reigns with you and the Holy Spirit, one God, now and forever.

Wednesday, April 27, 2011

Week of Easter I

Matthew 28:1-10
Proclaim the resurrection

[T]he angel said to the women, "Do not be afraid; I know that you are looking for Jesus who was crucified. He is not here; for he has been raised, as he said. Come, see the place where he lay. Then go quickly and tell his disciples, 'He has been raised from the dead, and indeed he is going ahead of you to Galilee; there you will see him.' This is my message for you." So they left the tomb quickly with fear and great joy, and ran to tell his disciples. Suddenly Jesus met them and said, "Greetings!" And they came to him, took hold of his feet, and worshiped him. Then Jesus said to them, "Do not be afraid; go and tell my brothers to go to Galilee; there they will see me." (Matt. 28:5-10)

Psalm
Psalm 118:1-2, 14-24
On this day God has acted

Additional Readings
Joshua 3:1-17
Israel crosses into the promised land

Hymn: The Day of Resurrection! ELW 361

Blessed are you, Holy One, for you send messengers with good news. Grant that we may always run to pass on that good news with great joy. We rejoice with our risen Lord Jesus Christ, who lives and reigns with you and the Holy Spirit, one God, now and forever.

Thursday, April 28, 2011

Week of Easter 1

Psalm 16
Fullness of joy

I bless the LORD who gives me counsel;
   in the night also my heart instructs me.
I keep the LORD always before me;
   because he is at my right hand, I shall not be moved.
Therefore my heart is glad, and my soul rejoices;
   my body also rests secure.
For you do not give me up to Sheol,
   or let your faithful one see the Pit.
You show me the path of life.
   In your presence there is fullness of joy;
   in your right hand are pleasures forevermore. (Ps. 16:7-11)

Additional Readings
Song of Solomon 2:8-15
Arise, for the winter is past

Colossians 4:2-5
The new life in Christ

Hymn: In Thee Is Gladness, ELW 867

Blessed are you, O God, for you are always at our right hand, and in your presence there is fullness of joy. We rejoice together with our risen Lord Jesus Christ, who lives and reigns with you and the Holy Spirit, one God, now and forever.

Friday, April 29, 2011

Week of Easter 1

Catherine of Siena, theologian, 1380

1 Corinthians 15:1-11

Witnesses to the risen Christ

For I handed on to you as of first importance what I in turn had received: that Christ died for our sins in accordance with the scriptures, and that he was buried, and that he was raised on the third day in accordance with the scriptures, and that he appeared to Cephas, then to the twelve. Then he appeared to more than five hundred brothers and sisters at one time, most of whom are still alive, though some have died. Then he appeared to James, then to all the apostles. Last of all, as to one untimely born, he appeared also to me. (1 Cor. 15:3-8)

Psalm

Psalm 16

Fullness of joy

Additional Reading

Song of Solomon 5:9—6:3

The beloved in the garden

Hymn: Now the Green Blade Rises, ELW 379

Blessed are you, ever-living God, for in the resurrection of your Son you have revealed your love. May we joyfully hand on the good news we have received, through our risen Lord Jesus Christ, who lives and reigns with you and the Holy Spirit, one God, now and forever.

Saturday, April 30, 2011

Week of Easter 1

Song of Solomon 8:6-7

Love is strong as death

Set me as a seal upon your heart,
   as a seal upon your arm;
for love is strong as death,
   passion fierce as the grave.
Its flashes are flashes of fire,
   a raging flame.
Many waters cannot quench love,
   neither can floods drown it.
If one offered for love
   all the wealth of his house,
    it would be utterly scorned. (Song of Sol. 8:6-7)

Psalm

Psalm 16

Fullness of joy

Additional Reading

John 20:11-20

The witness of Mary Magdalene

Hymn: Come, My Way, My Truth, My Life, ELW 816

Blessed are you, eternal God, for you have revealed that your love is stronger than death and fiercer than the grave. We praise you through our risen Lord Jesus Christ, who lives and reigns with you and the Holy Spirit, one God, now and forever.

Sunday, May 1, 2011

Second Sunday of Easter

Philip and James, Apostles (transferred to May 2)

John 20:19-31

Beholding the wounds of the risen Christ

A week later [Jesus'] disciples were again in the house, and Thomas was with them. Although the doors were shut, Jesus came and stood among them and said, "Peace be with you." Then he said to Thomas, "Put your finger here and see my hands. Reach out your hand and put it in my side. Do not doubt but believe." Thomas answered him, "My Lord and my God!" Jesus said to him, "Have you believed because you have seen me? Blessed are those who have not seen and yet have come to believe." (John 20:26-29)

Psalm	Additional Readings	
Psalm 16	Acts 2:14a, 22-32	1 Peter 1:3-9
Fullness of joy	*God fulfills the promise to David*	*New birth to a living hope*

Hymn: The Risen Christ, ELW 390

Almighty and eternal God, the strength of those who believe and the hope of those who doubt, may we, who have not seen, have faith in you and receive the fullness of Christ's blessing, who lives and reigns with you and the Holy Spirit, one God, now and forever.

Monday, May 2, 2011

Philip and James, Apostles *(transferred)*

Athanasius, Bishop of Alexandria, 373

John 14:8-14
The Son and the Father are one

Philip said to him, "Lord, show us the Father, and we will be satisfied." Jesus said to him, "Have I been with you all this time, Philip, and you still do not know me? Whoever has seen me has seen the Father. How can you say, 'Show us the Father'? Do you not believe that I am in the Father and the Father is in me? The words that I say to you I do not speak on my own; but the Father who dwells in me does his works." (John 14:8-10)

Psalm
Psalm 44:1-3, 20-26
Save us for the sake of your love

Additional Readings
Isaiah 30:18-21
God's mercy and justice

2 Corinthians 4:1-6
Proclaiming Jesus Christ as Lord

Hymn: Thine Is the Glory, ELW 376

Almighty God, you gave to your apostles Philip and James grace and strength to bear witness to your Son. Grant that we, remembering their victory of faith, may glorify in life and death the name of our Lord Jesus Christ, who lives and reigns and you and the Holy Spirit, one God, now and forever.

Tuesday, May 3, 2011

Week of Easter 2

1 Corinthians 15:19-28

Paul teaches the resurrection

For since death came through a human being, the resurrection of the dead has also come through a human being; for as all die in Adam, so all will be made alive in Christ. But each in his own order: Christ the first fruits, then at his coming those who belong to Christ. Then comes the end, when he hands over the kingdom to God the Father, after he has destroyed every ruler and every authority and power. For he must reign until he has put all his enemies under his feet. (1 Cor. 15:21-25)

Psalm

Psalm 114

God saves through water

Additional Reading

Jonah 1:1-17

Jonah saved from the sea

Hymn: This Joyful Eastertide, ELW 391

Lord God, you rule over heaven and earth. Renew our hope in the resurrection and the promise of life beyond the injustice, cruelty, and indifference of our human institutions, while also helping us to transform our world so it may better reflect your glory.

Wednesday, May 4, 2011

Week of Easter 2

Monica, mother of Augustine, 387

Matthew 12:38-42

Jesus speaks of the sign of Jonah

Then some of the scribes and Pharisees said to him, "Teacher, we wish to see a sign from you." But he answered them, "An evil and adulterous generation asks for a sign, but no sign will be given to it except the sign of the prophet Jonah. For just as Jonah was three days and three nights in the belly of the sea monster, so for three days and three nights the Son of Man will be in the heart of the earth. The people of Nineveh will rise up at the judgment with this generation and condemn it, because they repented at the proclamation of Jonah, and see, something greater than Jonah is here! The queen of the South will rise up at the judgment with this generation and condemn it, because she came from the ends of the earth to listen to the wisdom of Solomon, and see, something greater than Solomon is here!" (Matt. 12:38-42)

Psalm

Psalm 114
God saves through water

Additional Reading

Jonah 2:1-10
Jonah's praise for deliverance

Hymn: The Strife Is O'er, the Battle Done, ELW 366

God of life and light, guide us through this dark world. Grant us eyes to see all the wonder and mystery that your creation, incarnation, and resurrection contain so that we may trust in your word as we yearn for your kingdom.

Thursday, May 5, 2011

Week of Easter 2

Psalm 116:1-4, 12-19

I will call upon God

What shall I return to the LORD
   for all his bounty to me?
I will lift up the cup of salvation
   and call on the name of the LORD,
I will pay my vows to the LORD
   in the presence of all his people.
Precious in the sight of the LORD
   is the death of his faithful ones. (Ps. 116:12-15)

Additional Readings

Isaiah 25:1-5
Praise for deliverance

1 Peter 1:8b-12
The promised salvation comes

Hymn: Christ, the Life of All the Living, ELW 339

*We call on your name, O Lord. Assure us that our prayers, our pleas,
and even our cries are heard by you. May your promise of salvation
bring dawn to our darkness.*

Friday, May 6, 2011

Week of Easter 2

Isaiah 26:1-4
God sets up victory like bulwarks

On that day this song will be sung in the land of Judah:
We have a strong city;
   he sets up victory
   like walls and bulwarks.
Open the gates,
   so that the righteous nation that keeps faith
   may enter in.
Those of steadfast mind you keep in peace—
   in peace because they trust in you.
Trust in the LORD forever,
   for in the LORD GOD
   you have an everlasting rock. (Isa. 26:1-4)

Psalm
Psalm 116:1-4, 12-19
I will call upon God

Additional Reading
1 Peter 1:13-16
A holy life

Hymn: Dear Christians, One and All, Rejoice, ELW 594

Trusting in your promise and singing your song of victory, we rest in the peace that can only come through faith in your everlasting love. Place in our hearts the melody of your faithfulness so we may chant your praise without ceasing.

Saturday, May 7, 2011

Week of Easter 2

Luke 14:12-14

Welcome those in need to your table

He said also to the one who had invited him, "When you give a luncheon or a dinner, do not invite your friends or your brothers or your relatives or rich neighbors, in case they may invite you in return, and you would be repaid. But when you give a banquet, invite the poor, the crippled, the lame, and the blind. And you will be blessed, because they cannot repay you, for you will be repaid at the resurrection of the righteous." (Luke 14:12-14)

Psalm

Psalm 116:1-4, 12-19

I will call upon God

Additional Reading

Isaiah 25:6-9

The feast for all peoples

Hymn: Let Us Go Now to the Banquet, ELW 523

Stir in us, O God of the poor, a yearning for justice, for righteousness, and for fellowship. Embolden us to reach beyond our comfortable relationships to be beacons of hospitality, generosity, and humility, in your holy name.

Blessing for Mother's Day (May 8)

Under your wings, O Lord, you have held us,
as a mother holds her young.
Look with favor on all those women
who have sheltered children in their loving care.
Guide that they may lead;
strengthen that they may be tender;
grant wisdom that the people may live;
and hold all in your loving gaze
until we see you face to face.
Amen.

Sunday, May 8, 2011

Third Sunday of Easter

Julian of Norwich, renewer of the church, c. 1416

Luke 24:13-35

Eating with the risen Christ

As they came near the village to which they were going, walked ahead as if he were going on. But they urged him strongly, saying, "Stay with us, [Jesus] because it is almost evening and the day is now nearly over." So he went in to stay with them. When he was at the table with them, he took bread, blessed and broke it, and gave it to them. Then their eyes were opened, and they recognized him; and he vanished from their sight. They said to each other, "Were not our hearts burning within us while he was talking to us on the road, while he was opening the scriptures to us?" (Luke 24:28-32)

Psalm

Psalm 116:1-4, 12-19

I will call upon God

Additional Readings

Acts 2:14a, 36-41

Receiving God's promise through baptism

1 Peter 1:17-23

Born anew

Hymn: Day of Arising, ELW 374

O God, your Son makes himself known to all his disciples in the breaking of bread. Open the eyes of our faith, that we may see him in his redeeming work, who lives and reigns with you and the Holy Spirit, one God, now and forever.

Monday, May 9, 2011

Week of Easter 3

Nicolaus Ludwig von Zinzendorf, renewer of the church, hymnwriter, 1760

Psalm 134
Praise God day and night

Come, bless the LORD, all you servants of the LORD,
    who stand by night in the house of the LORD!
Lift up your hands to the holy place,
    and bless the LORD.
May the LORD, maker of heaven and earth,
    bless you from Zion. (Ps. 134:1-3)

Additional Readings
Genesis 18:1-14
Abraham and Sarah eat with God

1 Peter 1:23-25
The word of God endures

Hymn: The Trumpets Sound, the Angels Sing, ELW 531

Creator God, we come before you this day in celebration of all that you have given us. Continue to bless us with the fruits of the earth, the fruits of our labors, and the fruits of your Spirit.

Tuesday, May 10, 2011

Week of Easter 3

1 Peter 2:1-3

Long for the pure spiritual milk

Rid yourselves, therefore, of all malice, and all guile, insincerity, envy, and all slander. Like newborn infants, long for the pure, spiritual milk, so that by it you may grow into salvation—if indeed you have tasted that the Lord is good. (1 Peter 2:1-3)

Psalm

Psalm 134
Praise God day and night

Additional Reading

Proverbs 8:32—9:6
Wisdom serves a meal

Hymn: All Who Hunger, Gather Gladly, ELW 461

God, you who are both mother and father, cradle us in your arms. You who are both ruler and servant, guide us in our small steps toward maturity. You who are both bread and wine, nourish our bodies and purify our hearts.

Wednesday, May 11, 2011

Week of Easter 3

Exodus 24:1-11

Moses and the elders eat with God

Then Moses and Aaron, Nadab, and Abihu, and seventy of the elders of Israel went up, and they saw the God of Israel. Under his feet there was something like a pavement of sapphire stone, like the very heaven for clearness. God did not lay his hand on the chief men of the people of Israel; also they beheld God, and they ate and drank. (Exod. 24:9-11)

Psalm
Psalm 134
Praise God day and night

Additional Reading
John 21:1-14
The risen Christ eats with the disciples

Hymn: At the Lamb's High Feast We Sing, ELW 362

We long, O God of Moses and Aaron, for your presence in our world. Show us the heavenly banquet prepared for your children and give us a glimpse of the salvation that you have promised.

Thursday, May 12, 2011

Week of Easter 3

Psalm 23
God our shepherd

Even though I walk through the darkest valley,
   I fear no evil;
for you are with me;
   your rod and your staff—
   they comfort me.
You prepare a table before me
   in the presence of my enemies;
you anoint my head with oil;
   my cup overflows.
Surely goodness and mercy shall follow me
   all the days of my life,
and I shall dwell in the house of the Lord
   my whole life long. (Ps. 23:4-6)

Additional Readings
Exodus 2:15b-25
Moses the shepherd

1 Peter 2:9-12
Living as God's people

Hymn: Shepherd Me, O God, ELW 780

Shepherd us, O God. May we feel your direction, your protection, and even your correction when we go astray. We walk with the warmth of your goodness and mercy in our hearts; may it sustain us through even the darkest valleys.

Friday, May 13, 2011

Week of Easter 3

1 Peter 2:13-17

Living honorably in the world

For the Lord's sake accept the authority of every human institution, whether of the emperor as supreme, or of governors, as sent by him to punish those who do wrong and to praise those who do right. For it is God's will that by doing right you should silence the ignorance of the foolish. As servants of God, live as free people, yet do not use your freedom as a pretext for evil. Honor everyone. Love the family of believers. Fear God. Honor the emperor. (1 Peter 2:13-17)

Psalm

Psalm 23

God our shepherd

Additional Reading

Exodus 3:16-22; 4:18-20

Moses the shepherd of Israel

Hymn: What God Ordains Is Good Indeed, ELW 776

Lord God, ruler of the universe, we bow before you and you alone. You have given humanity gifts of mind and heart to care for one another and to protect your creation. Help us in our efforts to do justice, love kindness, and walk humbly in your ways.

Saturday, May 14, 2011

Matthias, Apostle

Luke 6:12-16
Jesus calls the Twelve

Now during those days he went out to the mountain to pray; and he spent the night in prayer to God. And when day came, he called his disciples and chose twelve of them, whom he also named apostles: Simon, whom he named Peter, and his brother Andrew, and James, and John, and Philip, and Bartholomew, and Matthew, and Thomas, and James son of Alphaeus, and Simon, who was called the Zealot, and Judas son of James, and Judas Iscariot, who became a traitor. (Luke 6:12-16)

Psalm

Psalm 56
*I am bound by the vow
I made to you*

Additional Readings

Isaiah 66:1-2
*Heaven is God's throne,
earth is God's footstool*

Acts 1:15-26
*The apostles cast lots for
Matthias*

Hymn: The Church of Christ, in Every Age, ELW 729

Almighty God, you chose your faithful servant Matthias to be numbered among the twelve. Grant that your church may always be taught and guided by faithful and true pastors, through Jesus Christ our shepherd, who lives and reigns with you and the Holy Spirit, one God, now and forever.

Sunday, May 15, 2011

Fourth Sunday of Easter

John 10:1-10
Christ the shepherd

So again Jesus said to them, "Very truly, I tell you, I am the gate for the sheep. All who came before me are thieves and bandits; but the sheep did not listen to them. I am the gate. Whoever enters by me will be saved, and will come in and go out and find pasture. The thief comes only to steal and kill and destroy. I came that they may have life, and have it abundantly." (John 10:7-10)

Psalm

Psalm 23
God our shepherd

Additional Readings

Acts 2:42-47
The believers' common life

1 Peter 2:19-25
Follow the shepherd, even in suffering

Hymn: The Lord's My Shepherd, ELW 778

O God our shepherd, you know your sheep by name and lead us to safety through the valleys of death. Guide us by your voice, that we may walk in certainty and security to the joyous feast prepared in your house, through Jesus Christ, our Savior and Lord, who lives and reigns with you and the Holy Spirit, one God, now and forever.

Monday, May 16, 2011

Week of Easter 4

Psalm 100
We are the sheep of God's pasture

Make a joyful noise to the LORD, all the earth.
　　Worship the LORD with gladness;
　　come into his presence with singing.
Know that the LORD is God.
　　It is he that made us, and we are his;
　　we are his people, and the sheep of his pasture.
Enter his gates with thanksgiving,
　　and his courts with praise.
　　Give thanks to him, bless his name.
For the LORD is good;
　　his steadfast love endures forever,
　　and his faithfulness to all generations. (Ps. 100:1-5)

Additional Readings
Ezekiel 34:17-23
God the true shepherd

1 Peter 5:1-5
Tend the flock of God

Hymn: All People That on Earth Do Dwell, ELW 883

God of all generations, we come into your presence this day with singing and gladness, with praise and thanksgiving! Renew our spirits with your steadfast love and faithfulness so we can join the song of our ancestors, the song of all creation, in your holy name.

Tuesday, May 17, 2011

Week of Easter 4

Hebrews 13:20-21

God's blessing through Christ the shepherd

Now may the God of peace, who brought back from the dead our
Lord Jesus, the great shepherd of the sheep, by the blood of the eternal
covenant, make you complete in everything good so that you may
do his will, working among us that which is pleasing in his sight,
through Jesus Christ, to whom be the glory forever and ever. Amen.
(Heb. 13:20-21)

Psalm
Psalm 100
We are the sheep of God's pasture

Additional Reading
Ezekiel 34:23-31
God provides perfect pasture

Hymn: Go, My Children, with My Blessing, ELW 543

God of peace, you have sheltered us, comforted us, and guided us
through your Son, Jesus Christ our Lord and shepherd. We thank you
for giving us the strength and skills to do your will and give glory to you
forever and ever.

Wednesday, May 18, 2011

Week of Easter 4

Erik, King of Sweden, martyr, 1160

Jeremiah 23:1-8
God will gather the flock

Woe to the shepherds who destroy and scatter the sheep of my pasture! says the Lord. Therefore thus says the Lord, the God of Israel, concerning the shepherds who shepherd my people: It is you who have scattered my flock, and have driven them away, and you have not attended to them. So I will attend to you for your evil doings, says the Lord. Then I myself will gather the remnant of my flock out of all the lands where I have driven them, and I will bring them back to their fold, and they shall be fruitful and multiply. I will raise up shepherds over them who will shepherd them, and they shall not fear any longer, or be dismayed, nor shall any be missing, says the Lord. (Jer. 23:1-4)

Psalm
Psalm 100
We are the sheep of God's pasture

Additional Reading
Matthew 20:17-28
Jesus came to serve

Hymn: Gather Us In, ELW 532

We look to you, O true Shepherd, to gather us together. Show us the path back to your flock, where we can leave our fears and failings behind, trusting that you will care for and preserve each of us in your everlasting mercy.

Thursday, May 19, 2011

Week of Easter 4

Psalm 31:1-5, 15-16
I commend my spirit

In you, O LORD, I seek refuge;
    do not let me ever be put to shame;
    in your righteousness deliver me.
Incline your ear to me;
    rescue me speedily.
Be a rock of refuge for me,
    a strong fortress to save me.
You are indeed my rock and my fortress;
    for your name's sake lead me and guide me,
take me out of the net that is hidden for me,
    for you are my refuge.
Into your hand I commit my spirit;
    you have redeemed me, O LORD, faithful God. (Ps. 31:1-5)

Additional Readings
Genesis 12:1-3
The call of Abram

Acts 6:8-15
Stephen is arrested

Hymn: Shout to the Lord, ELW 821

O Lord, our faithful God, protect us! Though we have fallen away, we take heart that you, O Redeemer, will never turn from us. Lead us and guide our spirits back to your holy, perfect, and eternal peace.

Friday, May 20, 2011

Week of Easter 4

Exodus 3:1-12
Moses at the burning bush

When the LORD saw that [Moses] had turned aside to see, God called to him out of the bush, "Moses, Moses!" And he said, "Here I am." Then he said, "Come no closer! Remove the sandals from your feet, for the place on which you are standing is holy ground." He said further, "I am the God of your father, the God of Abraham, the God of Isaac, and the God of Jacob." And Moses hid his face, for he was afraid to look at God. (Exod. 3:4-6)

Psalm
Psalm 31:1-5, 15-16
I commend my spirit

Additional Reading
Acts 7:1-16
Stephen addresses the council

Hymn: Christ Is Risen! Alleluia! ELW 382

God of our fathers and mothers, we call on your name and know that you hear us. Daily we walk on the holy ground of your creation, surrounded by your Spirit and strengthened by the promise of the resurrection of Jesus Christ.

Saturday, May 21, 2011

Week of Easter 4

Helena, mother of Constantine, c. 330

Jeremiah 26:20-24
A prophet of the Lord persecuted

There was another man prophesying in the name of the LORD, Uriah son of Shemaiah from Kiriath-jearim. He prophesied against this city and against this land in words exactly like those of Jeremiah. And when King Jehoiakim, with all his warriors and all the officials, heard his words, the king sought to put him to death; but when Uriah heard of it, he was afraid and fled and escaped to Egypt. Then King Jehoiakim sent Elnathan son of Achbor and men with him to Egypt, and they took Uriah from Egypt and brought him to King Jehoiakim, who struck him down with the sword and threw his dead body into the burial place of the common people.

But the hand of Ahikam son of Shaphan was with Jeremiah so that he was not given over into the hands of the people to be put to death. (Jer. 26:20-24)

Psalm
Psalm 31:1-5, 15-16
I commend my spirit

Additional Reading
John 8:48-59
Jesus the greater prophet

Hymn: Faith of Our Fathers, ELW 812/813

We follow your ways, O God, knowing that the world may turn against us. We ask you for the strength to persevere in the face of persecution, pain, or even death, confident in your promise of eternal life.

Sunday, May 22, 2011

Fifth Sunday of Easter

John 14:1-14

Christ the way, truth, life

Philip said to [Jesus], "Lord, show us the Father, and we will be satisfied." Jesus said to him, "Have I been with you all this time, Philip, and you still do not know me? Whoever has seen me has seen the Father. How can you say, 'Show us the Father'? Do you not believe that I am in the Father and the Father is in me? The words that I say to you I do not speak on my own; but the Father who dwells in me does his works. Believe me that I am in the Father and the Father is in me; but if you do not, then believe me because of the works themselves. Very truly, I tell you, the one who believes in me will also do the works that I do and, in fact, will do greater works than these, because I am going to the Father." (John 14:8-12)

Psalm	Additional Readings	
Psalm 31:1-5, 15-16	Acts 7:55-60	1 Peter 2:2-10
I commend my spirit	*Martyrdom of Stephen*	*God's chosen people*

Hymn: You Are the Way, ELW 758

Almighty God, your Son Jesus Christ is the way, the truth, and the life. Give us grace to love one another, to follow in the way of his commandments, and to share his risen life with all the world, for he lives and reigns with you and the Holy Spirit, one God, now and forever.

Monday, May 23, 2011

Week of Easter 5

Psalm 102:1-17
Prayer for deliverance

But you, O LORD, are enthroned forever;
  your name endures to all generations.
You will rise up and have compassion on Zion,
  for it is time to favor it;
  the appointed time has come.
For your servants hold its stones dear,
  and have pity on its dust.
The nations will fear the name of the LORD,
  and all the kings of the earth your glory.
For the LORD will build up Zion;
  he will appear in his glory. (Ps. 102:12-16)

Additional Readings

Exodus 13:17-22
God leads the way

Acts 7:17-40
Stephen addresses the council

Hymn: O God of Every Nation, ELW 713

Lord God, ruler of the universe, we bow before your throne. All creation sings your praise, all the earth trembles in your holy presence. Show compassion to us, your lowly and humble servants, and deliver us from evil, in your eternal and perfect mercy.

Tuesday, May 24, 2011

Week of Easter 5

Nicolaus Copernicus, 1543; Leonhard Euler, 1783; scientists

Proverbs 3:5-12
God, the truth and life

Trust in the LORD with all your heart,
   and do not rely on your own insight.
In all your ways acknowledge him,
   and he will make straight your paths.
Do not be wise in your own eyes;
   fear the LORD, and turn away from evil.
It will be a healing for your flesh
   and a refreshment for your body. (Prov. 3:5-8)

Psalm
Psalm 102:1-17
Prayer for deliverance

Additional Reading
Acts 7:44-56
Stephen confronts the council

Hymn: All My Hope on God Is Founded, ELW 757

*Lord God, we place our trust in you. Guide our steps, heal our flesh,
refresh our spirits. We ask this in the name of your Son, Jesus Christ,
our Lord, who perfectly trusted in you.*

Wednesday, May 25, 2011

Week of Easter 5

John 8:31-38
Jesus, the truth of God

Jesus answered them, "Very truly, I tell you, everyone who commits sin is a slave to sin. The slave does not have a permanent place in the household; the son has a place there forever. So if the Son makes you free, you will be free indeed. I know that you are descendants of Abraham; yet you look for an opportunity to kill me, because there is no place in you for my word. I declare what I have seen in the Father's presence; as for you, you should do what you have heard from the Father." (John 8:34-38)

Psalm
Psalm 102:1-17
Prayer for deliverance

Additional Reading
Proverbs 3:13-18
God, the truth and life

Hymn: Awake, My Heart, with Gladness, ELW 378

God the Father, you sent your Son to make us free. Because of Emmanuel, God-made-flesh, you have restored us from being slaves to sin into free, faithful followers of Jesus Christ. We praise your name and join the unending hymn of all creation: thanks be to God!

Thursday, May 26, 2011

Week of Easter 5

Psalm 66:8-20

Be joyful in God, all you lands

Bless our God, O peoples,
  let the sound of his praise be heard,
who has kept us among the living,
  and has not let our feet slip.
For you, O God, have tested us;
  you have tried us as silver is tried.
You brought us into the net;
  you laid burdens on our backs;
you let people ride over our heads;
  we went through fire and through water;
yet you have brought us out to a spacious place. (Ps. 66:8-12)

Additional Readings

Genesis 6:5-22
God's command to Noah

Acts 27:1-12
Paul sails for Rome

Hymn: Christ Jesus Lay in Death's Strong Bands, ELW 370

O God, we are a blessed people! We echo your blessings with our songs of praise and adoration. May our lives be a continuous demonstration of our thankfulness, our devotion, and the glory that is yours alone.

Friday, May 27, 2011

Week of Easter 5

John Calvin, renewer of the church, 1564

Genesis 7:1-24
The great flood

Then the LORD said to Noah, "Go into the ark, you and all your household, for I have seen that you alone are righteous before me in this generation. Take with you seven pairs of all clean animals, the male and its mate; and a pair of the animals that are not clean, the male and its mate; and seven pairs of the birds of the air also, male and female, to keep their kind alive on the face of all the earth. For in seven days I will send rain on the earth for forty days and forty nights; and every living thing that I have made I will blot out from the face of the ground." And Noah did all that the LORD had commanded him. (Gen. 7:1-5)

Psalm
Psalm 66:8-20
Be joyful in God, all you lands

Additional Reading
Acts 27:13-38
Paul survives shipwreck

Hymn: Thy Holy Wings, ELW 613

Lord of flood and famine, of water and wind, of creation and destruction: we plead for mercy. As you cared enough to save the animals and birds, inspire us to follow your commands and care for your whole creation.

Saturday, May 28, 2011

Week of Easter 5

John 14:27-29
Peace I leave with you

"Peace I leave with you; my peace I give to you. I do not give to you as the world gives. Do not let your hearts be troubled, and do not let them be afraid. You heard me say to you, 'I am going away, and I am coming to you.' If you loved me, you would rejoice that I am going to the Father, because the Father is greater than I. And now I have told you this before it occurs, so that when it does occur, you may believe." (John 14:27-29)

Psalm
Psalm 66:8-20
Be joyful in God, all you lands

Additional Reading
Genesis 8:13-19
The flood waters subside

Hymn: Alleluia! Sing to Jesus, ELW 392

God of peace, calm our hearts. How anxious we are! How we toss and turn, how we worry and fret about tomorrow, about yesterday, about eternity. Silence the voices of chaos and fear in our souls and still our minds that we may hear your word.

Sunday, May 29, 2011

Sixth Sunday of Easter

Jiří Tranovský, hymnwriter, 1637

John 14:15-21
Christ our advocate

"If you love me, you will keep my commandments. And I will ask the Father, and he will give you another Advocate, to be with you forever. This is the Spirit of truth, whom the world cannot receive, because it neither sees him nor knows him. You know him, because he abides with you, and he will be in you." (John 14:15-17)

Psalm
Psalm 66:8-20
Be joyful in God, all you lands

Additional Readings
Acts 17:22-31
Paul's message to the Athenians

1 Peter 3:13-22
The days of Noah, a sign of baptism

Hymn: O Spirit of Life, ELW 405

Almighty and ever-living God, you hold together all things in heaven and on earth. In your great mercy receive the prayers of all your children, and give to all the world the Spirit of your truth and peace, through Jesus Christ, our Savior and Lord, who lives and reigns with you and the Holy Spirit, one God, now and forever.

Monday, May 30, 2011

Week of Easter 6

Psalm 93

God reigns above the floods

The LORD is king, he is robed in majesty;
   the LORD is robed, he is girded with strength.
He has established the world; it shall never be moved;
   your throne is established from of old;
   you are from everlasting.
The floods have lifted up, O LORD,
   the floods have lifted up their voice;
   the floods lift up their roaring.
More majestic than the thunders of mighty waters,
   more majestic than the waves of the sea,
   majestic on high is the LORD!
Your decrees are very sure;
   holiness befits your house,
   O LORD, forevermore. (Ps. 93:1-5)

Additional Readings

Genesis 9:8-17
Sign of the covenant

Acts 27:39-44
Paul and companions come safely to land

Hymn: Come, Thou Almighty King, ELW 408

O Lord God, we praise your name. We are surrounded by your awesome majesty and power. Startle us with reminders of your omnipotence. Shock us with demonstrations of your might. Save us with your Son, Jesus Christ, our Redeemer and Lord.

Tuesday, May 31, 2011

Visit of Mary to Elizabeth

Luke 1:39-57
Mary greets Elizabeth

In those days Mary set out and went with haste to a Judean town in the hill country, where she entered the house of Zechariah and greeted Elizabeth. When Elizabeth heard Mary's greeting, the child leaped in her womb. And Elizabeth was filled with the Holy Spirit and exclaimed with a loud cry, "Blessed are you among women, and blessed is the fruit of your womb." (Luke 1:39-42)

Psalm
Psalm 113
God, the helper of the needy

Additional Readings
1 Samuel 2:1-10
Hannah's thanksgiving

Romans 12:9-16b
Rejoice with those who rejoice

Hymn: Unexpected and Mysterious, ELW 258

Mighty God, by whose grace Elizabeth rejoiced with Mary and greeted her as the mother of the Lord: look with favor on your lowly servants that, with Mary, we may magnify your holy name and rejoice to acclaim her Son as our Savior, who lives and reigns with you and the Holy Spirit, one God, now and forever.

_____

_____

_____

_____

_____

_____

_____

_____

_____

_____

Wednesday, June 1, 2011

Week of Easter 6

Justin, martyr at Rome, c. 165

John 16:16-24

A little while, and you shall see

"A little while, and you will no longer see me, and again a little while, and you will see me." Then some of his disciples said to one another, "What does he mean by saying to us, 'A little while, and you will no longer see me, and again a little while, and you will see me'; and 'Because I am going to the Father'?" They said, "What does he mean by this 'a little while'? We do not know what he is talking about." Jesus knew that they wanted to ask him, so he said to them, "Are you discussing among yourselves what I meant when I said, 'A little while, and you will no longer see me, and again a little while, and you will see me'? Very truly, I tell you, you will weep and mourn, but the world will rejoice; you will have pain, but your pain will turn into joy." (John 16:16-20)

Psalm

Psalm 93

God reigns above the floods

Additional Reading

Deuteronomy 31:1-13

Moses promises God's presence

Hymn: Lord, Thee I Love with All My Heart, ELW 750

God of mysteries, we confess that we hear your voice, but like the disciples we often do not understand what you are talking about. Reveal yourself when we weep and speak to our pain, that it may turn into the joy of your presence.

Thursday, June 2, 2011

Ascension of Our Lord

Luke 24:44-53

Christ present in all times and places

Then [Jesus] opened their minds to understand the scriptures, and he said to them, "Thus it is written, that the Messiah is to suffer and to rise from the dead on the third day, and that repentance and forgiveness of sins is to be proclaimed in his name to all nations, beginning from Jerusalem. You are witnesses of these things. And see, I am sending upon you what my Father promised; so stay here in the city until you have been clothed with power from on high." (Luke 24:45-49)

Psalm
Psalm 47
God has gone up with a shout

Additional Readings
Acts 1:1-11
Jesus sends the apostles

Ephesians 1:15-23
Seeing the risen and ascended Christ

Hymn: A Hymn of Glory Let Us Sing! ELW 393

Almighty God, your only Son was taken into the heavens and in your presence intercedes for us. Receive us and our prayers for all the world, and in the end bring everything into your glory, through Jesus Christ, our Sovereign and Lord, who lives and reigns with you and the Holy Spirit, one God, now and forever.

Friday, June 3, 2011

Week of Easter 6

The Martyrs of Uganda, 1886; John XXIII, Bishop of Rome, 1963

Psalm 93
Praise to God who reigns

The LORD is king, he is robed in majesty;
    the LORD is robed, he is girded with strength.
He has established the world; it shall never be moved;
    your throne is established from of old;
    you are from everlasting.
The floods have lifted up, O LORD,
    the floods have lifted up their voice;
    the floods lift up their roaring.
More majestic than the thunders of mighty waters,
    more majestic than the waves of the sea,
    majestic on high is the LORD!
Your decrees are very sure;
    holiness befits your house,
    O LORD, forevermore. (Ps. 93)

Additional Readings

2 Kings 2:1-12
Elijah ascends in a chariot of fire

Ephesians 2:1-7
Seated in the heavenly places with Christ

Hymn: Rejoice, for Christ Is King! ELW 430

O mighty king, your power creates and sustains all things. Bend our pride to your authority that we might acknowledge your majesty and power over our world.

Saturday, June 4, 2011

Week of Easter 6

2 Kings 2:13-15
The spirit rests on Elisha

He picked up the mantle of Elijah that had fallen from him, and went back and stood on the bank of the Jordan. He took the mantle of Elijah that had fallen from him, and struck the water, saying, "Where is the LORD, the God of Elijah?" When he had struck the water, the water was parted to the one side and to the other, and Elisha went over.

When the company of prophets who were at Jericho saw him at a distance, they declared, "The spirit of Elijah rests on Elisha." They came to meet him and bowed to the ground before him.
(2 Kings 2:13-15)

Psalm
Psalm 93
Praise to God who reigns

Additional Reading
John 8:21-30
Jesus speaks of going to the Father

Hymn: Give to Our God Immortal Praise! ELW 848

King of Israel, let your Spirit fall again on your people, that filled with your presence we may enter distant places of our world to announce that your kingdom has drawn near.

Sunday, June 5, 2011

Seventh Sunday of Easter

Boniface, Bishop of Mainz, missionary to Germany, martyr, 754

John 17:1-11

Christ's prayer for his disciples

"I have made your name known to those whom you gave me from the world. They were yours, and you gave them to me, and they have kept your word. Now they know that everything you have given me is from you; for the words that you gave to me I have given to them, and they have received them and know in truth that I came from you; and they have believed that you sent me. I am asking on their behalf; I am not asking on behalf of the world, but on behalf of those whom you gave me, because they are yours. All mine are yours, and yours are mine; and I have been glorified in them. And now I am no longer in the world, but they are in the world, and I am coming to you. Holy Father, protect them in your name that you have given me, so that they may be one, as we are one." (John 17:6-11)

Psalm

Psalm 68:1-10, 32-35

Sing to God

Additional Readings

Acts 1:6-14

Jesus' companions at prayer

1 Peter 4:12-14; 5:6-11

God sustains those who suffer

Hymn: Lord, Who the Night You Were Betrayed, ELW 463

O God of glory, your Son Jesus Christ suffered for us and ascended to your right hand. Unite us with Christ and each other, in suffering and in joy, that all the world may be drawn into your bountiful presence, through Jesus Christ, our Savior and Lord, who lives and reigns with you and the Holy Spirit, one God, now and forever.

Monday, June 6, 2011

Week of Easter 7

Psalm 99

Priests and people praise God

The LORD is king; let the peoples tremble!
　　He sits enthroned upon the cherubim; let the earth quake!
The LORD is great in Zion;
　　he is exalted over all the peoples.
Let them praise your great and awesome name.
　　Holy is he!
Mighty King, lover of justice,
　　you have established equity;
you have executed justice
　　and righteousness in Jacob.
Extol the LORD our God;
　　worship at his footstool.
　　Holy is he! (Ps. 99:1-5)

Additional Readings

Leviticus 9:1-11, 22-24　　　　　**1 Peter 4:1-6**
The high priest Aaron offers sacrifice　　*Live by the will of God*

Hymn: Oh, Worship the King, ELW 842

Eternal Trinity, you rule heaven and earth with both justice and mercy. May we, your people, not only proclaim your kingdom but also be a living sign of it in our daily lives and communities.

Tuesday, June 7, 2011

Week of Easter 7

Seattle, chief of the Duwamish Confederacy, 1866

1 Peter 4:7-11
Be good stewards of grace

The end of all things is near; therefore be serious and discipline yourselves for the sake of your prayers. Above all, maintain constant love for one another, for love covers a multitude of sins. Be hospitable to one another without complaining. Like good stewards of the manifold grace of God, serve one another with whatever gift each of you has received. Whoever speaks must do so as one speaking the very words of God; whoever serves must do so with the strength that God supplies, so that God may be glorified in all things through Jesus Christ. To him belong the glory and the power forever and ever. Amen. (1 Peter 4:7-11)

Psalm
Psalm 99
Priests and people praise God

Additional Reading
Numbers 16:41-50
The high priest Aaron makes atonement

Hymn: We All Are One in Mission, ELW 576

Giver of life, you have called us into community to share all that you have given us. Grant that we may be generous with the grace that you have first shown us, that in it Jesus might be glorified.

Wednesday, June 8, 2011

Week of Easter 7

1 Kings 8:54-65
Solomon offers sacrifice

Then the king, and all Israel with him, offered sacrifice before the LORD. Solomon offered as sacrifices of well-being to the LORD twenty-two thousand oxen and one hundred twenty thousand sheep. So the king and all the people of Israel dedicated the house of the LORD. The same day the king consecrated the middle of the court that was in front of the house of the LORD; for there he offered the burnt offerings and the grain offerings and the fat pieces of the sacrifices of well-being, because the bronze altar that was before the LORD was too small to receive the burnt offerings and the grain offerings and the fat pieces of the sacrifices of well-being.

So Solomon held the festival at that time, and all Israel with him— a great assembly, people from Lebo-hamath to the Wadi of Egypt— before the LORD our God, seven days. (1 Kings 8:62-65)

Psalm
Psalm 99
Priests and people praise God

Additional Reading
John 3:31-36
The Son and the Father

Hymn: Jesus Shall Reign, ELW 434

O Lord our God, too often our giving is reduced to sharing that which is left over. Help us learn to dedicate the entire possessions and talents of our lives to your glory.

Thursday, June 9, 2011

Week of Easter 7

Columba, 597; Aidan, 651; Bede, 735; renewers of the church

Psalm 33:12-22
Our help and our shield

Truly the eye of the LORD is on those who fear him,
   on those who hope in his steadfast love,
to deliver their soul from death,
   and to keep them alive in famine.
Our soul waits for the LORD;
   he is our help and shield.
Our heart is glad in him,
   because we trust in his holy name.
Let your steadfast love, O LORD, be upon us,
   even as we hope in you. (Ps. 33:18-22)

Additional Readings
Exodus 19:1-9a   Acts 2:1-11
The covenant at Sinai   *The giving of the Spirit*

Hymn: Jesus Lives, My Sure Defense, ELW 621

Look upon us, O Lord, and set us aflame with your Spirit. Preserve us from all harm and send us to proclaim your greatness to everyone, that you might be the hope of all people.

Friday, June 10, 2011

Week of Easter 7

Romans 8:14-17

Led by the Spirit of God

For all who are led by the Spirit of God are children of God. For you did not receive a spirit of slavery to fall back into fear, but you have received a spirit of adoption. When we cry, "Abba! Father!" it is that very Spirit bearing witness with our spirit that we are children of God, and if children, then heirs, heirs of God and joint heirs with Christ—if, in fact, we suffer with him so that we may also be glorified with him. (Rom. 8:14-17)

Psalm
Psalm 33:12-22
Our help and our shield

Additional Reading
Exodus 19:16-25
Moses and Aaron meet the Lord

Hymn: We All Believe in One True God, ELW 411

In a world of fears, grant us good courage, Father of us all. As your children, reveal your love to us that we may love others. As your heirs, may we acknowledge your authority as we proclaim your kingdom to the world.

Saturday, June 11, 2011

Barnabas, Apostle

Vigil of Pentecost

Acts 11:19-30; 13:1-3
Barnabas and Saul are set apart

Now in the church at Antioch there were prophets and teachers: Barnabas, Simeon who was called Niger, Lucius of Cyrene, Manaen a member of the court of Herod the ruler, and Saul. While they were worshiping the Lord and fasting, the Holy Spirit said, "Set apart for me Barnabas and Saul for the work to which I have called them." Then after fasting and praying they laid their hands on them and sent them off. (Acts 13:1-3)

Psalm
Psalm 112
Happy are the God-fearing

Additional Readings
Isaiah 42:5-12
The LORD calls us in righteousness

Matthew 10:7-16
Jesus sends out the Twelve

Hymn: Spread, Oh, Spread, Almighty Word, ELW 663

We praise you, O God, for the life of your faithful servant Barnabas, who, seeking not his own renown but the well-being of your church, gave generously of his life and possessions for the relief of the poor and the spread of the gospel. Grant that we may follow his example and by our actions give glory to you, Father, Son, and Holy Spirit, now and forever.

Pentecost

Christians pray to God "in the power of the Spirit." The gifts of the Spirit are faith, hope, and love. Whenever two or more gather in Jesus' name, the Spirit is present. At every baptism and communion, we pray for the Spirit's presence to forgive and strengthen, inspire and refresh. In the household, we pray for the Spirit's guidance, for the deepening of faith, hope, and love, for the patience and wisdom to live in peace with each other and our neighbors.

Table Prayer for Pentecost

Blessed are you, O Lord our God,
who gathers the whole world into the Spirit of your Son.
You have given us food for another day:
blessed be God forever!
We beg you to pour out food for the needy,
that all peoples and languages may praise your name,
through Jesus Christ our Lord.
Amen.

Thanksgiving for the Holy Spirit
Use this prayer during the week following Pentecost Sunday.

O Spirit of God, seek us;
Good Spirit, pray with us;
Spirit of counsel, inform us;
Spirit of might, free us;
Spirit of truth, enlighten us;
Spirit of Christ, raise us;
O Holy Spirit, dwell in us. Amen.

Sunday, June 12, 2011

Day of Pentecost

John 20:19-23
The Spirit poured out

When it was evening on that day, the first day of the week, and the doors of the house where the disciples had met were locked for fear of the Jews, Jesus came and stood among them and said, "Peace be with you." After he said this, he showed them his hands and his side. Then the disciples rejoiced when they saw the Lord. Jesus said to them again, "Peace be with you. As the Father has sent me, so I send you." When he had said this, he breathed on them and said to them, "Receive the Holy Spirit. If you forgive the sins of any, they are forgiven them; if you retain the sins of any, they are retained." (John 20:19-23)

Psalm
Psalm 104:24-34, 35b
Renewing the face of the earth

Additional Readings
Acts 2:1-21
Filled with the Spirit

1 Corinthians 12:3b-13
Varieties of gifts, the same Spirit

Hymn: O Day Full of Grace, ELW 627

O God, on this day you open the hearts of your faithful people by sending into us your Holy Spirit. Direct us by the light of that Spirit, that we may have a right judgment in all things and rejoice at all times in your peace, through Jesus Christ, your Son and our Lord, who lives and reigns with you and the Holy Spirit, one God, now and forever.

Monday, June 13, 2011

Time after Pentecost

Psalm 104:24-34, 35b

Renewing the face of the earth

O Lord, how manifold are your works!
    In wisdom you have made them all;
    the earth is full of your creatures.
These all look to you
    to give them their food in due season;
when you give to them, they gather it up;
    when you open your hand, they are filled with good things.
When you hide your face, they are dismayed;
    when you take away their breath, they die
    and return to their dust.
When you send forth your spirit, they are created;
    and you renew the face of the ground. (Ps. 104:24, 27-30)

Additional Readings

Joel 2:18-29
The promised spirit of God

Romans 8:18-24
We have the first fruits of the Spirit

Hymn: All Creatures, Worship God Most High! ELW 835

We acknowledge your creative bounty, O God. Guide us to be faithful stewards of the earth and all its creatures, that upheld by your Spirit we might be your instruments in renewing the world.

Tuesday, June 14, 2011

Time after Pentecost

**Basil the Great, Bishop of Caesarea, 379;
Gregory, Bishop of Nyssa, c. 385; Gregory of Nazianzus,
Bishop of Constantinople, c. 389; Macrina, teacher, c. 379**

Romans 8:26-27
Praying in the Spirit

Likewise the Spirit helps us in our weakness; for we do not know how to pray as we ought, but that very Spirit intercedes with sighs too deep for words. And God, who searches the heart, knows what is the mind of the Spirit, because the Spirit intercedes for the saints according to the will of God. (Rom. 8:26-27)

Psalm
Psalm 104:24-34, 35b
Renewing the face of the earth

Additional Reading
Ezekiel 39:7-8, 21-29
The promised spirit of God

Hymn: Healer of Our Every Ill, ELW 612

Lord, teach us to pray, not in proper words or in written formulas, but by the Spirit and from the heart you have set within us. Open our hearts and minds to your presence that our prayers may draw us closer to you.

Wednesday, June 15, 2011

Time after Pentecost

John 7:37-39

Jesus, the true living water

On the last day of the festival, the great day, while Jesus was standing there, he cried out, "Let anyone who is thirsty come to me, and let the one who believes in me drink. As the scripture has said, 'Out of the believer's heart shall flow rivers of living water.' " Now he said this about the Spirit, which believers in him were to receive; for as yet there was no Spirit, because Jesus was not yet glorified. (John 7:37-39)

Psalm
Psalm 104:24-34, 35b
Renewing the face of the earth

Additional Reading
Numbers 11:24-30
The spirit rests on Israel's elders

Hymn: Crashing Waters at Creation, ELW 455

Fountain of life, we thirst for justice and we thirst for peace. As we ever seek to be filled with your grace, strengthen our faith that we might quench the thirsts of a parched and dusty world.

Thursday, June 16, 2011

Time after Pentecost

Psalm 8
How exalted is your name

O Lord, our Sovereign,
  how majestic is your name in all the earth!
You have set your glory above the heavens.
  Out of the mouths of babes and infants
you have founded a bulwark because of your foes,
  to silence the enemy and the avenger.
When I look at your heavens, the work of your fingers,
  the moon and the stars that you have established;
what are human beings that you are mindful of them,
  mortals that you care for them?
Yet you have made them a little lower than God,
  and crowned them with glory and honor. (Ps. 8:1-5)

Additional Readings

Job 38:1-11
Creation story from Job

2 Timothy 1:8-12a
Grace revealed in Christ

Hymn: Many and Great, O God, ELW 837

God beyond us, gazing through telescopes we can only glimpse the universe you have created. God deep within us, peering through microscopes we can barely understand the intricacies of life. As you have claimed the entirety of our existence, we offer you ourselves.

Friday, June 17, 2011

Time after Pentecost

2 Timothy 1:12b-14

The treasure of the triune God

I am not ashamed, for I know the one in whom I have put my trust, and I am sure that he is able to guard until that day what I have entrusted to him. Hold to the standard of sound teaching that you have heard from me, in the faith and love that are in Christ Jesus. Guard the good treasure entrusted to you, with the help of the Holy Spirit living in us. (2 Tim. 1:12b-14)

Psalm

Psalm 8

How exalted is your name

Additional Reading

Job 38:12-21

Creation story from Job

Hymn: Praise the Almighty! ELW 877

Father, Son, and Holy Spirit, you are a mystery and a unity we cannot understand. Help us not only to proclaim your name but to share in that unity with all people, until the whole creation proclaims your glory.

Saturday, June 18, 2011

Time after Pentecost

John 14:15-17
Father, Son, Spirit

"If you love me, you will keep my commandments. And I will ask the Father, and he will give you another Advocate, to be with you forever. This is the Spirit of truth, whom the world cannot receive, because it neither sees him nor knows him. You know him, because he abides with you, and he will be in you." (John 14:15-17)

Psalm
Psalm 8
How exalted is your name

Additional Reading
Job 38:22-38
Creation story from Job

Hymn: Father Most Holy, ELW 415

As we pray to you, Father, grant us the blessings revealed in the fullness of the Trinity: the love of Christ, the truth of the Holy Spirit, and your abundant gifts in creation.

Time after Pentecost

Summer

The weeks and months following the Day of Pentecost coincide with the natural seasons of summer, autumn, and late autumn/November. Christian communities refer to this time in different ways. Whatever time is used to describe the many weeks between Pentecost and Christ the King (the last Sunday of the year), the seasons and calendars of North America offer some distinctive periods through which we may shape prayer in the household.

The Day of Pentecost is celebrated close to the end of the school year. A connection exists between graduations/new beginnings and our prayer for the Spirit's guidance in new endeavors. For many people, the months of June, July, and August signal a slightly altered schedule attuned to the weather, harvests, and vacations. Summer months offer their unique grace to those who spend time in discerning the many images which link the scriptures and the patient growth of the seed in the soil.

Table Prayer for Summer

O God of wonder,
the whole earth is full of your glory.
We give you thanks for the gifts of summer
and the blessings of this meal.
Teach us to share what we have received,
for you are the giver of all good things.
We ask this through Christ our Lord. Amen.

Table Prayer for Holy Trinity (June 19)

O God of love given, returned, and shared,
we praise you for the creation of this good earth
and for the food you gave to Adam and Eve,
a garden of delights.
And now, our Abba,
feed all your little children
from wherever they cry in fear and slavery.
Turn this bleak world into your garden again;
through Christ our Lord. Amen.

Blessing for Father's Day (June 19)

As a loving father cares for his children,
so you, O God, have compassion for us.
Look with favor on all those men
who guide and protect their children.
Hold them in your good care
and strengthen them for the holy task
which you have entrusted to them,
that all your children may flourish
in an atmosphere of wise love. Amen.

Sunday, June 19, 2011

The Holy Trinity

Matthew 28:16-20

Living in the community of the Trinity

Now the eleven disciples went to Galilee, to the mountain to which Jesus had directed them. When they saw him, they worshiped him; but some doubted. And Jesus came and said to them, "All authority in heaven and on earth has been given to me. Go therefore and make disciples of all nations, baptizing them in the name of the Father and of the Son and of the Holy Spirit, and teaching them to obey everything that I have commanded you. And remember, I am with you always, to the end of the age." (Matt. 28:16-20)

Psalm

Psalm 8
How exalted is your name

Additional Readings

Genesis 1:1—2:4a
Creation of the heavens and the earth

2 Corinthians 13:11-13
Paul's farewell

Hymn: Come, Join the Dance of Trinity, ELW 412

Almighty Creator and ever-living God, we worship your glory, eternal Three-in-One, and we praise your power, majestic One-in-Three. Keep us steadfast in this faith, defend us in all adversity, and bring us at last into your presence, where you live in endless joy and love, Father, Son, and Holy Spirit, one God, now and forever.

Monday, June 20, 2011

Time after Pentecost

Psalm 29
Praise the glory of God

Ascribe to the LORD, O heavenly beings,
    ascribe to the LORD glory and strength.
Ascribe to the LORD the glory of his name;
    worship the LORD in holy splendor.
The LORD sits enthroned over the flood;
    the LORD sits enthroned as king forever.
May the LORD give strength to his people!
    May the LORD bless his people with peace! (Ps. 29:1-2, 10-11)

Additional Readings
Job 38:39—39:12   I Corinthians 12:1-3
Creation story from Job   *Faith is a gift of the Spirit*

Hymn: Oh, That I Had a Thousand Voices, ELW 833

*God seems too short a name and human language too inadequate to
describe your greatness. In the poverty of our words give us faith to
acknowledge your presence in our lives.*

Tuesday, June 21, 2011

Time after Pentecost

Onesimos Nesib, translator, evangelist, 1931

1 Corinthians 12:4-13
The Spirit in the community

Now there are varieties of gifts, but the same Spirit; and there are varieties of services, but the same Lord; and there are varieties of activities, but it is the same God who activates all of them in everyone. To each is given the manifestation of the Spirit for the common good. (1 Cor. 12:4-7)

Psalm
Psalm 29
Praise the glory of God

Additional Reading
Job 39:13-25
Creation story from Job

Hymn: O Living Breath of God, ELW 407

Lord, you have knit us together by your hand. Unite our various gifts into the body of Christ, that as your hands we may serve the world for the common good.

Wednesday, June 22, 2011

Time after Pentecost

John 14:25-26

Father, Son, Spirit

"I have said these things to you while I am still with you. But the Advocate, the Holy Spirit, whom the Father will send in my name, will teach you everything, and remind you of all that I have said to you." (John 14:25-26)

Psalm
Psalm 29
Praise the glory of God

Additional Reading
Job 39:26—40:5
Creation story from Job; Job's response

Hymn: Come, Gracious Spirit, Heavenly Dove, ELW 404

Father, our memories are short and we are easily distracted by many cares. Send your Spirit as promised by Jesus, so that we might not only remember all that he taught, but conform our lives to his.

Thursday, June 23, 2011

Time after Pentecost

Psalm 89:1-4, 15-18
I sing of your love

I will sing of your steadfast love, O LORD, forever;
  with my mouth I will proclaim your faithfulness to all generations.
I declare that your steadfast love is established forever;
  your faithfulness is as firm as the heavens.
You said, "I have made a covenant with my chosen one,
  I have sworn to my servant David:
'I will establish your descendants forever,
  and build your throne for all generations.'" (Ps. 89:1-4)

Additional Readings
Jeremiah 25:1-7   **Galatians 5:2-6**
Israel provokes God's anger   *The nature of Christian freedom*

Hymn: Great Is Thy Faithfulness, ELW 733

Open our lips that we might sing of your praises. Help us to use our voices and all our creative arts to proclaim your gospel, speak of your greatness, and be a prelude to the great song of eternity.

Friday, June 24, 2011

John the Baptist

Luke 1:57-67 [68-80]
The birth and naming of John

On the eighth day [Elizabeth and her neighbors and relatives] came to circumcise the child, and they were going to name him Zechariah after his father. But his mother said, "No; he is to be called John." They said to her, "None of your relatives has this name." Then they began motioning to his father to find out what name he wanted to give him. He asked for a writing tablet and wrote, "His name is John." And all of them were amazed. Immediately his mouth was opened and his tongue freed, and he began to speak, praising God. (Luke 1:59-64)

Psalm
Psalm 141
My eyes are turned to God

Additional Readings
Malachi 3:1-4
My messenger, a refiner and purifier

Acts 13:13-26
The gospel for the descendents of Abraham

Hymn: Blessed Be the God of Israel, ELW 250

Almighty God, by your gracious providence your servant John the Baptist was born to Elizabeth and Zechariah. Grant to your people the wisdom to see your purpose and the openness to hear your will, that the light of Christ may increase in us, through Jesus Christ, our Savior and Lord, who lives and reigns with you and the Holy Spirit, one God, now and forever.

Saturday, June 25, 2011

Time after Pentecost

Presentation of the Augsburg Confession, 1530
Philipp Melanchthon, renewer of the church, 1560

Jeremiah 28:1-4

Hananiah prophesies falsely

In that same year, at the beginning of the reign of King Zedekiah of Judah, in the fifth month of the fourth year, the prophet Hananiah son of Azzur, from Gibeon, spoke to me in the house of the LORD, in the presence of the priests and all the people, saying, "Thus says the LORD of hosts, the God of Israel: I have broken the yoke of the king of Babylon. Within two years I will bring back to this place all the vessels of the LORD's house, which King Nebuchadnezzar of Babylon took away from this place and carried to Babylon. I will also bring back to this place King Jeconiah son of Jehoiakim of Judah, and all the exiles from Judah who went to Babylon, says the LORD, for I will break the yoke of the king of Babylon." (Jer. 28:1-4)

Psalm
Psalm 89:1-4, 15-18
I sing of your love

Additional Reading
Luke 17:1-4
Causing little ones to stumble

Hymn: God of Grace and God of Glory, ELW 705

Lord of the church, send us faithful leaders that we might be renewed in every part of our lives. Equip us to discern your will, to be generous with one another when we disagree, and to pass on the faith to future generations.

Sunday, June 26, 2011

Time after Pentecost

Matthew 10:40-42
Welcome Christ in those Christ sends

"Whoever welcomes you welcomes me, and whoever welcomes me welcomes the one who sent me. Whoever welcomes a prophet in the name of a prophet will receive a prophet's reward; and whoever welcomes a righteous person in the name of a righteous person will receive the reward of the righteous; and whoever gives even a cup of cold water to one of these little ones in the name of a disciple—truly I tell you, none of these will lose their reward." (Matt. 10:40-42)

Psalm
Psalm 89:1-4, 15-18
I sing of your love

Additional Readings
Jeremiah 28:5-9
Test of a true prophet

Romans 6:12-23
No longer under law but under grace

Hymn: O Christ, Your Heart, Compassionate, ELW 722

O God, you direct our lives by your grace, and your words of justice and mercy reshape the world. Mold us into a people who welcome your word and serve one another through Jesus Christ, our Savior and Lord.

Monday, June 27, 2011

Time after Pentecost

Cyril, Bishop of Alexandria, 444

Psalm 119:161-168
Loving God's law

Great peace have those who love your law;
    nothing can make them stumble.
I hope for your salvation, O LORD,
    and I fulfill your commandments.
My soul keeps your decrees;
    I love them exceedingly.
I keep your precepts and decrees,
    for all my ways are before you. (Ps. 119:165-168)

Additional Readings
I Kings 21:1-16   I Thessalonians 4:9-12
Ahab and Jezebel rob Naboth   *How to love one another*

Hymn: My God, How Wonderful Thou Art, ELW 863

Revealed Lord, you do not restrict us with rules that oppress or forgive us in ways that do not hold us unaccountable. Help us to comprehend the fullness of your love that reveals our sin but forgives us to serve you in freedom.

Tuesday, June 28, 2011

Time after Pentecost

Irenaeus, Bishop of Lyons, c. 202

1 John 4:1-6
Testing the spirits

Beloved, do not believe every spirit, but test the spirits to see whether they are from God; for many false prophets have gone out into the world. By this you know the Spirit of God: every spirit that confesses that Jesus Christ has come in the flesh is from God, and every spirit that does not confess Jesus is not from God. And this is the spirit of the antichrist, of which you have heard that it is coming; and now it is already in the world. (1 John 4:1-3)

Psalm
Psalm 119:161-168
Loving God's law

Additional Reading
1 Kings 21:17-29
Elijah confronts Ahab

Hymn: Let Us Ever Walk with Jesus, ELW 802

God of all wisdom, with so many voices seeking to convince us that we can exist without you, help us to test all things by your Spirit, that we might prove faithful by your power alone.

Wednesday, June 29, 2011

Peter and Paul, Apostles

John 21:15-19
Jesus says to Peter: Tend my sheep

When they had finished breakfast, Jesus said to Simon Peter, "Simon son of John, do you love me more than these?" He said to him, "Yes, Lord; you know that I love you." Jesus said to him, "Feed my lambs." A second time he said to him, "Simon son of John, do you love me?" He said to him, "Yes, Lord; you know that I love you." Jesus said to him, "Tend my sheep." He said to him the third time, "Simon son of John, do you love me?" Peter felt hurt because he said to him the third time, "Do you love me?" And he said to him, "Lord, you know everything; you know that I love you." Jesus said to him, "Feed my sheep. Very truly, I tell you, when you were younger, you used to fasten your own belt and to go wherever you wished. But when you grow old, you will stretch out your hands, and someone else will fasten a belt around you and take you where you do not wish to go." (He said this to indicate the kind of death by which he would glorify God.) After this he said to him, "Follow me." (John 21:15-19)

Psalm
Psalm 87:1-3, 5-7
Glorious things are spoken of you

Additional Readings
Acts 12:1-11
Peter released from prison

2 Timothy 4:6-8, 17-18
The good fight of faith

Hymn: Lord, You Give the Great Commission, ELW 579

Almighty God, we praise you that your blessed apostles Peter and Paul glorified you by their martyrdoms. Grant that your church throughout the world may always be instructed by their teaching and example, be knit together in unity by your Spirit, and ever stand firm upon the one foundation who is Jesus Christ our Lord, for he lives and reigns with you and the Holy Spirit, one God, now and forever.

Thursday, June 30, 2011

Time after Pentecost

Psalm 145:8-14
God is full of compassion

All your works shall give thanks to you, O Lord,
    and all your faithful shall bless you.
They shall speak of the glory of your kingdom,
    and tell of your power,
to make known to all people your mighty deeds,
    and the glorious splendor of your kingdom.
Your kingdom is an everlasting kingdom,
    and your dominion endures throughout all generations.
The Lord is faithful in all his words,
    and gracious in all his deeds. (Ps. 145:10-13)

Additional Readings
Zechariah 1:1-6
Israel urged to repent

Romans 7:1-6
Dying to the law through Christ

Hymn: Thine the Amen, ELW 826

*God of all faithfulness, your word is constant, speaking to every
generation in its time and place, that the gospel might be heard in new
languages and cultures. Enable us to proclaim your glory rather than
our own.*

_____

_____

_____

_____

_____

_____

_____

_____

_____

_____

_____

Friday, July 1, 2011

Time after Pentecost

Catherine Winkworth, 1878; John Mason Neale, 1866;
hymn translators

Zechariah 2:6-13

Exiles are the apple of God's eye

Up, up! Flee from the land of the north, says the LORD; for I have
spread you abroad like the four winds of heaven, says the LORD. Up!
Escape to Zion, you that live with daughter Babylon. For thus said
the LORD of hosts (after his glory sent me) regarding the nations that
plundered you: Truly, one who touches you touches the apple of my
eye. See now, I am going to raise my hand against them, and they
shall become plunder for their own slaves. Then you will know that
the LORD of hosts has sent me. Sing and rejoice, O daughter Zion! For
lo, I will come and dwell in your midst, says the LORD. (Zech. 2:6-10)

Psalm

Psalm 145:8-14
God is full of compassion

Additional Reading

Romans 7:7-20
Sin and the law kill us

Hymn: Let Streams of Living Justice, ELW 710

*God in our midst, as your presence fills us in this time after Pentecost,
lead us to discover anew your faithful love. Today make us bringers of
simple love into every situation where you lead us.*

Saturday, July 2, 2011

Time after Pentecost

Luke 10:21-24
Jesus rejoices in the Holy Spirit

At that same hour Jesus rejoiced in the Holy Spirit and said, "I thank you, Father, Lord of heaven and earth, because you have hidden these things from the wise and the intelligent and have revealed them to infants; yes, Father, for such was your gracious will. All things have been handed over to me by my Father; and no one knows who the Son is except the Father, or who the Father is except the Son and anyone to whom the Son chooses to reveal him."

Then turning to the disciples, Jesus said to them privately, "Blessed are the eyes that see what you see! For I tell you that many prophets and kings desired to see what you see, but did not see it, and to hear what you hear, but did not hear it." (Luke 10:21-24)

Psalm
Psalm 145:8-14
God is full of compassion

Additional Reading
Zechariah 4:1-7
By my Spirit, says God

Hymn: O God of Mercy, God of Light, ELW 714

O Holy One, as Jesus blessed the eyes of his dearest friends, bless our vision today. We gratefully welcome your gift of faith. As we open our hearts to your Holy Spirit, make way for renewal and change.

Sunday, July 3, 2011

Time after Pentecost

Thomas, Apostle (transferred to July 4)

Matthew 11:16-19, 25-30
The yoke of discipleship

"Come to me, all you that are weary and are carrying heavy burdens, and I will give you rest. Take my yoke upon you, and learn from me; for I am gentle and humble in heart, and you will find rest for your souls. For my yoke is easy, and my burden is light." (Matt. 11:28-30)

Psalm
Psalm 145:8-14
God is full of compassion

Additional Readings
Zechariah 9:9-12
The king comes in peace

Romans 7:15-25a
The struggle within the self

Hymn: Softly and Tenderly Jesus Is Calling, ELW 608

You are great, O God, and greatly to be praised. You have made us for yourself, and our hearts are restless until they rest in you. Grant that we may believe in you, call upon you, know you, and serve you through your Son, Jesus Christ, our Savior and Lord.

Monday, July 4, 2011

Thomas, Apostle *(transferred)*

John 14:1-7
Jesus, the way, the truth, the life

Thomas said to [Jesus], "Lord, we do not know where you are going. How can we know the way?" Jesus said to him, "I am the way, and the truth, and the life. No one comes to the Father except through me. If you know me, you will know my Father also. From now on you do know him and have seen him." (John 14:5-7)

Psalm
Psalm 136:1-4, 23-26
God's mercy endures forever

Additional Readings
Judges 6:36-40
God affirms Gideon's calling

Ephesians 4:11-16
The body of Christ has various gifts

Hymn: Come, My Way, My Truth, My Life, ELW 816

Ever-living God, you strengthened your apostle Thomas with firm and certain faith in the resurrection of your Son. Grant that we too may confess our faith in Jesus Christ, our Lord and our God, who lives and reigns with you and the Holy Spirit, one God, now and forever.

Tuesday, July 5, 2011

Time after Pentecost

Psalm 131

I rest like a weaned child on God

O LORD, my heart is not lifted up,
 my eyes are not raised too high;
I do not occupy myself with things
 too great and too marvelous for me.
But I have calmed and quieted my soul,
 like a weaned child with its mother;
 my soul is like the weaned child that is with me.
O Israel, hope in the LORD
 from this time on and forevermore. (Ps. 131:1-3)

Additional Readings

Jeremiah 28:10-17
Hananiah breaks Jeremiah's yoke

Romans 3:1-8
The faithfulness of God

Hymn: Come Down, O Love Divine, ELW 804

God, you care for us in the deepest of ways, even as a loving mother nurtures and protects her baby. Provide rest for us in your tender, strong love as we make the decisions before us as best we can.

Wednesday, July 6, 2011

Time after Pentecost

Jan Hus, martyr, 1415

Jeremiah 13:1-11
Jeremiah's loincloth

Then the word of the LORD came to me: Thus says the LORD: Just so I
will ruin the pride of Judah and the great pride of Jerusalem. This evil
people, who refuse to hear my words, who stubbornly follow their
own will and have gone after other gods to serve them and worship
them, shall be like this loincloth, which is good for nothing. For as
the loincloth clings to one's loins, so I made the whole house of Israel
and the whole house of Judah cling to me, says the LORD, in order
that they might be for me a people, a name, a praise, and a glory.
But they would not listen. (Jer. 13:8-11)

Psalm
Psalm 131
I rest like a weaned child on God

Additional Reading
John 13:1-17
Jesus washes the disciples' feet

Hymn: Abide with Me, ELW 629

*As this day unfolds, loving God, we surrender our lives once again to
your holy way with us. Where we have strength, welcome us. Where we
are weak, come and find us with your strength.*

Thursday, July 7, 2011

Time after Pentecost

Psalm 65:[1-8] 9-13
Your paths overflow with plenty

You visit the earth and water it,
   you greatly enrich it;
the river of God is full of water;
   you provide the people with grain,
   for so you have prepared it.
You water its furrows abundantly,
   settling its ridges,
softening it with showers,
   and blessing its growth.
You crown the year with your bounty;
   your wagon tracks overflow with richness.
The pastures of the wilderness overflow,
   the hills gird themselves with joy,
the meadows clothe themselves with flocks,
   the valleys deck themselves with grain,
   they shout and sing together for joy. (Ps. 65:9-13)

Additional Readings
Isaiah 48:1-5
What God declared long ago

Romans 2:12-16
God judges the secret thoughts

Hymn: This Is My Father's World, ELW 824

God of creation, in our planet's lakes, forests, and mountains we witness your awe-inspiring majesty. In lions, birds, and bugs, we discover your amazing creativity. Help us to honor you by valuing the blessings of your creation.

Friday, July 8, 2011

Time after Pentecost

Romans 15:14-21
Sanctified by the Holy Spirit

I myself feel confident about you, my brothers and sisters, that you yourselves are full of goodness, filled with all knowledge, and able to instruct one another. Nevertheless on some points I have written to you rather boldly by way of reminder, because of the grace given me by God to be a minister of Christ Jesus to the Gentiles in the priestly service of the gospel of God, so that the offering of the Gentiles may be acceptable, sanctified by the Holy Spirit. In Christ Jesus, then, I have reason to boast of my work for God. (Rom. 15:14-17)

Psalm
Psalm 65:[1-8] 9-13
Your paths overflow with plenty

Additional Reading
Isaiah 48:6-11
You will hear new, hidden things

Hymn: The Son of God, Our Christ, ELW 584

When you speak, God, we will listen. In our moments of doubt and wondering, we long for your promise of new life and purpose. Today fill us with bold confidence in your unconditional claim on us.

Saturday, July 9, 2011

Time after Pentecost

Isaiah 52:1-6
Sold, redeemed without money

For thus says the LORD: You were sold for nothing, and you shall be redeemed without money. For thus says the Lord GOD: Long ago, my people went down into Egypt to reside there as aliens; the Assyrian, too, has oppressed them without cause. Now therefore what am I doing here, says the LORD, seeing that my people are taken away without cause? Their rulers howl, says the LORD, and continually, all day long, my name is despised. Therefore my people shall know my name; therefore in that day they shall know that it is I who speak; here am I. (Isa. 52:3-6)

Psalm
Psalm 65:[1-8] 9-13
Your paths overflow with plenty

Additional Reading
John 12:44-50
I have come as light into the world

Hymn: O God of Every Nation, ELW 713

You are our God and we are your people. As we listen to the sound of your voice, wake us up to your promise! You are our God and we are your people.

Sunday, July 10, 2011

Time after Pentecost

Matthew 13:1-9, 18-23

The parable of the sower and the seed

And he told them many things in parables, saying: "Listen! A sower went out to sow. And as he sowed, some seeds fell on the path, and the birds came and ate them up. Other seeds fell on rocky ground, where they did not have much soil, and they sprang up quickly, since they had no depth of soil. But when the sun rose, they were scorched; and since they had no root, they withered away. Other seeds fell among thorns, and the thorns grew up and choked them. Other seeds fell on good soil and brought forth grain, some a hundredfold, some sixty, some thirty. Let anyone with ears listen!" (Matt. 13:3-9)

Psalm

Psalm 65:[1-8] 9-13
Your paths overflow with plenty

Additional Readings

Isaiah 55:10-13
The growth of the word

Romans 8:1-11
Living according to the Spirit

Hymn: Lord, Let My Heart Be Good Soil, ELW 512

Almighty God, we thank you for planting in us the seed of your word. By your Holy Spirit help us to receive it with joy, live according to it, and grow in faith and hope and love, through Jesus Christ, our Savior and Lord.

Monday, July 11, 2011

Time after Pentecost

Benedict of Nursia, Abbot of Monte Cassino, c. 540

Psalm 92
The righteous as a tree

The righteous flourish like the palm tree,
   and grow like a cedar in Lebanon.
They are planted in the house of the LORD;
   they flourish in the courts of our God.
In old age they still produce fruit;
   they are always green and full of sap,
showing that the LORD is upright;
   he is my rock, and there is no unrighteousness in him.
(Ps. 92:12-15)

Additional Readings
Leviticus 26:3-20
A rich and a poor harvest

I Thessalonians 4:1-8
A life pleasing to God

Hymn: My Hope Is Built on Nothing Less, ELW 596/597

O God, help our lives be faithful to you as a tree is true to the seed from which it sprouted and to the gardener who tended it. We belong to you. Tend us now.

Tuesday, July 12, 2011

Time after Pentecost

Nathan Söderblom, Bishop of Uppsala, 1931

Ephesians 4:17—5:2

The old life and the new

Let no evil talk come out of your mouths, but only what is useful for building up, as there is need, so that your words may give grace to those who hear. And do not grieve the Holy Spirit of God, with which you were marked with a seal for the day of redemption. Put away from you all bitterness and wrath and anger and wrangling and slander, together with all malice, and be kind to one another, tenderhearted, forgiving one another, as God in Christ has forgiven you. (Eph. 4:29-32)

Psalm

Psalm 92
The righteous as a tree

Additional Reading

Deuteronomy 28:1-14
The blessings of obedience

Hymn: God, When Human Bonds Are Broken, ELW 603

God of reclaiming love, nothing is wasted in your world. Help us to return your love among the neediest people where Christ dwells. We are your love moving in the world today.

Wednesday, July 13, 2011

Time after Pentecost

Proverbs 11:23-30
The fruit of righteousness

Whoever diligently seeks good seeks favor,
  but evil comes to the one who searches for it.
Those who trust in their riches will wither,
  but the righteous will flourish like green leaves.
Those who trouble their households will inherit wind,
  and the fool will be servant to the wise.
The fruit of the righteous is a tree of life,
  but violence takes lives away. (Prov. 11:27-30)

Psalm
Psalm 92
The righteous as a tree

Additional Reading
Matthew 13:10-17
The purpose of parable

Hymn: Be Thou My Vision, ELW 793

God, ground us in Christ like a tree is anchored in the soil. Grow our roots deep so that the fruit for the world will be your new life shared with every person we encounter.

Thursday, July 14, 2011

Time after Pentecost

Psalm 86:11-17
Teach me your ways

Teach me your way, O LORD,
   that I may walk in your truth;
   give me an undivided heart to revere your name.
I give thanks to you, O LORD my God, with my whole heart,
   and I will glorify your name forever.
For great is your steadfast love toward me;
   you have delivered my soul from the depths of Sheol.
(Ps. 86:11-13)

Additional Readings
Isaiah 41:21-29
The futility of idols

Hebrews 2:1-9
Warning to pay attention

Hymn: O Master, Let Me Walk with You, ELW 818

Holy One, it is your way that we desire. In the silence of this moment, help us to notice anything that is in the way between us and you. Give us understanding and courage to follow you more nearly.

Friday, July 15, 2011

Time after Pentecost

Hebrews 6:13-20
The certainty of God's promises

When God made a promise to Abraham, because he had no one greater by whom to swear, he swore by himself, saying, "I will surely bless you and multiply you." And thus Abraham, having patiently endured, obtained the promise. (Heb. 6:13-15)

Psalm
Psalm 86:11-17
Teach me your ways

Additional Reading
Isaiah 44:9-17
Those who make idols are nothing

Hymn: The God of Abraham Praise, ELW 831

God of Abraham, God of Sarah, you are a God of promise. Even before we breathed our first breath, you had been faithful for generations of people just like us. What promise do you have for us today?

Saturday, July 16, 2011

Time after Pentecost

Matthew 7:15-20

A tree and its fruit

"Beware of false prophets, who come to you in sheep's clothing but inwardly are ravenous wolves. You will know them by their fruits. Are grapes gathered from thorns, or figs from thistles? In the same way, every good tree bears good fruit, but the bad tree bears bad fruit. A good tree cannot bear bad fruit, nor can a bad tree bear good fruit. Every tree that does not bear good fruit is cut down and thrown into the fire. Thus you will know them by their fruits." (Matt. 7:15-20)

Psalm

Psalm 86:11-17

Teach me your ways

Additional Reading

Isaiah 44:18-20

Idols do not know or comprehend

Hymn: If God My Lord Be for Me, ELW 788

Make our hearts simpler, God: authentic, clear, true. Let our witness be natural: kindness flowing from the kindness of Christ; justice flowing from the justice of Christ. May our presence carry your presence through the Holy Spirit of Christ.

Sunday, July 17, 2011

Time after Pentecost

Bartolomé de Las Casas, missionary to the Indies, 1566

Matthew 13:24-30, 36-43

The parable of the weeds

He put before them another parable: "The kingdom of heaven may be compared to someone who sowed good seed in his field; but while everybody was asleep, an enemy came and sowed weeds among the wheat, and then went away. So when the plants came up and bore grain, then the weeds appeared as well. And the slaves of the householder came and said to him, 'Master, did you not sow good seed in your field? Where, then, did these weeds come from?' He answered, 'An enemy has done this.' The slaves said to him, 'Then do you want us to go and gather them?' But he replied, 'No; for in gathering the weeds you would uproot the wheat along with them. Let both of them grow together until the harvest; and at harvest time I will tell the reapers, Collect the weeds first and bind them in bundles to be burned, but gather the wheat into my barn.'"
(Matt. 13:24-30)

Psalm

Psalm 86:11-17
Teach me your ways

Additional Readings

Isaiah 44:6-8
There is no other God

Romans 8:12-25
The revealing of the children of God

Hymn: Come, Ye Thankful People, Come, ELW 693

Faithful God, most merciful judge, you care for your children with firmness and compassion. By your Spirit nurture us who live in your kingdom, that we may be rooted in the way of your Son, Jesus Christ, our Savior and Lord.

Monday, July 18, 2011

Time after Pentecost

Psalm 75
God's judgment

We give thanks to you, O God;
   we give thanks; your name is near.
People tell of your wondrous deeds.
At the set time that I appoint
   I will judge with equity.
When the earth totters, with all its inhabitants,
   it is I who keep its pillars steady. (Ps. 75:1-3)

Additional Readings
Nahum 1:1-13
The wrath and mercy of God

Revelation 14:12-20
The harvest at the end of time

Hymn: How Great Thou Art, ELW 856

Bring us clarity, God of justice; clarity to understand when to speak up and when to be quiet, clarity to know when to act and when to step out of the way. You are shaping us. We are ready.

Tuesday, July 19, 2011

Time after Pentecost

Galatians 4:21—5:1
An allegory about those saved

Now you, my friends, are children of the promise, like Isaac. But just as at that time the child who was born according to the flesh persecuted the child who was born according to the Spirit, so it is now also. But what does the scripture say? "Drive out the slave and her child; for the child of the slave will not share the inheritance with the child of the free woman." So then, friends, we are children, not of the slave but of the free woman. For freedom Christ has set us free. Stand firm, therefore, and do not submit again to a yoke of slavery. (Gal. 4:28—5:1)

Psalm
Psalm 75
God's judgment

Additional Reading
Zephaniah 3:1-13
The wicked convert to God

Hymn: We Are Called, ELW 720

Holy One, we have much more freedom in your grace than we will ever allow our minds to accept. Open to us a renewed confidence in your claim on us through Jesus Christ, our friend, our leader, and our Lord.

Wednesday, July 20, 2011

Time after Pentecost

Daniel 12:1-13
The righteous will shine

"At that time Michael, the great prince, the protector of your people, shall arise. There shall be a time of anguish, such as has never occurred since nations first came into existence. But at that time your people shall be delivered, everyone who is found written in the book. Many of those who sleep in the dust of the earth shall awake, some to everlasting life, and some to shame and everlasting contempt. Those who are wise shall shine like the brightness of the sky, and those who lead many to righteousness, like the stars forever and ever. But you, Daniel, keep the words secret and the book sealed until the time of the end. Many shall be running back and forth, and evil shall increase." (Dan. 12:1-4)

Psalm
Psalm 75
God's judgment

Additional Reading
Matthew 12:15-21
God's chosen servant

Hymn: I'm So Glad Jesus Lifted Me, ELW 860

In the mystery of your promise we live, O God. Where there is suffering anywhere, we all suffer because we are all connected. Create in us a heart for both justice and compassion, and give us patience with this world.

Thursday, July 21, 2011

Time after Pentecost

Psalm 119:129-136
Light and understanding

Your decrees are wonderful;
   therefore my soul keeps them.
The unfolding of your words gives light;
   it imparts understanding to the simple.
With open mouth I pant,
   because I long for your commandments.
Turn to me and be gracious to me,
   as is your custom toward those who love your name.
Keep my steps steady according to your promise,
   and never let iniquity have dominion over me. (Ps. 119:129-133)

Additional Readings
1 Kings 1:28-37
Solomon designated as king

1 Corinthians 4:14-20
Reign of God depends not on talk but power

Hymn: Let All Things Now Living, ELW 881

Keep our steps steady with you, Holy One, guide and helper. For the decisions before us this day, grant clarity and your light of understanding. Give us peace to rest our choices as they are held in your grace.

Friday, July 22, 2011

Mary Magdalene, Apostle

John 20:1-2, 11-18

Mary Magdalene meets Jesus in the garden

Jesus said to [Mary Magdalene], "Woman, why are you weeping? Whom are you looking for?" Supposing him to be the gardener, she said to him, "Sir, if you have carried him away, tell me where you have laid him, and I will take him away." Jesus said to her, "Mary!" She turned and said to him in Hebrew, "Rabbouni!" (which means Teacher). Jesus said to her, "Do not hold on to me, because I have not yet ascended to the Father. But go to my brothers and say to them, 'I am ascending to my Father and your Father, to my God and your God.'" Mary Magdalene went and announced to the disciples, "I have seen the Lord"; and she told them that he had said these things to her. (John 20:15-18)

Psalm

Psalm 73:23-28

I will speak of all God's works

Additional Readings

Ruth 1:6-18

Ruth stays with Naomi

Acts 13:26-33a

The raising of Jesus fulfills God's promise

Hymn: Signs and Wonders, ELW 672

Almighty God, your Son first entrusted the apostle Mary Magdalene with the joyful news of his resurrection. Following the example of her witness, may we proclaim Christ as our living Lord and one day see him in glory, for he lives and reigns with you and the Holy Spirit, one God, now and forever.

Saturday, July 23, 2011

Time after Pentecost

Birgitta of Sweden, renewer of the church, 1373

1 Kings 2:1-4
David's instructions to Solomon

When David's time to die drew near, he charged his son Solomon, saying: "I am about to go the way of all the earth. Be strong, be courageous, and keep the charge of the LORD your God, walking in his ways and keeping his statutes, his commandments, his ordinances, and his testimonies, as it is written in the law of Moses, so that you may prosper in all that you do and wherever you turn. Then the LORD will establish his word that he spoke concerning me: 'If your heirs take heed to their way, to walk before me in faithfulness with all their heart and with all their soul, there shall not fail you a successor on the throne of Israel.' " (1 Kings 2:1-4)

Psalm
Psalm 119:129-136
Light and understanding

Additional Reading
Matthew 12:38-42
Something greater than Solomon is here

Hymn: Lord of All Nations, Grant Me Grace, ELW 716

Give us attentive hearts, open as a delicate lotus, open as a hungry baby bird's mouth, open as sails full of the powerful wind. We are teachable and we are listening, God. Speak to us.

Sunday, July 24, 2011

Time after Pentecost

Matthew 13:31-33, 44-52

Parables of the reign of heaven

[Jesus] told them another parable: "The kingdom of heaven is like yeast that a woman took and mixed in with three measures of flour until all of it was leavened."

"The kingdom of heaven is like treasure hidden in a field, which someone found and hid; then in his joy he goes and sells all that he has and buys that field.

"Again, the kingdom of heaven is like a merchant in search of fine pearls; on finding one pearl of great value, he went and sold all that he had and bought it." (Matt. 13:33, 44-46)

Psalm

Psalm 119:129-136

Light and understanding

Additional Readings

1 Kings 3:5-12

Solomon's prayer for wisdom

Romans 8:26-39

Nothing can separate us from God's love

Hymn: You Are the Way, ELW 758

Beloved and sovereign God, through the death and resurrection of your Son you bring us into your kingdom of justice and mercy. By your Spirit, give us your wisdom, that we may treasure the life that comes from Jesus Christ, our Savior and Lord.

Monday, July 25, 2011

James, Apostle

Mark 10:35-45

Whoever wishes to be great must serve

James and John, the sons of Zebedee, came forward to him and said to him, "Teacher, we want you to do for us whatever we ask of you." And he said to them, "What is it you want me to do for you?" And they said to him, "Grant us to sit, one at your right hand and one at your left, in your glory." But Jesus said to them, "You do not know what you are asking. Are you able to drink the cup that I drink, or be baptized with the baptism that I am baptized with?" They replied, "We are able." Then Jesus said to them, "The cup that I drink you will drink; and with the baptism with which I am baptized, you will be baptized; but to sit at my right hand or at my left is not mine to grant, but it is for those for whom it has been prepared." (Mark 10:35-40)

Psalm
Psalm 7:1-10
God, my shield and defense

Additional Readings
1 Kings 19:9-18
Elijah hears God in the midst of silence

Acts 11:27—12:3a
James is killed by Herod

Hymn: Will You Let Me Be Your Servant, ELW 659

Gracious God, we remember before you today your servant and apostle James, the first among the twelve to be martyred for the name of Jesus Christ. Pour out on the leaders of your church that spirit of self-denying service which is the true mark of authority among your people, through Jesus Christ our servant, who lives and reigns with you and the Holy Spirit, one God, now and forever.

Tuesday, July 26, 2011

Time after Pentecost

Psalm 119:121-128
Give me understanding

I am your servant; give me understanding,
    so that I may know your decrees.
It is time for the LORD to act,
    for your law has been broken.
Truly I love your commandments
    more than gold, more than fine gold.
Truly I direct my steps by all your precepts;
    I hate every false way. (Ps. 119:125-128)

Additional Readings
1 Kings 4:29-34
God gave Solomon wisdom

Ephesians 6:10-18
The allegory of the armor of God

Hymn: Lord Jesus, You Shall Be My Song, ELW 808

Your way to live is better than money. Your way with us is greater than our own attempts at smartness. In the rich silence of this moment, we give our whole attention to you. Help us to be faithful today.

Wednesday, July 27, 2011

Time after Pentecost

Proverbs 1:1-7, 20-33
The call of wisdom

Wisdom cries out in the street;
   in the squares she raises her voice.
At the busiest corner she cries out;
   at the entrance of the city gates she speaks:
"How long, O simple ones, will you love being simple?
How long will scoffers delight in their scoffing
   and fools hate knowledge?
Give heed to my reproof;
I will pour out my thoughts to you;
   I will make my words known to you." (Prov. 1:20-23)

Psalm
Psalm 119:121-128
Give me understanding

Additional Reading
Mark 4:30-34
Jesus' use of parables

Hymn: We Eat the Bread of Teaching, ELW 518

God, our world is full of words. Some days our minds are cluttered with opinions that confuse us and facts that overwhelm us. Clear our minds with the mind of Christ. Be our wisdom, O God.

Thursday, July 28, 2011

Time after Pentecost

Johann Sebastian Bach, 1750; Heinrich Schütz, 1672;
George Frederick Handel, 1759; musicians

Psalm 145:8-9, 14-21
You open wide your hand

The LORD upholds all who are falling,
    and raises up all who are bowed down.
The eyes of all look to you,
    and you give them their food in due season.
You open your hand,
    satisfying the desire of every living thing. (Ps. 145:14-16)

Additional Readings
Proverbs 10:1-5
The righteous will not go hungry

Philippians 4:10-15
Being well fed and yet hungry

Hymn: O Bread of Life from Heaven, ELW 480

God our provider, everything we have and everything we are has been given to us as a pure gift. As today we ask again for our daily bread, open our lives to receive, and make us ever more grateful people.

Friday, July 29, 2011

Time after Pentecost

Mary, Martha, and Lazarus of Bethany; Olaf, King of Norway, martyr, 1030

Isaiah 51:17-23

Drink no more from the bowl of wrath

Therefore hear this, you who are wounded,
   who are drunk, but not with wine:
Thus says your Sovereign, the LORD,
   your God who pleads the cause of his people:
See, I have taken from your hand the cup of staggering;
you shall drink no more
   from the bowl of my wrath.
And I will put it into the hand of your tormentors,
   who have said to you,
   "Bow down, that we may walk on you";
and you have made your back like the ground
   and like the street for them to walk on. (Isa. 51:21-23)

Psalm
Psalm 145:8-9, 14-21
You open wide your hand

Additional Reading
Romans 9:6-13
True descendants of Abraham

Hymn: All Are Welcome, ELW 641

When there is pain, we pray differently. We use different names for you, God. We use a different tone of voice when there is suffering. Hear our prayers with your world-wide heart and be with us.

Saturday, July 30, 2011

Time after Pentecost

Isaiah 44:1-5

God's blessing on Israel

But now hear, O Jacob my servant,
  Israel whom I have chosen!
Thus says the LORD who made you,
  who formed you in the womb and will help you:
Do not fear, O Jacob my servant,
  Jeshurun whom I have chosen.
For I will pour water on the thirsty land,
  and streams on the dry ground;
I will pour my spirit upon your descendants,
  and my blessing on your offspring.
They shall spring up like a green tamarisk,
  like willows by flowing streams.
This one will say, "I am the LORD's,"
  another will be called by the name of Jacob,
yet another will write on the hand, "The LORD's,"
  and adopt the name of Israel. (Isa. 44:1-5)

Psalm
Psalm 145:8-9, 14-21
You open wide your hand

Additional Reading
Matthew 7:7-11
Bread and stones

Hymn: Bread of Life, Our Host and Meal, ELW 464

*God, you have chosen us and called us your own. You must see the
possibility in our lives where we cannot. Drench our deserts in your
time, and tend the seeds of faith that you have planted.*

Sunday, July 31, 2011

Time after Pentecost

Matthew 14:13-21

Jesus feeds 5000

Then [Jesus] ordered the crowds to sit down on the grass. Taking the five loaves and the two fish, he looked up to heaven, and blessed and broke the loaves, and gave them to the disciples, and the disciples gave them to the crowds. And all ate and were filled; and they took up what was left over of the broken pieces, twelve baskets full. And those who ate were about five thousand men, besides women and children. (Matt. 14:19-21)

Psalm

Psalm 145:8-9, 14-21
You open wide your hand

Additional Readings

Isaiah 55:1-5
Eat and drink what truly satisfies

Romans 9:1-5
The glory of God's people in Israel

Hymn: We Come to the Hungry Feast, ELW 479

Glorious God, your generosity waters the world with goodness, and you cover creation with abundance. Awaken in us a hunger for the food that satisfies both body and spirit, and with this food fill all the starving world; through your Son, Jesus Christ, our Savior and Lord.

_____

_____

_____

_____

_____

_____

_____

_____

_____

_____

_____

_____

Monday, August 1, 2011

Time after Pentecost

Psalm 78:1-8, 17-29

God fed the people with manna

Yet he commanded the skies above,
  and opened the doors of heaven;
he rained down on them manna to eat,
  and gave them the grain of heaven.
Mortals ate of the bread of angels;
  he sent them food in abundance. (Ps. 78:23-25)

Additional Readings
Deuteronomy 8:1-10
God will feed the people

Romans 1:8-15
A harvest among the Gentiles

Hymn: Break Now the Bread of Life, ELW 515

Gracious God, you sent down manna from heaven. Make us ever-mindful of those who will go hungry this day. As you give us daily bread, create in us a hunger for justice until all people are fed by your abundant gifts.

Tuesday, August 2, 2011

Time after Pentecost

Acts 2:37-47

The believers breaking bread

Awe came upon everyone, because many wonders and signs were being done by the apostles. All who believed were together and had all things in common; they would sell their possessions and goods and distribute the proceeds to all, as any had need. Day by day, as they spent much time together in the temple, they broke bread at home and ate their food with glad and generous hearts, praising God and having the goodwill of all the people. And day by day the Lord added to their number those who were being saved. (Acts 2:43-47)

Psalm
Psalm 78:1-8, 17-29
God fed the people with manna

Additional Reading
Deuteronomy 26:1-15
A tithe from God's harvest

Hymn: Draw Us in the Spirit's Tether, ELW 470

Loving God, you gather your people together around food and drink. Be present with us also in our common meals and gatherings in our homes, in workplaces and schools, and also when we rest.

Wednesday, August 3, 2011

Time after Pentecost

Exodus 16:2-15, 31-35
God feeds the people manna

The whole congregation of the Israelites complained against Moses and Aaron in the wilderness. The Israelites said to them, "If only we had died by the hand of the LORD in the land of Egypt, when we sat by the fleshpots and ate our fill of bread; for you have brought us out into this wilderness to kill this whole assembly with hunger."
Then the LORD said to Moses, "I am going to rain bread from heaven for you, and each day the people shall go out and gather enough for that day. In that way I will test them, whether they will follow my instruction or not." (Exod. 16:2-4)

Psalm
Psalm 78:1-8, 17-29
God fed the people with manna

Additional Reading
Matthew 15:32-39
Jesus feeds 4000

Hymn: Glorious Things of You Are Spoken, ELW 647

God our provider, you give us all that we need. With glad hearts make us thankful for the things we have. Shower us with peace and confidence that we might always put our trust in you.

Thursday, August 4, 2011

Time after Pentecost

Psalm 85:8-13
I will listen to God

Let me hear what God the LORD will speak,
    for he will speak peace to his people,
    to his faithful, to those who turn to him in their hearts.
Surely his salvation is at hand for those who fear him,
    that his glory may dwell in our land.
Steadfast love and faithfulness will meet;
    righteousness and peace will kiss each other.
Faithfulness will spring up from the ground,
    and righteousness will look down from the sky.
The LORD will give what is good,
    and our land will yield its increase.
Righteousness will go before him,
    and will make a path for his steps. (Ps. 85:8-13)

Additional Readings
1 Kings 18:1-16
God promises relief from drought

Acts 17:10-15
The good news is shared

Hymn: Lord, Speak to Us, That We May Speak, ELW 676

Almighty God, the whole creation knows your goodness. You bring life even to the most hostile of places. Guide us in our care for every plant and animal on this earth.

Friday, August 5, 2011

Time after Pentecost

Acts 18:24-28

A new disciple preaches

Now there came to Ephesus a Jew named Apollos, a native of Alexandria. He was an eloquent man, well-versed in the scriptures. He had been instructed in the Way of the Lord; and he spoke with burning enthusiasm and taught accurately the things concerning Jesus, though he knew only the baptism of John. He began to speak boldly in the synagogue; but when Priscilla and Aquila heard him, they took him aside and explained the Way of God to him more accurately. And when he wished to cross over to Achaia, the believers encouraged him and wrote to the disciples to welcome him. On his arrival he greatly helped those who through grace had become believers, for he powerfully refuted the Jews in public, showing by the scriptures that the Messiah is Jesus. (Acts 18:24-28)

Psalm
Psalm 85:8-13
I will listen to God

Additional Reading
1 Kings 18:17-19, 30-40
God's flooded altar burns

Hymn: In Christ Called to Baptize, ELW 575

Lord God, you strengthen the faith of your people. Cure us of our apathy. Fan the flame of the gospel within each of us that we may proclaim boldly the good news to everyone we meet.

Saturday, August 6, 2011

Time after Pentecost

1 Kings 18:41-46

From drought to heavy rain

Elijah said to Ahab, "Go up, eat and drink; for there is a sound of rushing rain." So Ahab went up to eat and to drink. Elijah went up to the top of Carmel; there he bowed himself down upon the earth and put his face between his knees. He said to his servant, "Go up now, look toward the sea." He went up and looked, and said, "There is nothing." Then he said, "Go again seven times." At the seventh time he said, "Look, a little cloud no bigger than a person's hand is rising out of the sea." Then he said, "Go say to Ahab, 'Harness your chariot and go down before the rain stops you.'" In a little while the heavens grew black with clouds and wind; there was a heavy rain. Ahab rode off and went to Jezreel. But the hand of the LORD was on Elijah; he girded up his loins and ran in front of Ahab to the entrance of Jezreel. (1 Kings 18:41-46)

Psalm
Psalm 85:8-13
I will listen to God

Additional Reading
Matthew 16:1-4
The sign of Jonah

Hymn: Crashing Waters at Creation, ELW 455

Living God, you bring forth waters that nourish the earth. Bring clean drinking water to all who thirst. Shower our farmers' crops with sufficient rains that they may yield bountiful harvests. Bathe all creation in the waters of life.

Sunday, August 7, 2011

Time after Pentecost

Matthew 14:22-33

Jesus walking on the sea

Immediately [Jesus] made the disciples get into the boat and go on ahead to the other side, while he dismissed the crowds. And after he had dismissed the crowds, he went up the mountain by himself to pray. When evening came, he was there alone, but by this time the boat, battered by the waves, was far from the land, for the wind was against them. And early in the morning he came walking toward them on the sea. But when the disciples saw him walking on the sea, they were terrified, saying, "It is a ghost!" And they cried out in fear. But immediately Jesus spoke to them and said, "Take heart, it is I; do not be afraid." (Matt. 14:22-27)

Psalm

Psalm 85:8-13
I will listen to God

Additional Readings

1 Kings 19:9-18
Elijah on Mount Horeb

Romans 10:5-15
The word of faith

Hymn: Calm to the Waves, ELW 794

O God our defender, storms rage around and within us and cause us to be afraid. Rescue your people from despair, deliver your sons and daughters from fear, and preserve us all in the faith of your Son, Jesus Christ, our Savior and Lord.

Monday, August 8, 2011

Time after Pentecost

Dominic, founder of the Order of Preachers (Dominicans), 1221

Psalm 18:1-19
God saves from the waters

He reached down from on high, he took me;
   he drew me out of mighty waters.
He delivered me from my strong enemy,
   and from those who hated me;
   for they were too mighty for me.
They confronted me in the day of my calamity;
   but the LORD was my support.
He brought me out into a broad place;
   he delivered me, because he delighted in me. (Ps. 18:16-19)

Additional Readings
Genesis 7:11—8:5
God saves Noah from the flood

2 Peter 2:4-10
God judges and rescues

Hymn: Eternal Father, Strong to Save, ELW 756

God our protector, watch over the vulnerable children who are bullied in our schools. Keep safe those who serve in the military and other challenging missions. Use us to keep people from dangerous situations around us.

Tuesday, August 9, 2011

Time after Pentecost

Genesis 19:1-29
God saves Lot

Abraham went early in the morning to the place where he had stood before the LORD; and he looked down toward Sodom and Gomorrah and toward all the land of the Plain and saw the smoke of the land going up like the smoke of a furnace.

So it was that, when God destroyed the cities of the Plain, God remembered Abraham, and sent Lot out of the midst of the overthrow, when he overthrew the cities in which Lot had settled. (Gen. 19:27-29)

Psalm
Psalm 18:1-19
God saves from the waters

Additional Reading
Romans 9:14-29
God's wrath, God's mercy

Hymn: In All Our Grief, ELW 615

Merciful God, you remember your people and lead them to safety. Bless our firefighters and police who work tirelessly to keep us safe. Guide them in their work and keep them from danger.

Wednesday, August 10, 2011

Time after Pentecost

Lawrence, deacon, martyr, 258

Matthew 8:23-27

Jesus stills the storm

And when he got into the boat, his disciples followed him. A windstorm arose on the sea, so great that the boat was being swamped by the waves; but he was asleep. And they went and woke him up, saying, "Lord, save us! We are perishing!" And he said to them, "Why are you afraid, you of little faith?" Then he got up and rebuked the winds and the sea; and there was a dead calm. They were amazed, saying, "What sort of man is this, that even the winds and the sea obey him?" (Matt. 8:23-27)

Psalm
Psalm 18:1-19
God saves from the waters

Additional Reading
Job 36:24-33; 37:14-24
The waters of God's creation

Hymn: Jesus, Savior, Pilot Me, ELW 755

Eternal God, you command the winds and seas and they obey. Strengthen our faith, especially in seemingly hopeless moments. Be near to us so that we do not fear perishing and give us your peace that we may know life.

Thursday, August 11, 2011

Time after Pentecost

Clare, Abbess of San Damiano, 1253

Psalm 67
Let all the peoples praise God

May God be gracious to us and bless us
   and make his face to shine upon us,
that your way may be known upon earth,
   your saving power among all nations.
Let the peoples praise you, O God;
   let all the peoples praise you.
Let the nations be glad and sing for joy,
   for you judge the peoples with equity
   and guide the nations upon earth.
Let the peoples praise you, O God;
   let all the peoples praise you. (Ps. 67:1-5)

Additional Readings
Isaiah 45:20-25
All the ends of the earth shall be saved

Revelation 15:1-4
All nations will worship God

Hymn: Praise to the Lord, the Almighty, ELW 858

Gracious God, you have blessed all your children of every tribe and race. Help us to reflect your goodness throughout our daily lives. Shine upon our faces and in our hearts until all people join together in praising you.

Friday, August 12, 2011

Time after Pentecost

Isaiah 63:15-19

A plea for God's attention

> Why, O LORD, do you make us stray from your ways
> > and harden our heart, so that we do not fear you?
> Turn back for the sake of your servants,
> > for the sake of the tribes that are your heritage.
> Your holy people took possession for a little while;
> > but now our adversaries have trampled down your sanctuary.
> We have long been like those whom you do not rule,
> > like those not called by your name. (Isa. 63:17-19)

Psalm

Psalm 67

Let all the peoples praise God

Additional Reading

Acts 14:19-28

God opens the door to Gentiles

Hymn: By Gracious Powers, ELW 626

Lord God, you promise to have mercy on all who call upon your name. When it appears you are silent, help us to listen. Grant us healing and wholeness. Make your presence known among us, especially all who are sick, suffering, or dying.

Saturday, August 13, 2011

Time after Pentecost

Florence Nightengale, 1910; Clara Maass, 1901; renewers of society

Isaiah 56:1-5
A covenant for all who obey

Thus says the LORD:
Maintain justice, and do what is right,
for soon my salvation will come,
    and my deliverance be revealed.
Happy is the mortal who does this,
    the one who holds it fast,
who keeps the sabbath, not profaning it,
    and refrains from doing any evil.
Do not let the foreigner joined to the LORD say,
    "The LORD will surely separate me from his people";
and do not let the eunuch say,
    "I am just a dry tree." (Isa. 56:1-3)

Psalm
Psalm 67
Let all the peoples praise God

Additional Reading
Matthew 14:34-36
Jesus heals the sick

Hymn: Let Justice Flow like Streams, ELW 717

Lord God, you grant salvation and deliverance to your people. Give us a passion for justice. Teach us to recognize the poor, the outcast, and the marginalized that live among us. Help us put an end to racist and oppressive thoughts and actions.

Sunday, August 14, 2011

Time after Pentecost

Maximilian Kolbe, 1941;
Kaj Munk, 1944, martyrs

Matthew 15:[10-20] 21-28

The Canaanite woman's daughter is healed

[The Canaanite woman] came and knelt before [Jesus], saying, "Lord, help me." He answered, "It is not fair to take the children's food and throw it to the dogs." She said, "Yes, Lord, yet even the dogs eat the crumbs that fall from their masters' table." Then Jesus answered her, "Woman, great is your faith! Let it be done for you as you wish." And her daughter was healed instantly. (Matt. 15:25-28)

Psalm
Psalm 67
Let all the peoples praise God

Additional Readings
Isaiah 56:1, 6-8
A house of prayer for all people

Romans 11:1-2a, 29-32
God's mercy to all, Jew and Gentile

Hymn: We Come to You for Healing, Lord, ELW 617

God of all peoples, your arms reach out to embrace all those who call upon you. Teach us as disciples of your Son to love the world with compassion and constancy, that your name may be known throughout the earth, through Jesus Christ, our Savior and Lord.

Monday, August 15, 2011

Mary, Mother of Our Lord

Luke 1:46-55
Mary's thanksgiving

And Mary said,
"My soul magnifies the Lord,
    and my spirit rejoices in God my Savior,
for he has looked with favor on the lowliness of his servant.
    Surely, from now on all generations will call me blessed;
for the Mighty One has done great things for me,
    and holy is his name." (Luke 1:46-49)

Psalm
Psalm 34:1-9
O magnify the Lord with me

Additional Readings
Isaiah 61:7-11
God will cause righteousness to spring up

Galatians 4:4-7
We are no longer slaves, but children

Hymn: Canticle of the Turning, 723

Almighty God, in choosing the virgin Mary to be the mother of your Son, you made known your gracious regard for the poor, the lowly, and the despised. Grant us grace to receive your word in humility, and so to be made one with your Son, Jesus Christ our Savior and Lord, who lives and reigns with you and the Holy Spirit, one God, now and forever.

Tuesday, August 16, 2011

Time after Pentecost

Romans 11:13-29

God saves Jews and Gentiles

So that you may not claim to be wiser than you are, brothers and sisters, I want you to understand this mystery: a hardening has come upon part of Israel, until the full number of the Gentiles has come in. And so all Israel will be saved; as it is written,

"Out of Zion will come the Deliverer;
   he will banish ungodliness from Jacob."
"And this is my covenant with them,
   when I take away their sins."

As regards the gospel they are enemies of God for your sake; but as regards election they are beloved, for the sake of their ancestors; for the gifts and the calling of God are irrevocable. (Rom. 11:25-29)

Psalm

Psalm 87

Foreigners praise God in Zion

Additional Reading

Isaiah 43:8-13

Let all the nations gather

Hymn: Alleluia! Sing to Jesus, ELW 392

Everlasting God, you unite us as one body. Unfold the mystery of our lives that we may more fully discover our inter-connected relationships as brothers and sisters in Christ. In all things, give us patience and understanding.

Wednesday, August 17, 2011

Time after Pentecost

Matthew 8:1-13

Jesus heals many people

When [Jesus] entered Capernaum, a centurion came to him, appealing to him and saying, "Lord, my servant is lying at home paralyzed, in terrible distress." And he said to him, "I will come and cure him." The centurion answered, "Lord, I am not worthy to have you come under my roof; but only speak the word, and my servant will be healed. For I also am a man under authority, with soldiers under me; and I say to one, 'Go,' and he goes, and to another, 'Come,' and he comes, and to my slave, 'Do this,' and the slave does it." When Jesus heard him, he was amazed and said to those who followed him, "Truly I tell you, in no one in Israel have I found such faith." (Matt. 8:5-10)

Psalm
Psalm 87
Foreigners praise God in Zion

Additional Reading
Isaiah 66:18-23
All nations shall come to worship

Hymn: O Christ, the Healer, We Have Come, ELW 610

Lord God, you grant healing to all who are in distress. Comfort those living with mental illness, those who are alienated, depressed, or suffering with low self-esteem. Speak your word of life and peace to them.

Thursday, August 18, 2011

Time after Pentecost

Psalm 138
Your love endures forever

All the kings of the earth shall praise you, O LORD,
    for they have heard the words of your mouth.
They shall sing of the ways of the LORD,
    for great is the glory of the LORD.
For though the LORD is high, he regards the lowly;
    but the haughty he perceives from far away.
Though I walk in the midst of trouble,
    you preserve me against the wrath of my enemies;
you stretch out your hand,
    and your right hand delivers me.
The LORD will fulfill his purpose for me;
    your steadfast love, O LORD, endures forever.
    Do not forsake the work of your hands. (Ps. 138:4-8)

Additional Readings
Ezekiel 28:11-19
Disobedience and the loss of Eden

I Corinthians 6:1-11
When believers disagree

Hymn: Holy God, Holy and Glorious, ELW 637

Creating God, like a potter you give shape and purpose to our lives. Give us the gifts of space and time to discern your will. Guide our work and our play that you may be glorified in all that we do.

Friday, August 19, 2011

Time after Pentecost

Ezekiel 31:15-18
Israel like the cedars of Lebanon

Thus says the Lord God: On the day it went down to Sheol I closed the deep over it and covered it; I restrained its rivers, and its mighty waters were checked. I clothed Lebanon in gloom for it, and all the trees of the field fainted because of it. I made the nations quake at the sound of its fall, when I cast it down to Sheol with those who go down to the Pit; and all the trees of Eden, the choice and best of Lebanon, all that were well watered, were consoled in the world below. They also went down to Sheol with it, to those killed by the sword, along with its allies, those who lived in its shade among the nations. Which among the trees of Eden was like you in glory and in greatness? Now you shall be brought down with the trees of Eden to the world below; you shall lie among the uncircumcised, with those who are killed by the sword. This is Pharaoh and all his horde, says the Lord God. (Ezek. 31:15-18)

Psalm
Psalm 138
Your love endures forever

Additional Reading
2 Corinthians 10:12-18
Let those who boast, boast in the Lord

Hymn: Light Dawns on a Weary World, ELW 726

Almighty God, your creation extends to all corners of the earth. Strengthen our faith like the great cedars of Lebanon, firmly planted with deep roots. Enliven our faith like the vibrantly colored flowers of the garden of Eden.

Saturday, August 20, 2011

Time after Pentecost

Bernard, Abbot of Clairvaux, 1153

Ezekiel 36:33-38

A desolate land becomes like Eden

Thus says the Lord GOD: On the day that I cleanse you from all your iniquities, I will cause the towns to be inhabited, and the waste places shall be rebuilt. The land that was desolate shall be tilled, instead of being the desolation that it was in the sight of all who passed by. And they will say, "This land that was desolate has become like the garden of Eden; and the waste and desolate and ruined towns are now inhabited and fortified." Then the nations that are left all around you shall know that I, the LORD, have rebuilt the ruined places, and replanted that which was desolate; I, the LORD, have spoken, and I will do it. (Ezek. 36:33-36)

Psalm	**Additional Reading**
Psalm 138	Matthew 16:5-12
Your love endures forever	*Bread as a sign of other things*

Hymn: Come, Ye Disconsolate, ELW 607

God of new beginnings, you bring restoration to that which is desolate. Accompany those struggling with addiction. Turn their dependence toward you alone and bring them reconciliation within their communities.

Sunday, August 21, 2011

Time after Pentecost

Matthew 16:13-20
The profession of Peter's faith

[Jesus] said to [the disciples], "But who do you say that I am?" Simon Peter answered, "You are the Messiah, the Son of the living God." And Jesus answered him, "Blessed are you, Simon son of Jonah! For flesh and blood has not revealed this to you, but my Father in heaven. And I tell you, you are Peter, and on this rock I will build my church, and the gates of Hades will not prevail against it. I will give you the keys of the kingdom of heaven, and whatever you bind on earth will be bound in heaven, and whatever you loose on earth will be loosed in heaven." (Matt. 16:15-19)

Psalm
Psalm 138
Your love endures forever

Additional Readings
Isaiah 51:1-6
God's enduring salvation

Romans 12:1-8
One body in Christ, with gifts that differ

Hymn: Built on a Rock, ELW 652

O God, with all your faithful followers of every age, we praise you, the rock of our life. Be our strong foundation and form us into the body of your Son, that we may gladly minister to all the world, through Jesus Christ, our Savior and Lord.

Monday, August 22, 2011

Time after Pentecost

Psalm 18:1-3, 20-32
God the rock

I love you, O LORD, my strength.
The LORD is my rock, my fortress, and my deliverer,
   my God, my rock in whom I take refuge,
   my shield, and the horn of my salvation, my stronghold.
I call upon the LORD, who is worthy to be praised,
   so I shall be saved from my enemies. (Ps. 18:1-3)

Additional Readings
1 Samuel 7:3-13
Samuel raises the Ebenezer stone

Romans 2:1-11
The righteous judgment of God

Hymn: How Sweet the Name of Jesus Sounds, ELW 620

Loving God, you are our shelter and strength. Hear the voiceless cries from the men, women, and children whose lives are threatened by domestic violence. Deliver them to safe refuge where they may find peaceful rest and a loving embrace.

Tuesday, August 23, 2011

Time after Pentecost

Romans 11:33-36
The riches, wisdom, and knowledge of God

O the depth of the riches and wisdom and knowledge of God! How unsearchable are his judgments and how inscrutable his ways!
"For who has known the mind of the Lord?
Or who has been his counselor?"
"Or who has given a gift to him,
to receive a gift in return?"
For from him and through him and to him are all things. To him be the glory forever. Amen. (Rom. 11:33-36)

Psalm
Psalm 18:1-3, 20-32
God the rock

Additional Reading
Deuteronomy 32:18-20, 28-39
Praise the rock that is God

Hymn: He Comes to Us as One Unknown, ELW 737

Majestic God, all wisdom and knowledge comes from you alone. Bless the minds of students and teachers in their pursuit of wisdom. Grace the minds of scientists and doctors who seek to promote healthy living.

Wednesday, August 24, 2011

Bartholomew, Apostle

John 1:43-51

Jesus says: Follow me

When Jesus saw Nathanael coming toward him, he said of him, "Here is truly an Israelite in whom there is no deceit!" Nathanael asked him, "Where did you get to know me?" Jesus answered, "I saw you under the fig tree before Philip called you." Nathanael replied, "Rabbi, you are the Son of God! You are the King of Israel!" Jesus answered, "Do you believe because I told you that I saw you under the fig tree? You will see greater things than these." And he said to him, "Very truly, I tell you, you will see heaven opened and the angels of God ascending and descending upon the Son of Man." (John 1:47-51)

Psalm

Psalm 12
A plea for help in evil times

Additional Readings

Exodus 19:1-6
Israel is God's priestly kingdom

I Corinthians 12:27-31a
The body of Christ

Hymn: O God, My Faithful God, ELW 806

Almighty and everlasting God, you gave to your apostle Bartholomew grace truly to believe and courageously to preach your word. Grant that your church may proclaim the good news to the ends of the earth, through Jesus Christ, our Savior and Lord, who lives and reigns with you and the Holy Spirit, one God, now and forever.

Thursday, August 25, 2011

Time after Pentecost

Psalm 26:1-8
Your love is before my eyes

Vindicate me, O LORD,
   for I have walked in my integrity,
     and I have trusted in the LORD without wavering.
Prove me, O LORD, and try me;
   test my heart and mind.
For your steadfast love is before my eyes,
   and I walk in faithfulness to you. (Ps. 26:1-3)

Additional Readings

Jeremiah 14:13-18
Denunciation of lying prophets

Ephesians 5:1-6
Do not be deceived by empty words

Hymn: We Praise You, O God, ELW 870

Faithful God, you give strength to all who look to you. Help us to acknowledge the unique gifts of those living with physical limitations that we might recognize your sacred beauty in all its richest diversity.

Friday, August 26, 2011

Time after Pentecost

2 Thessalonians 2:7-12
Refusal to love the truth

For the mystery of lawlessness is already at work, but only until the one who now restrains it is removed. And then the lawless one will be revealed, whom the Lord Jesus will destroy with the breath of his mouth, annihilating him by the manifestation of his coming. The coming of the lawless one is apparent in the working of Satan, who uses all power, signs, lying wonders, and every kind of wicked deception for those who are perishing, because they refused to love the truth and so be saved. For this reason God sends them a powerful delusion, leading them to believe what is false, so that all who have not believed the truth but took pleasure in unrighteousness will be condemned. (2 Thess. 2:7-12)

Psalm
Psalm 26:1-8
Your love is before my eyes

Additional Reading
Jeremiah 15:1-9
The consequences of sin

Hymn: Abide, O Dearest Jesus, ELW 539

Lord God, you sent your Son, Jesus, to restore all creation from the bonds of sin. Turn our lives away from wickedness and deceit. Teach us to recognize your divine love in the world.

Saturday, August 27, 2011

Time after Pentecost

Jeremiah 15:10-14
Jeremiah's complaint to God

Woe is me, my mother, that you ever bore me, a man of strife and contention to the whole land! I have not lent, nor have I borrowed, yet all of them curse me. The LORD said: Surely I have intervened in your life for good, surely I have imposed enemies on you in a time of trouble and in a time of distress. Can iron and bronze break iron from the north?

Your wealth and your treasures I will give as plunder, without price, for all your sins, throughout all your territory. I will make you serve your enemies in a land that you do not know, for in my anger a fire is kindled that shall burn forever. (Jer. 15:10-14)

Psalm
Psalm 26:1-8
Your love is before my eyes

Additional Reading
Matthew 8:14-17
Jesus heals many at Peter's house

Hymn: If You But Trust in God to Guide You, ELW 769

Almighty God, you have rescued us from times of trouble. Grant us wisdom to make tough decisions on the most challenging events and situations of our lives. Bring us the peace that only you can give.

Sunday, August 28, 2011

Time after Pentecost

Augustine, Bishop of Hippo, 430;
Moses the Black, monk, martyr, c. 400

Matthew 16:21-28

The rebuke to Peter

From that time on, Jesus began to show his disciples that he must go to Jerusalem and undergo great suffering at the hands of the elders and chief priests and scribes, and be killed, and on the third day be raised. And Peter took him aside and began to rebuke him, saying, "God forbid it, Lord! This must never happen to you." But he turned and said to Peter, "Get behind me, Satan! You are a stumbling block to me; for you are setting your mind not on divine things but on human things." (Matt. 16:21-23)

Psalm

Psalm 26:1-8
Your love is before my eyes

Additional Readings

Jeremiah 15:15-21
God fortifies the prophet

Romans 12:9-21
Live in harmony

Hymn: Take Up Your Cross, the Savior Said, ELW 667

O God, we thank you for your Son who chose the path of suffering for the sake of the world. Humble us by his example, point us to the path of obedience, and give us strength to follow your commands, through Jesus Christ, our Savior and Lord.

Monday, August 29, 2011

Time after Pentecost

Psalm 17

The righteous shall see God

I call upon you, for you will answer me, O God;
   incline your ear to me, hear my words.
Wondrously show your steadfast love,
   O savior of those who seek refuge
   from their adversaries at your right hand.
Guard me as the apple of the eye;
   hide me in the shadow of your wings,
from the wicked who despoil me,
   my deadly enemies who surround me. (Ps. 17:6-9)

Additional Readings

2 Samuel 11:2-26
David sins

Revelation 3:1-6
Wake up to your faithlessness

Hymn: What Wondrous Love Is This, ELW 666

Everlasting God, you have promised to hear the cries of your people. Teach us to listen when you speak your word to us. Awaken us to the joys and beauty of this wondrous life that we may know your love.

Tuesday, August 30, 2011

Time after Pentecost

Revelation 3:7-13

Facing the hour of trial

"And to the angel of the church in Philadelphia write:
These are the words of the holy one, the true one,
who has the key of David,
who opens and no one will shut,
who shuts and no one opens:
Because you have kept my word of patient endurance, I will keep
you from the hour of trial that is coming on the whole world to test
the inhabitants of the earth. I am coming soon; hold fast to what
you have, so that no one may seize your crown. If you conquer, I will
make you a pillar in the temple of my God; you will never go out of
it. I will write on you the name of my God, and the name of the city
of my God, the new Jerusalem that comes down from my God out of
heaven, and my own new name." (Rev. 3:7, 10-12)

Psalm
Psalm 17
The righteous shall see God

Additional Reading
2 Samuel 11:27b—12:15
Nathan rebukes David

Hymn: Just As I Am, without One Plea, ELW 592

*Eternal God, you have inscribed your name on our hearts. Give us
constant faith to stand up against any trial and test that may challenge
our endless devotion to you. Bring us home at last to the place you have
prepared for us.*

Wednesday, August 31, 2011

Time after Pentecost

Jeremiah 17:5-18
The vindication of the righteous

Thus says the LORD:
Cursed are those who trust in mere mortals
    and make mere flesh their strength,
    whose hearts turn away from the LORD.
They shall be like a shrub in the desert,
    and shall not see when relief comes.
They shall live in the parched places of the wilderness,
    in an uninhabited salt land.
Blessed are those who trust in the LORD,
    whose trust is the LORD.
They shall be like a tree planted by water,
    sending out its roots by the stream.
It shall not fear when heat comes,
    and its leaves shall stay green;
in the year of drought it is not anxious,
    and it does not cease to bear fruit. (Jer. 17:5-8)

Psalm	**Additional Reading**
Psalm 17	Matthew 12:22-32
The righteous shall see God	*Jesus comes to cast out Satan*

Hymn: Come to Me, All Pilgrims Thirsty, ELW 777

Lord God, you strengthen the faint-hearted. Give us courage to face our fears. When the future seems rocky and barren, bring forth streams of water, gushing full of life.

TIME AFTER PENTECOST

AUTUMN

The days of early autumn (September and October) herald the resumption of a more regular schedule: school begins, church education programs commence, and the steady rhythms of work are accompanied by cooling breezes and the changing colors of the landscape. During these months, various crops are harvested and appear on roadside stands and in grocery stores. In many countries the harvest days of September and October are marked with prayer, feasting, and special care for the poor and hungry.

Table Prayer for Autumn

We praise you and bless you, O God,
for autumn days,
and for the gifts of this table.
Grant us grace to share your goodness,
until all people are fed by the harvest of the earth.
We ask this through Christ our Lord. Amen.

_____

_____

_____

_____

_____

_____

_____

_____

_____

_____

_____

Thursday, September 1, 2011

Time after Pentecost

Psalm 119:33-40
The path of your commandments

Teach me, O Lord, the way of your statutes,
    and I will observe it to the end.
Give me understanding, that I may keep your law
    and observe it with my whole heart.
Lead me in the path of your commandments,
    for I delight in it.
Turn my heart to your decrees,
    and not to selfish gain. (Ps. 119:33-36)

Additional Readings
Ezekiel 24:1-14   2 Corinthians 12:11-21
God judges unrepentant Israel   *Sinners warned but unrepentant*

Hymn: O God of Light, ELW 507

*Lord God, in your gracious law and commandments is your vision for
our life together. Forgive us in our failures to follow your ways, and set
our hearts on what is good, through Jesus Christ our Lord.*

Friday, September 2, 2011

Time after Pentecost

Nikolai Frederik Severin Grundtvig, bishop, renewer of the church, 1872

Romans 10:15b-21
God reaches out to erring Israel

As it is written, "How beautiful are the feet of those who bring good news!" But not all have obeyed the good news; for Isaiah says, "Lord, who has believed our message?" So faith comes from what is heard, and what is heard comes through the word of Christ. (Rom. 10:15b-17)

Psalm
Psalm 119:33-40
The path of your commandments

Additional Reading
Ezekiel 24:15-27
God opens the prophet's mouth

Hymn: God's Word Is Our Great Heritage, ELW 509

Gracious God, your gospel is a treasury of wealth beyond measure, open to all people. By your Spirit empower us to share the good news with those who have yet to hear it, through Christ Jesus our Savior and Lord.

Saturday, September 3, 2011

Time after Pentecost

Ezekiel 33:1-6
The prophet's vocation

The word of the LORD came to me: O Mortal, speak to your people and say to them, If I bring the sword upon a land, and the people of the land take one of their number as their sentinel; and if the sentinel sees the sword coming upon the land and blows the trumpet and warns the people; then if any who hear the sound of the trumpet do not take warning, and the sword comes and takes them away, their blood shall be upon their own heads. They heard the sound of the trumpet and did not take warning; their blood shall be upon themselves. But if they had taken warning, they would have saved their lives. But if the sentinel sees the sword coming and does not blow the trumpet, so that the people are not warned, and the sword comes and takes any of them, they are taken away in their iniquity, but their blood I will require at the sentinel's hand. (Ezek. 33:1-6)

Psalm
Psalm 119:33-40
The path of your commandments

Additional Reading
Matthew 23:29-36
The martyrdom of the prophets

Hymn: Lo! He Comes with Clouds Descending, ELW 435

God of all, in every age you send faithful prophets and preachers to call us back to you. Give us ears to hear their message, that we may live in your justice and peace, in Christ Jesus the incarnate Word.

Sunday, September 4, 2011

Time after Pentecost

Matthew 18:15-20
Reconciliation in the community of faith

"If another member of the church sins against you, go and point out the fault when the two of you are alone. If the member listens to you, you have regained that one. But if you are not listened to, take one or two others along with you, so that every word may be confirmed by the evidence of two or three witnesses. If the member refuses to listen to them, tell it to the church; and if the offender refuses to listen even to the church, let such a one be to you as a Gentile and a tax collector." (Matt. 18:15-17)

Psalm
Psalm 119:33-40
The path of your commandments

Additional Readings
Ezekiel 33:7-11
The prophet's responsibility

Romans 13:8-14
Live honorably as in the day

Hymn: Forgive Our Sins As We Forgive, ELW 605

O Lord God, enliven and preserve your church with your perpetual mercy. Without your help, we mortals will fail; remove far from us everything that is harmful, and lead us toward all that gives life and salvation, through Jesus Christ, our Savior and Lord.

Monday, September 5, 2011

Time after Pentecost

Psalm 119:65-72
The law humbles me

You have dealt well with your servant,
  O Lord, according to your word.
Teach me good judgment and knowledge,
  for I believe in your commandments.
Before I was humbled I went astray,
  but now I keep your word. (Ps. 119:65-67)

Additional Readings
Leviticus 4:27-31; 5:14-16
Atoning for sin in the community

1 Peter 2:11-17
Live as servants of God

Hymn: O Word of God Incarnate, ELW 514

Lord of life, your word is ever near us, humbling us when we stray and comforting us with your love. As servants of your word, inspire us to grow daily in your grace, through Jesus Christ our Lord.

Tuesday, September 6, 2011

Time after Pentecost

Romans 13:1-7
Obeying authority

Let every person be subject to the governing authorities; for there is no authority except from God, and those authorities that exist have been instituted by God. Therefore whoever resists authority resists what God has appointed, and those who resist will incur judgment. For rulers are not a terror to good conduct, but to bad. Do you wish to have no fear of the authority? Then do what is good, and you will receive its approval; for it is God's servant for your good. But if you do what is wrong, you should be afraid, for the authority does not bear the sword in vain! It is the servant of God to execute wrath on the wrongdoer. (Rom. 13:1-4)

Psalm
Psalm 119:65-72
The law humbles me

Additional Reading
Deuteronomy 17:2-13
Punishment for sin in community

Hymn: Let the Whole Creation Cry, ELW 876

Lord God, you have provided authorities and governments for the common good of the people. Empower them to care for the needs of all, and when they fail, correct them, in our Lord Jesus Christ.

Wednesday, September 7, 2011

Time after Pentecost

Matthew 21:18-22

Jesus teaches about praying in faith

In the morning, when he returned to the city, he was hungry. And seeing a fig tree by the side of the road, he went to it and found nothing at all on it but leaves. Then he said to it, "May no fruit ever come from you again!" And the fig tree withered at once. When the disciples saw it, they were amazed, saying, "How did the fig tree wither at once?" Jesus answered them, "Truly I tell you, if you have faith and do not doubt, not only will you do what has been done to the fig tree, but even if you say to this mountain, 'Be lifted up and thrown into the sea,' it will be done. Whatever you ask for in prayer with faith, you will receive." (Matt. 21:18-22)

Psalm

Psalm 119:65-72

The law humbles me

Additional Reading

Leviticus 16:1-5, 20-28

The scapegoat cleanses the community

Hymn: Lord, Teach Us How to Pray Aright, ELW 745

Creator God, from your hand we receive abundant gifts for our well-being. Stir up in us the faith to ask for what we need and to receive your blessings with thanksgiving, in Christ's name.

Thursday, September 8, 2011

Time after Pentecost

Psalm 103:[1-7] 8-13
God's compassion and mercy

The LORD is merciful and gracious,
    slow to anger and abounding in steadfast love.
He will not always accuse,
    nor will he keep his anger forever.
He does not deal with us according to our sins,
    nor repay us according to our iniquities.
For as the heavens are high above the earth,
    so great is his steadfast love toward those who fear him;
as far as the east is from the west,
    so far he removes our transgressions from us. (Ps. 103:8-12)

Additional Readings
Genesis 37:12-36
Joseph's brothers sin against him

1 John 3:11-16
Love one another

Hymn: Praise, My Soul, the God of Heaven, ELW 864

Forgiving God, you remain faithful to us even when we are faithless. Remind us always of your steadfast love, that our lives may reflect your goodness and mercy, through our Lord Jesus Christ.

Friday, September 9, 2011

Time after Pentecost

Peter Claver, priest, missionary to Colombia, 1654

Genesis 41:53—42:17

Joseph acts harshly against his brothers

But Joseph said to [his brothers], "It is just as I have said to you; you are spies! Here is how you shall be tested: as Pharaoh lives, you shall not leave this place unless your youngest brother comes here! Let one of you go and bring your brother, while the rest of you remain in prison, in order that your words may be tested, whether there is truth in you; or else, as Pharaoh lives, surely you are spies." And he put them all together in prison for three days. (Gen. 42:14-17)

Psalm

Psalm 103:[1-7] 8-13

God's compassion and mercy

Additional Reading

Acts 7:9-16

Joseph's family is fed in Egypt

Hymn: Lord of Glory, You Have Bought Us, ELW 707

Lord of life, in times of testing you provide relief in surprising ways. Renew our minds to see your saving work in the world, and grant us the strength to persevere, in the name of Christ Jesus.

Saturday, September 10, 2011

Time after Pentecost

Matthew 6:7-15

Forgiving one another

"Pray then in this way:
Our Father in heaven,
hallowed be your name.
Your kingdom come.
Your will be done,
on earth as it is in heaven.
Give us this day our daily bread.
And forgive us our debts,
as we also have forgiven our debtors.
And do not bring us to the time of trial,
but rescue us from the evil one." (Matt. 6:9-13)

Psalm

Psalm 103:[1-7] 8-13
God's compassion and mercy

Additional Reading

Genesis 45:1-20
Joseph forgives his brothers

Hymn: Our Father, God in Heaven Above, ELW 746/747

Forgiving God, while we were still your enemies you sent your Son to reconcile us to you. Open our hearts to forgive those who wrong us, just as we have been forgiven through the work of our Lord Jesus Christ.

Sunday, September 11, 2011

Time after Pentecost

Matthew 18:21-35

A parable of forgiveness

Then Peter came and said to him, "Lord, if another member of the church sins against me, how often should I forgive? As many as seven times?" Jesus said to him, "Not seven times, but, I tell you, seventy-seven times." (Matt. 18:21-22)

Psalm
Psalm 103:[1-7] 8-13
God's compassion and mercy

Additional Readings
Genesis 50:15-21
Joseph reconciles with his brothers

Romans 14:1-12
When brothers and sisters judge each other

Hymn: Listen, God Is Calling, ELW 513

O Lord God, merciful judge, you are the inexhaustible fountain of forgiveness. Replace our hearts of stone with hearts that love and adore you, that we may delight in doing your will, through Jesus Christ, our Savior and Lord.

Monday, September 12, 2011

Time after Pentecost

Psalm 133
How good it is to live in unity

How very good and pleasant it is
    when kindred live together in unity!
It is like the precious oil on the head,
    running down upon the beard,
on the beard of Aaron,
    running down over the collar of his robes.
It is like the dew of Hermon,
    which falls on the mountains of Zion.
For there the LORD ordained his blessing,
    life forevermore. (Ps. 133)

Additional Readings

Genesis 48:8-22
Jacob blesses Joseph's sons

Hebrews 11:23-29
The faith of Moses

Hymn: Behold, How Pleasant, ELW 649

God of all peoples, you establish families and communities for the purpose of supporting their members as well as newcomers and strangers. Repair any rifts in our society, and teach us to work for the good of all, though our Lord Jesus Christ.

Tuesday, September 13, 2011

Time after Pentecost

John Chrysostom, Bishop of Constantinople, 407

Romans 14:13—15:2

Building each other up

Let us therefore no longer pass judgment on one another, but resolve instead never to put a stumbling block or hindrance in the way of another. I know and am persuaded in the Lord Jesus that nothing is unclean in itself; but it is unclean for anyone who thinks it unclean. If your brother or sister is being injured by what you eat, you are no longer walking in love. Do not let what you eat cause the ruin of one for whom Christ died. So do not let your good be spoken of as evil. For the kingdom of God is not food and drink but righteousness and peace and joy in the Holy Spirit. The one who thus serves Christ is acceptable to God and has human approval. Let us then pursue what makes for peace and for mutual upbuilding. (Rom. 14:13-19)

Psalm
Psalm 133
How good it is to live in unity

Additional Reading
Genesis 49:29—50:14
Honoring Jacob's burial wishes

Hymn: Beloved, God's Chosen, ELW 648

Gracious God, in your promises we find true freedom to serve one another in love. By your liberating word, empower us to bear each other's burdens for the sake of Christ Jesus, our Lord.

Wednesday, September 14, 2011

Holy Cross Day

John 3:13-17
The Son of Man will be lifted up

"No one has ascended into heaven except the one who descended from heaven, the Son of Man. And just as Moses lifted up the serpent in the wilderness, so must the Son of Man be lifted up, that whoever believes in him may have eternal life.

"For God so loved the world that he gave his only Son, so that everyone who believes in him may not perish but may have eternal life.

"Indeed, God did not send the Son into the world to condemn the world, but in order that the world might be saved through him." (John 3:13-17)

Psalm
Psalm 98:1-4
The LORD has done marvelous things

Additional Readings
Numbers 21:4b-9
A bronze serpent in the wilderness

1 Corinthians 1:18-24
The cross is the power of God

Hymn: Lift High the Cross, ELW 660

Almighty God, your Son Jesus Christ was lifted high upon the cross so that he might draw the whole world to himself. To those who look upon the cross, grant your wisdom, healing, and eternal life, through Jesus Christ, our Savior and Lord, who lives and reigns with you and the Holy Spirit, one God, now and forever.

Thursday, September 15, 2011

Time after Pentecost

Psalm 145:1-8

God is slow to anger

I will extol you, my God and King,
   and bless your name forever and ever.
Every day I will bless you,
   and praise your name forever and ever.
Great is the LORD, and greatly to be praised;
   his greatness is unsearchable.
The LORD is gracious and merciful,
   slow to anger and abounding in steadfast love. (Ps. 145:1-3, 8)

Additional Readings

Nahum 1:1, 14—2:2
God's wrath toward Nineveh

2 Corinthians 13:1-4
Dissent among believers

Hymn: Before You, Lord, We Bow, ELW 893

Lord God, every day you shower us with the riches of your grace. Soften our hearts to receive your blessings with gratitude and to share them with others in faith, trusting in our Lord Jesus Christ.

Friday, September 16, 2011

Time after Pentecost

Cyprian, Bishop of Carthage, martyr, c. 258

2 Corinthians 13:5-10

Correction that builds up

But we pray to God that you may not do anything wrong—not that we may appear to have met the test, but that you may do what is right, though we may seem to have failed. For we cannot do anything against the truth, but only for the truth. For we rejoice when we are weak and you are strong. This is what we pray for, that you may become perfect. So I write these things while I am away from you, so that when I come, I may not have to be severe in using the authority that the Lord has given me for building up and not for tearing down. (2 Cor. 13:7-10)

Psalm

Psalm 145:1-8
God is slow to anger

Additional Reading

Nahum 2:3-13
Nineveh under siege

Hymn: Just a Closer Walk with Thee, ELW 697

God of all, you have appointed leaders of manifold gifts and abilities to serve your church. Sustain and uphold them by your Spirit, that their efforts may build faith in your people, in and through Christ our Lord.

Saturday, September 17, 2011

Time after Pentecost

Hildegard, Abbess of Bingen, 1179

Zephaniah 2:13-15

Judgment on Nineveh

And he will stretch out his hand against the north,
  and destroy Assyria;
and he will make Nineveh a desolation,
  a dry waste like the desert.
Herds shall lie down in it, every wild animal;
the desert owl and the screech owl shall lodge on its capitals;
the owl shall hoot at the window,
  the raven croak on the threshold;
  for its cedar work will be laid bare.
Is this the exultant city that lived secure,
that said to itself, "I am, and there is no one else"?
What a desolation it has become,
  a lair for wild animals!
Everyone who passes by it
  hisses and shakes the fist. (Zeph. 2:13-15)

Psalm
Psalm 145:1-8
God is slow to anger

Additional Reading
Matthew 19:23-30
The last will be first

Hymn: All Who Love and Serve Your City, ELW 724

*God our protector, in your bountiful goodness you nourish and provide
security for our cities and communities. Preserve them from all threats,
internal and external, that your peace may reign in them, through our
Lord Jesus Christ.*

Sunday, September 18, 2011

Time after Pentecost

Dag Hammarskjöld, renewer of society, 1961

Matthew 20:1-16

The parable of the vineyard workers

But [the landowner] replied to one of [the laborers], "Friend, I am doing you no wrong; did you not agree with me for the usual daily wage? Take what belongs to you and go; I choose to give to this last the same as I give to you. Am I not allowed to do what I choose with what belongs to me? Or are you envious because I am generous?" So the last will be first, and the first will be last." (Matt. 20:13-16)

Psalm

Psalm 145:1-8

God is slow to anger

Additional Readings

Jonah 3:10—4:11

God's concern for Nineveh

Philippians 1:21-30

Standing firm in the gospel

Hymn: Praise and Thanksgiving, ELW 689

Almighty and eternal God, you show perpetual lovingkindness to us your servants. Because we cannot rely on our own abilities, grant us your merciful judgment, and train us to embody the generosity of your Son, Jesus Christ, our Savior and Lord.

Monday, September 19, 2011

Time after Pentecost

Psalm 106:1-12
God's mercy

Praise the LORD!
O give thanks to the LORD, for he is good;
for his steadfast love endures forever.
Who can utter the mighty doings of the LORD,
or declare all his praise?
Happy are those who observe justice,
who do righteousness at all times.
Remember me, O LORD, when you show favor to your people;
help me when you deliver them;
that I may see the prosperity of your chosen ones,
that I may rejoice in the gladness of your nation,
that I may glory in your heritage. (Ps. 106:1-5)

Additional Readings
Genesis 27:1-29
The younger son gets the blessing

Romans 16:1-16
Diverse women and men are coworkers in Christ

Hymn: Praise and Thanks and Adoration, ELW 783

God of abundance, daily you multiply blessings among your people in surprising and life-giving ways. Help us not to squander your goodness, but to bless others with your mercy and peace, following the example of our Lord Jesus Christ.

Tuesday, September 20, 2011

Time after Pentecost

Romans 16:17-20

A warning about troublemakers

I urge you, brothers and sisters, to keep an eye on those who cause dissensions and offenses, in opposition to the teaching that you have learned; avoid them. For such people do not serve our Lord Christ, but their own appetites, and by smooth talk and flattery they deceive the hearts of the simple-minded. For while your obedience is known to all, so that I rejoice over you, I want you to be wise in what is good and guileless in what is evil. The God of peace will shortly crush Satan under your feet. The grace of our Lord Jesus Christ be with you. (Rom. 16:17-20)

Psalm
Psalm 106:1-12
God's mercy

Additional Reading
Genesis 28:10-17
God blesses the runaway Jacob

Hymn: Lord, Take My Hand and Lead Me, ELW 767

Lord God, you desire your peace to reign among nations, cities, and neighborhoods. Teach us the ways of peace, that we may shun bitterness and resentment, and open doors for reconciliation and understanding, in Christ our Savior.

Wednesday, September 21, 2011

Matthew, Apostle and Evangelist

Matthew 9:9-13

Jesus calls to Matthew: Follow me

As Jesus was walking along, he saw a man called Matthew sitting at
the tax booth; and he said to him, "Follow me." And he got up and
followed him.

And as he sat at dinner in the house, many tax collectors and sinners
came and were sitting with him and his disciples. When the Pharisees
saw this, they said to his disciples, "Why does your teacher eat with
tax collectors and sinners?" But when he heard this, he said, "Those
who are well have no need of a physician, but those who are sick. Go
and learn what this means, 'I desire mercy, not sacrifice.' For I have
come to call not the righteous but sinners." (Matt. 9:9-13)

Psalm

Psalm 119:33-40
Give me understanding

Additional Readings

Ezekiel 2:8—3:11
A prophet to the house of Israel

Ephesians 2:4-10
By grace you have been saved

Hymn: Jesus Calls Us; o'er the Tumult, ELW 696

*Almighty God, your Son our Savior called a despised tax collector to
become one of his apostles. Help us, like Matthew, to respond to the
transforming call of Jesus Christ, who lives and reigns with you and the
Holy Spirit, one God, now and forever.*

Thursday, September 22, 2011

Time after Pentecost

Psalm 25:1-9
God's compassion and love

Make me to know your ways, O Lord;
    teach me your paths.
Lead me in your truth, and teach me,
    for you are the God of my salvation;
    for you I wait all day long.
Be mindful of your mercy, O Lord, and of your steadfast love,
    for they have been from of old.
Do not remember the sins of my youth or my transgressions;
    according to your steadfast love remember me,
    for your goodness' sake, O Lord! (Ps. 25:4-7)

Additional Readings

Ezekiel 12:17-28
God's judgment is timely

James 4:11-16
We do not know what tomorrow will bring

Hymn: Rise Up, O Saints of God! ELW 669

Loving God, we give you thanks that in your mercy you overlook our sins, known and unknown to us. Reassure us of your never-failing love, that we may freely confess our wrongdoings to you, and receive forgiveness through our Lord Jesus Christ.

Friday, September 23, 2011

Time after Pentecost

Ezekiel 18:5-18

Those who repent shall live

If a man is righteous and does what is lawful and right—if he does not eat upon the mountains or lift up his eyes to the idols of the house of Israel, does not defile his neighbor's wife or approach a woman during her menstrual period, does not oppress anyone, but restores to the debtor his pledge, commits no robbery, gives his bread to the hungry and covers the naked with a garment, does not take advance or accrued interest, withholds his hand from iniquity, executes true justice between contending parties, follows my statutes, and is careful to observe my ordinances, acting faithfully—such a one is righteous; he shall surely live, says the Lord GOD. (Ezek. 18:5-9)

Psalm

Psalm 25:1-9

God's compassion and love

Additional Readings

Acts 13:32-41

Through Jesus forgiveness is proclaimed

Hymn: Thy Strong Word, ELW 511

Almighty God, you desire all to enter your kingdom of justice and peace. By your grace, strengthen us to live according to your vision, and forgive us when we fail. This we ask through Christ our Lord.

Saturday, September 24, 2011

Time after Pentecost

Ezekiel 18:19-24

A child does not suffer for a parent's sin

Yet you say, "Why should not the son suffer for the iniquity of the father?" When the son has done what is lawful and right, and has been careful to observe all my statutes, he shall surely live. The person who sins shall die. A child shall not suffer for the iniquity of a parent, nor a parent suffer for the iniquity of a child; the righteousness of the righteous shall be his own, and the wickedness of the wicked shall be his own. (Ezek. 18:19-20)

Psalm
Psalm 25:1-9
God's compassion and love

Additional Reading
Mark 11:27-33
Jesus' authority is questioned

Hymn: Christ, Whose Glory Fills the Skies, ELW 553

O God, your ways are just, and you call your servants to follow them and live. Enliven our spirits, that our desires may be your own, and our actions in keeping with them, in Christ our Lord.

Sunday, September 25, 2011

Time after Pentecost

Matthew 21:23-32

A parable of doing God's will

"What do you think? A man had two sons; he went to the first and said, 'Son, go and work in the vineyard today.' He answered, 'I will not'; but later he changed his mind and went. The father went to the second and said the same; and he answered, 'I go, sir'; but he did not go. Which of the two did the will of his father?" They said, "The first." Jesus said to them, "Truly I tell you, the tax collectors and the prostitutes are going into the kingdom of God ahead of you. For John came to you in the way of righteousness and you did not believe him, but the tax collectors and the prostitutes believed him; and even after you saw it, you did not change your minds and believe him." (Matt. 21:28-32)

Psalm	Additional Readings	
Psalm 25:1-9	Ezekiel 18:1-4, 25-32	Philippians 2:1-13
God's compassion and love	*The fairness of God's way*	*Christ humbled to the point of death*

Hymn: All My Hope on God Is Founded, ELW 757

God of love, giver of life, you know our frailties and failings. Give us your grace to overcome them, keep us from those things that harm us, and guide us in the way of salvation, through Jesus Christ, our Savior and Lord.

Monday, September 26, 2011

Time after Pentecost

Psalm 28
Prayer to do God's will

To you, O LORD, I call;
   my rock, do not refuse to hear me,
for if you are silent to me,
   I shall be like those who go down to the Pit.
Hear the voice of my supplication,
   as I cry to you for help,
as I lift up my hands
   toward your most holy sanctuary.
Blessed be the LORD,
   for he has heard the sound of my pleadings.
The LORD is my strength and my shield;
   in him my heart trusts;
so I am helped, and my heart exults,
   and with my song I give thanks to him. (Ps. 28:1-2, 6-7)

Additional Readings

Judges 14:1-20
Samson's riddle explained

Philippians 1:3-14
Paul prays for the Philippians

Hymn: All Depends on Our Possessing, ELW 589

Lord of our salvation, we come to you with hearts and hands open to receive your gracious presence among us. Loosen our lips to give you praise for your ongoing faithfulness and works of mercy, through our Savior Jesus Christ.

Tuesday, September 27, 2011

Time after Pentecost

Psalm 28
Prayer to do God's will

Blessed be the LORD,
    for he has heard the sound of my pleadings.
The LORD is my strength and my shield;
    in him my heart trusts;
so I am helped, and my heart exults,
    and with my song I give thanks to him.
The LORD is the strength of his people;
    he is the saving refuge of his anointed.
O save your people, and bless your heritage;
    be their shepherd, and carry them forever. (Ps. 28:6-9)

Additional Readings
Judges 16:1-22
Samson asked about his strength

Philippians 1:15-21
Christ is proclaimed regardless of the motive

Hymn: Jesus Lives, My Sure Defense, ELW 621

Almighty God, amid the fears and anxieties of this world we run to you for safe-keeping. Bind us to Christ, so that we may take comfort in his life-giving death and resurrection, and be at peace.

Wednesday, September 28, 2011

Time after Pentecost

Judges 16:23-31
Samson prays to do God's will

Then Samson called to the LORD and said, "Lord GOD, remember me and strengthen me only this once, O God, so that with this one act of revenge I may pay back the Philistines for my two eyes." And Samson grasped the two middle pillars on which the house rested, and he leaned his weight against them, his right hand on the one and his left hand on the other. Then Samson said, "Let me die with the Philistines." He strained with all his might; and the house fell on the lords and all the people who were in it. So those he killed at his death were more than those he had killed during his life. Then his brothers and all his family came down and took him and brought him up and buried him between Zorah and Eshtaol in the tomb of his father Manoah. He had judged Israel twenty years. (Judg. 16:28-31)

Psalm
Psalm 28
Prayer to do God's will

Additional Reading
Matthew 9:2-8
Jesus' authority to forgive and heal

Hymn: Lead On, O King Eternal! ELW 805

God of steadfast love, in times of weakness and despair you give us strength to face our trials. Keep us mindful of your constant care, that we may endure times of testing, trusting in the victory of Christ our Lord.

Thursday, September 29, 2011

Michael and all Angels

Revelation 12:7-12

Michael defeats Satan in a cosmic battle

And war broke out in heaven; Michael and his angels fought against
the dragon. The dragon and his angels fought back, but they were
defeated, and there was no longer any place for them in heaven. The
great dragon was thrown down, that ancient serpent, who is called
the Devil and Satan, the deceiver of the whole world—he was thrown
down to the earth, and his angels were thrown down with him.
(Rev. 12:7-9)

Psalm
Psalm 103:1-5, 20-22
Bless the Lord, you angels

Additional Readings
Daniel 10:10-14; 12:1-3
Michael shall arise

Luke 10:17-20
Jesus gives his followers authority

Hymn: Blessing and Honor, ELW 854

*Everlasting God, you have wonderfully established the ministries of
angels and mortals. Mercifully grant that as Michael and the angels
contend against the cosmic forces of evil, so by your direction they may
help and defend us here on earth, through your Son, Jesus Christ our
Lord, who lives and reigns with you and the Holy Spirit, one God whom
we worship and praise with angels and archangels and all the company
of heaven, now and forever.*

Friday, September 30, 2011

Time after Pentecost

Jerome, translator, teacher, 420

Philippians 2:14-18; 3:1-4a

Boast only in Jesus Christ

Do all things without murmuring and arguing, so that you may be blameless and innocent, children of God without blemish in the midst of a crooked and perverse generation, in which you shine like stars in the world. It is by your holding fast to the word of life that I can boast on the day of Christ that I did not run in vain or labor in vain. But even if I am being poured out as a libation over the sacrifice and the offering of your faith, I am glad and rejoice with all of you— and in the same way you also must be glad and rejoice with me. (Phil. 2:14-18)

Psalm

Psalm 80:7-15

Look down from heaven, O God

Additional Reading

Jeremiah 2:23-37

Israel shall be shamed

Hymn: O Savior, Precious Savior, ELW 820

Holy God, by your command you bring light from darkness, life from death. Embolden our confession of your word, that we may shine like stars in the world, reflecting the radiance of our Lord Jesus Christ.

PRAYER LIST FOR OCTOBER

_____

_____

_____

_____

_____

_____

_____

_____

_____

_____

_____

Saturday, October 1, 2011

Time after Pentecost

Jeremiah 6:1-10
Gleaning a remnant from the vine

Thus says the LORD of hosts:
Glean thoroughly as a vine
   the remnant of Israel;
like a grape-gatherer, pass your hand again
   over its branches.
To whom shall I speak and give warning,
   that they may hear?
See, their ears are closed,
   they cannot listen.
The word of the LORD is to them an object of scorn;
   they take no pleasure in it. (Jer. 6:9-10)

Psalm
Psalm 80:7-15
Look down from heaven, O God

Additional Reading
John 7:40-52
Some accept, others reject Jesus Christ

Hymn: Dearest Jesus, at Your Word, ELW 520

Make our ears and our hearts receptive to your saving word, O Lord, that it may take root in our lives. Cause faith to spring forth within us and bear fruit for the sake of the world.

Sunday, October 2, 2011

Time after Pentecost

Matthew 21:33-46

The parable of the vineyard owner's son

Jesus said to them, "Have you never read in the scriptures:
'The stone that the builders rejected
   has become the cornerstone;
this was the Lord's doing,
   and it is amazing in our eyes'?
Therefore I tell you, the kingdom of God will be taken away from you
and given to a people that produces the fruits of the kingdom. The
one who falls on this stone will be broken to pieces; and it will crush
anyone on whom it falls."

When the chief priests and the Pharisees heard his parables, they
realized that he was speaking about them. They wanted to arrest him,
but they feared the crowds, because they regarded him as a prophet.
(Matt. 21:42-46)

Psalm
Psalm 80:7-15
*Look down from heaven,
O God*

Additional Readings
Isaiah 5:1-7
The song of the vineyard

Philippians 3:4b-14
*Nothing surpasses knowing
Christ*

Hymn: Build Us Up, Lord, ELW 670

*Beloved God, from you come all things that are good. Lead us by the
inspiration of your Spirit to know those things that are right, and by
your merciful guidance, help us to do them, through Jesus Christ, our
Savior and Lord.*

Monday, October 3, 2011

Time after Pentecost

Psalm 144
Prayer for blessing

Blessed be the LORD, my rock,
    who trains my hands for war, and my fingers for battle;
my rock and my fortress,
    my stronghold and my deliverer,
my shield, in whom I take refuge,
    who subdues the peoples under me.
O LORD, what are human beings that you regard them,
    or mortals that you think of them?
They are like a breath;
    their days are like a passing shadow. (Ps. 144:1-4)

Additional Readings
Ezekiel 19:10-14
A lament for Israel the vine

1 Peter 2:4-10
Christ the cornerstone

Hymn: My Hope Is Built on Nothing Less, ELW 596/597

Lord, you are our refuge amid life's storms and struggles. Though we are weak, you are strong. When we are tossed about, you stand fast. Remember us, O Lord, in your mercy, and keep us safe in your love.

Tuesday, October 4, 2011

Time after Pentecost

Francis of Assisi, renewer of the church, 1226; Theodor Fliedner, renewer of society, 1864

2 Corinthians 5:17-21

God reconciles us through Christ

So if anyone is in Christ, there is a new creation: everything old has passed away; see, everything has become new! All this is from God, who reconciled us to himself through Christ, and has given us the ministry of reconciliation; that is, in Christ God was reconciling the world to himself, not counting their trespasses against them, and entrusting the message of reconciliation to us. So we are ambassadors for Christ, since God is making his appeal through us; we entreat you on behalf of Christ, be reconciled to God. For our sake he made him to be sin who knew no sin, so that in him we might become the righteousness of God. (2 Cor. 5:17-21)

Psalm
Psalm 144
Prayer for blessing

Additional Reading
Isaiah 27:1-6
God will save Israel the vine

Hymn: Rise, Shine, You People! ELW 665

God, through Jesus Christ, you have reconciled the world to yourself and opened the way for us to new life. Help us to lay aside the old ways of sin and walk in the ways of your righteousness.

Wednesday, October 5, 2011

Time after Pentecost

John 11:45-57
Critics plan to silence Jesus

Now the Passover of the Jews was near, and many went up from the country to Jerusalem before the Passover to purify themselves. They were looking for Jesus and were asking one another as they stood in the temple, "What do you think? Surely he will not come to the festival, will he?" Now the chief priests and the Pharisees had given orders that anyone who knew where Jesus was should let them know, so that they might arrest him. (John 11:55-57)

Psalm
Psalm 144
Prayer for blessing

Additional Reading
Song of Solomon 8:5-14
A love song for the vineyard

Hymn: Oh, Love, How Deep, ELW 322

Lord, your Son walked amid the turmoil of this world and willingly made his way to the cross. Give us the courage to join him on the path of sacrifice and service, so that others might know of your love.

Thursday, October 6, 2011

Time after Pentecost

William Tyndale, translator, martyr, 1536

Psalm 23
You spread a table before me

The LORD is my shepherd, I shall not want.
   He makes me lie down in green pastures;
he leads me beside still waters;
   he restores my soul.
He leads me in right paths for his name's sake.
Even though I walk through the darkest valley,
   I fear no evil;
for you are with me;
   your rod and your staff—they comfort me.
You prepare a table before me
   in the presence of my enemies;
you anoint my head with oil;
   my cup overflows.
Surely goodness and mercy shall follow me all the days of my life,
and I shall dwell in the house of the LORD
   my whole life long. (Ps. 23)

Additional Readings
Isaiah 22:1-8a
A futile cry to the mountains for help

1 Peter 5:1-5, 12-14
Stand fast, the chief shepherd is coming

Hymn: Savior, like a Shepherd Lead Us, ELW 789

O Lord, great shepherd of the sheep, lead us to green pastures and still waters. Guide us along right pathways and through the darkest of valleys. Comfort us with your presence and with the hope of life with you forever.

Friday, October 7, 2011

Time after Pentecost

Henry Melchior Muhlenberg, pastor in North America, 1787

James 4:4-10
Humble yourselves before God

Submit yourselves therefore to God. Resist the devil, and he will flee from you. Draw near to God, and he will draw near to you. Cleanse your hands, you sinners, and purify your hearts, you double-minded. Lament and mourn and weep. Let your laughter be turned into mourning and your joy into dejection. Humble yourselves before the Lord, and he will exalt you. (James 4:7-10)

Psalm
Psalm 23
You spread a table before me

Additional Reading
Isaiah 22:8b-14
False joy instead of repentance

Hymn: Lord, Whose Love in Humble Service, ELW 712

Almighty God, as lost and condemned sinners we are not worthy to stand in your presence or ask for your salvation, yet the open arms of your mercy and love bid us to come. Help us draw close to you.

Saturday, October 8, 2011

Time after Pentecost

Isaiah 24:17-23

God judges the earth from Mount Zion

On that day the LORD will punish
   the host of heaven in heaven,
     and on earth the kings of the earth.
They will be gathered together
   like prisoners in a pit;
they will be shut up in a prison,
   and after many days they will be punished.
Then the moon will be abashed,
   and the sun ashamed;
for the LORD of hosts will reign
   on Mount Zion and in Jerusalem,
and before his elders he will manifest his glory. (Isa. 24:21-23)

Psalm
Psalm 23
You spread a table before me

Additional Reading
Mark 2:18-22
No fasting when the bridegroom is present

Hymn: Oh, Happy Day When We Shall Stand, ELW 441

Lord, your judgments are righteous and your decrees are just. For our own misdeeds we deserve nothing but punishment. May the light of your glorious mercy shine on us, and may your love turn our hearts to you.

Matthew 22:1-14

The parable of the unwelcome guest

"But when the king came in to see the guests, he noticed a man there who was not wearing a wedding robe, and he said to him, 'Friend, how did you get in here without a wedding robe?' And he was speechless. Then the king said to the attendants, 'Bind him hand and foot, and throw him into the outer darkness, where there will be weeping and gnashing of teeth.' For many are called, but few are chosen." (Matt. 22:11-14)

Psalm

Psalm 23

You spread a table before me

Additional Readings

Isaiah 25:1-9

The feast of victory

Philippians 4:1-9

Rejoice in the Lord always

Hymn: All Who Hunger, Gather Gladly, ELW 461

Lord of the feast, you have prepared a table before all peoples and poured out your life with abundance. Call us again to your banquet. Strengthen us by what is honorable, just, and pure, and transform us into a people of righteousness and peace, through Jesus Christ, our Savior and Lord.

Monday, October 10, 2011

Day of Thanksgiving (Canada)

A Blessing of the Household for Thanksgiving Day can be found on page 367.

Psalm 34
Taste and see

O taste and see that the LORD is good;
  happy are those who take refuge in him.
O fear the LORD, you his holy ones,
  for those who fear him have no want.
The young lions suffer want and hunger,
  but those who seek the LORD lack no good thing. (Ps. 34:8-10)

Additional Readings
Exodus 19:7-20
God meets Moses on the mountain

Jude 17-25
Prepare for the Lord's coming

Hymn: Taste and See, ELW 493

Lord, your goodness fills our world and our lives abound with blessings. Open our eyes to see your wonders around us. Open our hearts to receive your good gifts with thanksgiving. Open our hands to share your abundance with others.

Tuesday, October 11, 2011

Time after Pentecost

Amos 9:5-15

Sweet wine from the mountains

The time is surely coming, says the LORD,
    when the one who plows shall overtake the one who reaps,
    and the treader of grapes the one who sows the seed;
the mountains shall drip sweet wine,
    and all the hills shall flow with it.
I will restore the fortunes of my people Israel,
    and they shall rebuild the ruined cities and inhabit them;
they shall plant vineyards and drink their wine,
    and they shall make gardens and eat their fruit.
I will plant them upon their land,
    and they shall never again be plucked up
    out of the land that I have given them,
                says the LORD your God. (Amos 9:13-15)

Psalm	**Additional Reading**
Psalm 34	Philippians 3:13—4:1
Taste and see	*Hold fast to Christ*

Hymn: Sing to the Lord of Harvest, ELW 694

The earth bears testimony to your abundance, O Lord, and you fill our lives with good things. Help us not to forsake you in the vain pursuit of earthly blessings, nor lose sight of the hope that only you can give.

Wednesday, October 12, 2011

Time after Pentecost

Song of Solomon 7:10—8:4
Love like rich fruit

I am my beloved's,
 and his desire is for me.
Come, my beloved,
 let us go forth into the fields,
 and lodge in the villages;
let us go out early to the vineyards,
 and see whether the vines have budded,
whether the grape blossoms have opened
 and the pomegranates are in bloom.
There I will give you my love.
The mandrakes give forth fragrance,
 and over our doors are all choice fruits,
new as well as old,
 which I have laid up for you, O my beloved. (Song of Sol. 7:10-13)

Psalm
Psalm 34
Taste and see

Additional Reading
John 6:25-35
God will feed the believer

Hymn: Come, Beloved of the Maker, ELW 306

Loving God, you take delight in us and desire to live in relationship with us. May your love blossom in our hearts as we seek to love you in return and share your love with those around us.

Thursday, October 13, 2011

Time after Pentecost

Psalm 96:1-9 [10-13]
God's glory among the nations

O sing to the LORD a new song;
  sing to the LORD, all the earth.
Sing to the LORD, bless his name;
  tell of his salvation from day to day.
Declare his glory among the nations,
  his marvelous works among all the peoples.
For great is the LORD, and greatly to be praised;
  he is to be revered above all gods. (Ps. 96:1-4)

Additional Readings
Judges 17:1-6
Before Israel had a king

3 John 9-12
Imitate what is good

Hymn: Earth and All Stars! ELW 731

Heaven and earth resound with the sound of your praise, O Lord, and your greatness fills the land. Accept our praises as we join our voices with those of every place and time, and sing of your marvelous works.

Friday, October 14, 2011

Time after Pentecost

1 Peter 5:1-5

Exemplary leadership

Now as an elder myself and a witness of the sufferings of Christ, as well as one who shares in the glory to be revealed, I exhort the elders among you to tend the flock of God that is in your charge, exercising the oversight, not under compulsion but willingly, as God would have you do it—not for sordid gain but eagerly. Do not lord it over those in your charge, but be examples to the flock. And when the chief shepherd appears, you will win the crown of glory that never fades away. In the same way, you who are younger must accept the authority of the elders. And all of you must clothe yourselves with humility in your dealings with one another, for

"God opposes the proud,
    but gives grace to the humble." (1 Peter 5:1-5)

Psalm
Psalm 96:1-9 [10-13]
God's glory among the nations

Additional Reading
Deuteronomy 17:14-20
The limitations of royal authority

Hymn: We All Are One in Mission, ELW 576

Lord, you have blessed your people with a variety of gifts and entrusted us with many responsibilities. Guide us as we humbly use our talents and gifts in service to one another and for the good of your world.

Saturday, October 15, 2011

Time after Pentecost

Teresa of Avila, teacher, renewer of the church, 1582

Isaiah 14:3-11
The king of Babylon will fall

When the LORD has given you rest from your pain and turmoil and the hard service with which you were made to serve, you will take up this taunt against the king of Babylon:

How the oppressor has ceased!
How his insolence has ceased!
The LORD has broken the staff of the wicked,
the scepter of rulers,
that struck down the peoples in wrath
with unceasing blows,
that ruled the nations in anger
with unrelenting persecution. (Isa. 14:3-6)

Psalm
Psalm 96:1-9 [10-13]
God's glory among the nations

Additional Reading
Matthew 14:1-12
King Herod's misuse of power

Hymn: O Day of Peace, ELW 711

O God of the nations, we pray for governmental leaders and all those entrusted with worldly authority. Instill in them your wisdom, so that the downtrodden might be uplifted, justice might be served, and all people might live in peace.

Sunday, October 16, 2011

Time after Pentecost

Matthew 22:15-22

A teaching about the emperor and God

But Jesus, aware of their malice, said, "Why are you putting me to the test, you hypocrites? Show me the coin used for the tax." And they brought him a denarius. Then he said to them, "Whose head is this, and whose title?" They answered, "The emperor's." Then he said to them, "Give therefore to the emperor the things that are the emperor's, and to God the things that are God's." When they heard this, they were amazed; and they left him and went away. (Matt. 22:18-22)

Psalm

Psalm 96:1-9 [10-13]

God's glory among the nations

Additional Readings

Isaiah 45:1-7

An earthly ruler works God's will

1 Thessalonians 1:1-10

Thanksgiving for the church at Thessalonica

Hymn: We Give Thee but Thine Own, ELW 686

Sovereign God, raise your throne in our hearts. Created by you, let us live in your image; created for you, let us act for your glory; redeemed by you, let us give you what is yours, through Jesus Christ, our Savior and Lord.

Monday, October 17, 2011

Time after Pentecost

Ignatius, Bishop of Antioch, martyr, c. 115

Psalm 98
God reigns over the nations

O sing to the LORD a new song,
  for he has done marvelous things.
His right hand and his holy arm
  have gotten him victory.
The LORD has made known his victory;
  he has revealed his vindication in the sight of the nations.
He has remembered his steadfast love and faithfulness
  to the house of Israel.
All the ends of the earth have seen
  the victory of our God. (Ps. 98:1-3)

Additional Readings
Daniel 3:1-18
Three disobey Nebuchadnezzar

Revelation 18:1-10, 19-20
The fall of Babylon

Hymn: Oh, Sing to the Lord, ELW 822

Your rule is love, O Lord, and you reign with justice. Let your righteousness fill the earth. Keep us steadfast in faith as we await the final victory on that day when your kingdom will come in all its fullness.

Tuesday, October 18, 2011

Luke, Evangelist

Luke 1:1-4; 24:44-53
Luke witnesses to the ministry of Jesus

Since many have undertaken to set down an orderly account of the events that have been fulfilled among us, just as they were handed on to us by those who from the beginning were eyewitnesses and servants of the word, I too decided, after investigating everything carefully from the very first, to write an orderly account for you, most excellent Theophilus, so that you may know the truth concerning the things about which you have been instructed. (Luke 1:1-4)

Psalm
Psalm 124
Our help is in God

Additional Readings
Isaiah 43:8-13
You are my witness

2 Timothy 4:5-11
The good fight of faith

Hymn: I Love to Tell the Story, ELW 661

Almighty God, you inspired your servant Luke to reveal in his gospel the love and healing power of your Son. Give your church the same love and power to heal, and to proclaim your salvation to the nations, to the glory of your name, through Jesus Christ, your Son, our healer, who lives and reigns with you and the Holy Spirit, one God, now and forever.

Wednesday, October 19, 2011

Time after Pentecost

Matthew 17:22-27
Jesus pays the temple tax

When they reached Capernaum, the collectors of the temple tax came to Peter and said, "Does your teacher not pay the temple tax?" He said, "Yes, he does." And when he came home, Jesus spoke of it first, asking, "What do you think, Simon? From whom do kings of the earth take toll or tribute? From their children or from others?" When Peter said, "From others," Jesus said to him, "Then the children are free. However, so that we do not give offense to them, go to the sea and cast a hook; take the first fish that comes up; and when you open its mouth, you will find a coin; take that and give it to them for you and me." (Matt. 17:24-27)

Psalm
Psalm 98
God reigns over the nations

Additional Reading
Daniel 6:1-28
Daniel disobeys King Darius

Hymn: Oh, Praise the Gracious Power, ELW 651

O God of both heaven and earth, you have placed us on earth, yet planted within us the hope of heavenly glory. Help us carry out our earthly responsibilities faithfully while we await the coming of your heavenly kingdom.

Thursday, October 20, 2011

Time after Pentecost

Psalm 1
Their delight is in the law

Happy are those
  who do not follow the advice of the wicked,
or take the path that sinners tread,
  or sit in the seat of scoffers;
but their delight is in the law of the LORD,
  and on his law they meditate day and night.
They are like trees
  planted by streams of water,
which yield their fruit in its season,
  and their leaves do not wither.
In all that they do, they prosper. (Ps. 1:1-3)

Additional Readings
Numbers 5:5-10
Restitution for wronged neighbors

Titus 1:5-16
Troublemakers deny God

Hymn: Oh, That the Lord Would Guide My Ways, ELW 772

O Lord, your decrees are just and your law is life giving. Help us to delight in your law of love and your gospel of salvation. Through your word guide us to abundant life, both now and eternally.

Friday, October 21, 2011

Time after Pentecost

Titus 2:7-8, 11-15
A life devoted to good works

For the grace of God has appeared, bringing salvation to all, training us to renounce impiety and worldly passions, and in the present age to live lives that are self-controlled, upright, and godly, while we wait for the blessed hope and the manifestation of the glory of our great God and Savior, Jesus Christ. He it is who gave himself for us that he might redeem us from all iniquity and purify for himself a people of his own who are zealous for good deeds. (Titus 2:11-14)

Psalm
Psalm 1
Their delight is in the law

Additional Reading
Deuteronomy 9:25—10:5
The second set of commandments

Hymn: Salvation unto Us Has Come, ELW 590

O God, in Christ you have redeemed us and brought about our salvation. As we wait for Christ's return, help us to glorify you and do good things for others.

Saturday, October 22, 2011

Time after Pentecost

John 5:39-47
Moses judges the disobedient

[Jesus said to the Jews:] "I have come in my Father's name, and you do not accept me; if another comes in his own name, you will accept him. How can you believe when you accept glory from one another and do not seek the glory that comes from the one who alone is God? Do not think that I will accuse you before the Father; your accuser is Moses, on whom you have set your hope. If you believed Moses, you would believe me, for he wrote about me. But if you do not believe what he wrote, how will you believe what I say?" (John 5:43-47)

Psalm
Psalm 1
Their delight is in the law

Additional Reading
Proverbs 24:23-34
Rise above retribution

Hymn: We All Believe in One True God, ELW 411

In the face of your Son Jesus Christ, we have seen your face of love and mercy. Give us faith to see in him the fulfillment of that which the law and the prophets spoke and the glory of your salvation.

Sunday, October 23, 2011

Time after Pentecost

James of Jerusalem, martyr, c. 62

Matthew 22:34-46

Loving God and neighbor

When the Pharisees heard that [Jesus] had silenced the Sadducees, they gathered together, and one of them, a lawyer, asked him a question to test him. "Teacher, which commandment in the law is the greatest?" He said to him, "'You shall love the Lord your God with all your heart, and with all your soul, and with all your mind.' This is the greatest and first commandment. And a second is like it: 'You shall love your neighbor as yourself.' On these two commandments hang all the law and the prophets." (Matt. 22:34-40)

Psalm

Psalm 1

Their delight is in the law

Additional Readings

Leviticus 19:1-2, 15-18

Acts of justice

1 Thessalonians 2:1-8

The apostle's concern

Hymn: We Are Called, ELW 720

O Lord God, you are the holy lawgiver, you are the salvation of your people. By your Spirit renew us in your covenant of love, and train us to care tenderly for all our neighbors, through Jesus Christ, our Savior and Lord.

Monday, October 24, 2011

Time after Pentecost

Psalm 119:41-48
I will keep God's law

Let your steadfast love come to me, O LORD,
   your salvation according to your promise.
Then I shall have an answer for those who taunt me,
   for I trust in your word.
Do not take the word of truth utterly out of my mouth,
   for my hope is in your ordinances.
I will keep your law continually,
   forever and ever. (Ps. 119:41-44)

Additional Readings
Deuteronomy 6:1-9, 20-25   James 2:8-13
The great commandment   *Fulfilling the royal law*

Hymn: O Jesus, I Have Promised, ELW 810

Doubts assail us, Lord, and threaten to draw us away from you. Help us to trust your word, that we may be secure in your love. When we are tempted to forsake you, keep us steadfast in your promised salvation.

Tuesday, October 25, 2011

Time after Pentecost

James 2:14-26

Faith without works is dead

What good is it, my brothers and sisters, if you say you have faith but do not have works? Can faith save you? If a brother or sister is naked and lacks daily food, and one of you says to them, "Go in peace; keep warm and eat your fill," and yet you do not supply their bodily needs, what is the good of that? So faith by itself, if it has no works, is dead. (James 2:14-17)

Psalm

Psalm 119:41-48
I will keep God's law

Additional Reading

Deuteronomy 10:10-22
Moses urges the people to obey

Hymn: Where Cross the Crowded Ways of Life, ELW 719

Lord, your word of salvation rings out in our world. Increase in us the gift of faith so we may trust in that word. Increase in us the gift of love so we might serve our neighbors in need.

Wednesday, October 26, 2011

Time after Pentecost

Philipp Nicolai, 1608; Johann Heermann, 1647; Paul Gerhardt, 1676;
hymnwriters

Matthew 19:16-22

Keeping the commandments

Then someone came to him and said, "Teacher, what good deed must I do to have eternal life?" And he said to him, "Why do you ask me about what is good? There is only one who is good. If you wish to enter into life, keep the commandments." He said to him, "Which ones?" And Jesus said, "You shall not murder; You shall not commit adultery; You shall not steal; You shall not bear false witness; Honor your father and mother; also, You shall love your neighbor as yourself." The young man said to him, "I have kept all these; what do I still lack?" Jesus said to him, "If you wish to be perfect, go, sell your possessions, and give the money to the poor, and you will have treasure in heaven; then come, follow me." When the young man heard this word, he went away grieving, for he had many possessions. (Matt. 19:16-22)

Psalm

Psalm 119:41-48
I will keep God's law

Additional Reading

Proverbs 16:1-20
It is good to obey

Hymn: O God, My Faithful God, ELW 806

Good and gracious God, you gave us your commandments to guide our earthly lives. You gave us your love that we might have eternal life. Give us your grace so that your commandments might guide us in loving one another.

Thursday, October 27, 2011

Time after Pentecost

Psalm 43
Send out your light and truth

Vindicate me, O God, and defend my cause
   against an ungodly people;
from those who are deceitful and unjust
   deliver me!
For you are the God in whom I take refuge;
   why have you cast me off?
Why must I walk about mournfully
   because of the oppression of the enemy?
O send out your light and your truth;
   let them lead me;
let them bring me to your holy hill
   and to your dwelling.
Then I will go to the altar of God,
   to God my exceeding joy;
and I will praise you with the harp,
   O God, my God. (Ps. 43:1-4)

Additional Readings
1 Samuel 2:27-36
Hope for a better priesthood

Romans 2:17-29
Real circumcision a matter of the heart

Hymn: Christ, Be Our Light, ELW 715

Evil and deceit surround us, O Lord, and threaten to make us stumble in our walk of faith. Be our refuge and protector along the journey, and may the light of your word lead us into your eternal presence.

Friday, October 28, 2011

Simon and Jude, Apostles

John 14:21-27

Those who love Jesus will keep his word

They who have my commandments and keep them are those who love me; and those who love me will be loved by my Father, and I will love them and reveal myself to them." Judas (not Iscariot) said to him, "Lord, how is it that you will reveal yourself to us, and not to the world?" Jesus answered him, "Those who love me will keep my word, and my Father will love them, and we will come to them and make our home with them. Whoever does not love me does not keep my words; and the word that you hear is not mine, but is from the Father who sent me." (John 14:21-24)

Psalm
Psalm 11
Take refuge in God

Additional Readings
Jeremiah 26:[1-6] 7-16
Jeremiah promises the judgment of God

1 John 4:1-6
Do not believe every spirit of this world

Hymn: Here, O Lord, Your Servants Gather, ELW 530

O God, we thank you for the glorious company of the apostles, and especially on this day for Simon and Jude. We pray that, as they were faithful and zealous in your mission, so we may with ardent devotion make known the love and mercy of our Savior Jesus Christ, who lives and reigns with you and the Holy Spirit, one God, now and forever.

Saturday, October 29, 2011

Time after Pentecost

Malachi 1:6—2:9
False and true priests

Oh, that someone among you would shut the temple doors, so that you would not kindle fire on my altar in vain! I have no pleasure in you, says the LORD of hosts, and I will not accept an offering from your hands. For from the rising of the sun to its setting my name is great among the nations, and in every place incense is offered to my name, and a pure offering; for my name is great among the nations, says the LORD of hosts. But you profane it when you say that the Lord's table is polluted, and the food for it may be despised. "What a weariness this is," you say, and you sniff at me, says the LORD of hosts. You bring what has been taken by violence or is lame or sick, and this you bring as your offering! Shall I accept that from your hand? says the LORD. (Mal. 1:10-13)

Psalm
Psalm 43
Send out your light and truth

Additional Reading
Matthew 23:13-28
Woe to the scribes and pharisees

Hymn: God of Tempest, God of Whirlwind, ELW 400

You pour out your blessings upon us, O Lord, and we live from the abundance of your generosity. Forgive our greedy hoarding of your good gifts. Open our hearts and our hands to share with those in need.

Sunday, October 30, 2011

Time after Pentecost

Matthew 23:1-12

Humble yourselves

Then Jesus said to the crowds and to his disciples, "The scribes and the Pharisees sit on Moses' seat; therefore, do whatever they teach you and follow it; but do not do as they do, for they do not practice what they teach. They tie up heavy burdens, hard to bear, and lay them on the shoulders of others; but they themselves are unwilling to lift a finger to move them. They do all their deeds to be seen by others; for they make their phylacteries broad and their fringes long." (Matt. 23:1-5)

Psalm

Psalm 43
Send out your light and truth

Additional Readings

Micah 3:5-12
Judgment upon corrupt leaders

1 Thessalonians 2:9-13
The apostle's teaching

Hymn: Will You Let Me Be Your Servant, ELW 659

O God, generous and supreme, your loving Son lived among us, instructing us in the ways of humility and justice. Continue to ease our burdens, and train us to serve alongside of him, Jesus Christ, our Savior and Lord.

Monday, October 31, 2011

Reformation Day

John 8:31-36

The truth will set you free

Then Jesus said to the Jews who had believed in him, "If you continue in my word, you are truly my disciples; and you will know the truth, and the truth will make you free." They answered him, "We are descendants of Abraham and have never been slaves to anyone. What do you mean by saying, 'You will be made free'?"

Jesus answered them, "Very truly, I tell you, everyone who commits sin is a slave to sin. The slave does not have a permanent place in the household; the son has a place there forever. So if the Son makes you free, you will be free indeed." (John 8:31-36)

Psalm

Psalm 46
The God of Jacob is our stronghold

Additional Readings

Jeremiah 31:31-34
I will write my law in their hearts

Romans 3:19-28
Justified by God's grace as a gift

Hymn: Lord, Keep Us Steadfast in Your Word, ELW 517

Almighty God, gracious Lord, we thank you that your Holy Spirit renews the church in every age. Pour out your Holy Spirit on your faithful people. Keep them steadfast in your Word, protect and comfort them in times of trial, defend them against all enemies of the gospel, and bestow on the church your saving peace, through Jesus Christ, our Savior and Lord, who lives and reigns with you and the Holy Spirit, one God, now and forever.

TIME AFTER PENTECOST

NOVEMBER

The month of November is unique in that it begins with All Saints Day (November 1) and ends with the feast of Christ the King (often the last Sunday of November). The Sunday and daily readings seem to extend the harvest, but in a new way: They speak of God's harvest of *human beings* into their heavenly home.

Perhaps it is no coincidence that November's scriptural emphasis on the consummation of all things in Christ is reflected in the landscape and the chilling temperatures. Yet in the midst of this turning of the seasons and the reminders of death's presence, Christians hold forth the central feast of the year: the death and resurrection of Christ present in baptism and the holy supper. In these last days of the church's year, Christians are invited to celebrate the reign of Christ, whose death on the cross has transformed our deaths into the gate of everlasting life.

Table Prayer for November

Stay with us, God of life,
as we share the bounty of this food and drink.
We give you thanks for those who have gone before us in faith.
Bring us, with them, to the harvest of everlasting life,
where all people will feast forever at your abundant table.
We ask this through Christ our Lord. Amen.

_____

_____

_____

_____

_____

_____

_____

_____

_____

_____

_____

Remembering Those Who Have Died
Use this prayer in the home or at the grave.

O God, our help in ages past and our hope for years to come:
We give you thanks for all your faithful people
who have followed the light of your word throughout the centuries
into our time and place.

Here individual names may be spoken.

As we remember these people,
strengthen us to follow Christ through this world
until we are carried into the harvest of eternal life,
where suffering and death will be no more.
Hear our prayer in the name of the good and gracious shepherd,
Jesus Christ, our Savior and Lord. Amen.

or

With reverence and affection we remember before you,
O everlasting God,
all our departed friends and relatives.
Keep us in union with them here
through faith and love toward you,
that hereafter we may enter into your presence
and be numbered with those who serve you
and look upon your face in glory everlasting,
through your Son, Jesus Christ our Lord. Amen.

Tuesday, November 1, 2011

All Saints Day

Matthew 5:1-12
Blessed are the poor in spirit

"Blessed are those who are persecuted for righteousness' sake, for theirs is the kingdom of heaven.

"Blessed are you when people revile you and persecute you and utter all kinds of evil against you falsely on my account. Rejoice and be glad, for your reward is great in heaven, for in the same way they persecuted the prophets who were before you." (Matt. 5:10-12)

Psalm
Psalm 34:1-10, 22
Fear the Lord, you saints

Additional Readings
Revelation 7:9-17
The multitude of heaven worship the Lamb

1 John 3:1-3
We are God's children

Hymn: Blest Are They, ELW 728

Almighty God, you have knit your people together in one communion in the mystical body of your Son, Jesus Christ our Lord. Grant us grace to follow your blessed saints in lives of faith and commitment, and to know the inexpressible joys you have prepared for those who love you, through Jesus Christ, our Savior and Lord, who lives and reigns with you and the Holy Spirit, one God, now and forever.

Wednesday, November 2, 2011

Time after Pentecost

Proverbs 16:21-33

The wise heart and persuasive lips

The wise of heart is called perceptive,
  and pleasant speech increases persuasiveness.
Wisdom is a fountain of life to one who has it,
  but folly is the punishment of fools.
The mind of the wise makes their speech judicious,
  and adds persuasiveness to their lips. (Prov. 16:21-23)

Psalm

Psalm 5
God blesses the righteous

Additional Reading

Matthew 15:1-9
Lips that misrepresent the heart

Hymn: Holy God, Holy and Glorious, ELW 637

Source and spring of understanding, in the hearts of the baptized you cause rivers of living water to flow. With your Spirit bring forth refreshing and gracious words from us that reflect your holy wisdom and word, Jesus Christ.

Thursday, November 3, 2011

Time after Pentecost

Martín de Porres, renewer of society, 1639

Psalm 70

You are my helper and deliverer

Be pleased, O God, to deliver me.
　O Lord, make haste to help me!
Let those be put to shame and confusion
　who seek my life.
Let those be turned back and brought to dishonor
　who desire to hurt me.
Let those who say, "Aha, Aha!"
　turn back because of their shame.
Let all who seek you
　rejoice and be glad in you.
Let those who love your salvation
　say evermore, "God is great!"
But I am poor and needy;
　hasten to me, O God!
You are my help and my deliverer;
　O Lord, do not delay! (Ps. 70:1-5)

Additional Readings

Amos 1:1—2:5
God judges Israel's neighbors

Revelation 8:6—9:12
The trumpet of God's judgment

Hymn: Immortal, Invisible, God Only Wise, ELW 834

God our defender, forces outside and within ourselves wear us down and threaten harm. Pain makes every moment seem longer than it is. Push away danger and fear and be swift to save us.

Friday, November 4, 2011

Time after Pentecost

Amos 3:1-12
Israel's guilt and punishment

Proclaim to the strongholds in Ashdod,
   and to the strongholds in the land of Egypt,
and say, "Assemble yourselves on Mount Samaria,
   and see what great tumults are within it,
   and what oppressions are in its midst."
They do not know how to do right, says the LORD,
   those who store up violence and robbery in their strongholds.
Therefore thus says the Lord GOD:
An adversary shall surround the land,
   and strip you of your defense;
   and your strongholds shall be plundered. (Amos 3:9-11)

Psalm	Additional Reading
Psalm 70	Revelation 9:13-21
You are my helper and deliverer	*Unrepentant humankind persists in sin*

Hymn: My Life Flows On in Endless Song, ELW 763

Righteous God, greed and injustice beget their own destruction. In time of tumult, when all else is stripped away, help us to discover you as our enduring stronghold and priceless treasure.

Saturday, November 5, 2011

Time after Pentecost

Matthew 24:1-14
Jesus foretells the end

When [Jesus] was sitting on the Mount of Olives, the disciples came to him privately, saying, "Tell us, when will this be, and what will be the sign of your coming and of the end of the age?" Jesus answered them, "Beware that no one leads you astray. For many will come in my name, saying, 'I am the Messiah!' and they will lead many astray. And you will hear of wars and rumors of wars; see that you are not alarmed; for this must take place, but the end is not yet." (Matt. 24:3-6)

Psalm
Psalm 70
You are my helper and deliverer

Additional Reading
Amos 4:6-13
Israel, prepare to meet your God

Hymn: Lord Christ, When First You Came to Earth, ELW 727

Creator of heaven and earth, you make all things new. Amid wars and rumors of wars keep us steadfast in your word, that we not be distracted by what we hear but centered and sustained by what we know: friendship with Jesus Christ.

Sunday, November 6, 2011

Time after Pentecost

Matthew 25:1-13

Wise and foolish bridesmaids

"Then the kingdom of heaven will be like this. Ten bridesmaids took their lamps and went to meet the bridegroom. Five of them were foolish, and five were wise. When the foolish took their lamps, they took no oil with them; but the wise took flasks of oil with their lamps." (Matt. 25:1-4)

Psalm	Additional Readings	
Psalm 70	Amos 5:18-24	1 Thessalonians 4:13-18
You are my helper and deliverer	*Let justice roll down like waters*	*The promise of the resurrection*

Hymn: Rejoice, Rejoice, Believers, ELW 244

O God of justice and love, you illumine our way through life with the words of your Son. Give us the light we need, awaken us to the needs of others, through Jesus Christ, our Savior and Lord.

Monday, November 7, 2011

Time after Pentecost

John Christian Frederick Heyer, 1873; Bartholomaeus Ziegenbalg, 1719;
Ludwig Nommensen, 1918; missionaries

Psalm 63
God is a rich feast

My soul is satisfied as with a rich feast,
    and my mouth praises you with joyful lips
when I think of you on my bed,
    and meditate on you in the watches of the night;
for you have been my help,
    and in the shadow of your wings I sing for joy.
My soul clings to you;
    your right hand upholds me. (Ps. 63:5-8)

Additional Readings
Amos 8:7-14   1 Corinthians 14:20-25
A famine of hearing God's word   *They will not listen to me*

Hymn: Thy Holy Wings, ELW 613

*Giver of bread and cup, of life and breath: you grant sanctuary in the
shadow of your wings. May we praise you with silence and song, at table
and rest, by day and night.*

Tuesday, November 8, 2011

Time after Pentecost

I Thessalonians 3:6-13

Stand firm in the faith

Now may our God and Father himself and our Lord Jesus direct our way to you. And may the Lord make you increase and abound in love for one another and for all, just as we abound in love for you. And may he so strengthen your hearts in holiness that you may be blameless before our God and Father at the coming of our Lord Jesus with all his saints. (1 Thess. 3:11-13)

Psalm

Psalm 63

God is a rich feast

Additional Reading

Joel 1:1-14

Call to repentance

Hymn: Blest Be the Tie That Binds, ELW 656

God and Father, you direct our ways and help us to grow strong in love. Lead us to find the holiness in one another. Develop the richness of our capacity to love until at last you call us to yourself.

Wednesday, November 9, 2011

Time after Pentecost

Matthew 24:29-35
My words will not pass away

"From the fig tree learn its lesson: as soon as its branch becomes tender and puts forth its leaves, you know that summer is near. So also, when you see all these things, you know that he is near, at the very gates. Truly I tell you, this generation will not pass away until all these things have taken place. Heaven and earth will pass away, but my words will not pass away." (Matt. 24:32-35)

Psalm
Psalm 63
God is a rich feast

Additional Reading
Joel 3:9-21
Promise of a glorious future

Hymn: My Lord, What a Morning, ELW 438

Maker of branch and tree, sign and season: as darkness gathers, your word reminds us of summer's light and warmth. Encourage us with the promise of our future in Christ, whose words and love will never pass away.

Thursday, November 10, 2011

Time after Pentecost

Psalm 90:1-8 [9-11] 12
Number your days

Lord, you have been our dwelling place
    in all generations.
Before the mountains were brought forth,
    or ever you had formed the earth and the world,
    from everlasting to everlasting you are God.
You turn us back to dust,
    and say, "Turn back, you mortals."
For a thousand years in your sight
    are like yesterday when it is past,
    or like a watch in the night. (Ps. 90:1-4)

Additional Readings
Ezekiel 6:1-14
Judgment on idolatrous Israel

Revelation 16:1-7
God's judgments are true and just

Hymn: How Small Our Span of Life, ELW 636

God our dwelling, beyond all that we can touch and imagine, you provide eternal shelter and home. Draw us to deep trust in Jesus Christ, to whom belong all the ages, and who goes to prepare a place for us.

Friday, November 11, 2011

Time after Pentecost

Martin, Bishop of Tours, 397; Søren Aabye Kierkegaard, teacher, 1855

Ezekiel 7:1-9
The end is upon us

The word of the LORD came to me: You, O mortal, thus says the Lord
GOD to the land of Israel:
An end! The end has come
upon the four corners of the land.
Now the end is upon you,
I will let loose my anger upon you;
I will judge you according to your ways,
I will punish you for all your abominations.
My eye will not spare you, I will have no pity.
I will punish you for your ways,
while your abominations are among you.
Then you shall know that I am the LORD. (Ezek. 7:1-4)

Psalm
Psalm 90:1-8 [9-11] 12
Number your days

Additional Reading
Revelation 16:8-21
The judged curse God

Hymn: My God, How Wonderful Thou Art, ELW 863

*O God, outrage is the index of your heartbreak, from the time of Cain
and Abel until now. Make a true end of the abomination of brother
killing brother by binding our wounds, reconciling enemies, and
bringing warriors to peace.*

Saturday, November 12, 2011

Time after Pentecost

Matthew 12:43-45

From bad to worse

"When the unclean spirit has gone out of a person, it wanders through waterless regions looking for a resting place, but it finds none. Then it says, 'I will return to my house from which I came.' When it comes, it finds it empty, swept, and put in order. Then it goes and brings along seven other spirits more evil than itself, and they enter and live there; and the last state of that person is worse than the first. So will it be also with this evil generation." (Matt. 12:43-45)

Psalm
Psalm 90:1-8 [9-11] 12
Number your days

Additional Reading
Ezekiel 7:10-27
You shall know that the Lord is God

Hymn: Goodness Is Stronger than Evil, ELW 721

Compassionate God, you understand the effort of keeping house and tending soul. Breathe into us a spirit that resists harshness, that our zeal for purity neither destroys what merely seems unclean nor invites false comparisons. Fill all our rooms with your love.

Sunday, November 13, 2011

Time after Pentecost

Matthew 25:14-30

Slaves entrusted with talents

"Then the [slave] who had received the one talent also came forward, saying, 'Master, I knew that you were a harsh man, reaping where you did not sow, and gathering where you did not scatter seed; so I was afraid, and I went and hid your talent in the ground. Here you have what is yours.' But his master replied, 'You wicked and lazy slave! You knew, did you, that I reap where I did not sow, and gather where I did not scatter? Then you ought to have invested my money with the bankers, and on my return I would have received what was my own with interest. So take the talent from him, and give it to the one with the ten talents.'" (Matt. 25:24-28)

Psalm

Psalm 90:1-8 [9-11] 12

Number your days

Additional Readings

Zephaniah 1:7, 12-18

The day of the Lord

1 Thessalonians 5:1-11

Be alert for the day of the Lord

Hymn: God, Whose Giving Knows No Ending, ELW 678

Righteous God, our merciful master, you own the earth and all its peoples, and you give us all that we have. Inspire us to serve you with justice and wisdom, and prepare us for the joy of the day of your coming, through Jesus Christ, our Savior and Lord.

Monday, November 14, 2011

Time after Pentecost

Psalm 9:1-14
God's reward for the righteous

I will give thanks to the LORD with my whole heart;
   I will tell of all your wonderful deeds.
I will be glad and exult in you;
   I will sing praise to your name, O Most High.
When my enemies turned back,
   they stumbled and perished before you.
For you have maintained my just cause;
   you have sat on the throne giving righteous judgment. (Ps. 9:1-4)

Additional Readings
Zechariah 1:7-17
God's judgment and mercy

Romans 2:1-11
The righteous judgment of God

Hymn: Lord, I Lift Your Name on High, ELW 857

We praise and bless you, O Most High, for in a world of shifting loyalties you alone remain constant in keeping our best interests at heart. Teach us to maintain integrity, relying upon you as advocate and judge.

Tuesday, November 15, 2011

Time after Pentecost

Zechariah 2:1-5; 5:1-4
Visions of mercy and judgment

I looked up and saw a man with a measuring line in his hand. Then I asked, "Where are you going?" He answered me, "To measure Jerusalem, to see what is its width and what is its length." Then the angel who talked with me came forward, and another angel came forward to meet him, and said to him, "Run, say to that young man: Jerusalem shall be inhabited like villages without walls, because of the multitude of people and animals in it. For I will be a wall of fire all around it, says the LORD, and I will be the glory within it." (Zech. 2:1-5)

Psalm
Psalm 9:1-14
God's reward for the righteous

Additional Reading
1 Thessalonians 5:12-18
The Christian life

Hymn: Jerusalem, My Happy Home, ELW 628

O God, architect of our hope, when all is in ruins you design restoration. From loneliness and desolation you bring abundant life. Shape us into your holy city with your Spirit.

Wednesday, November 16, 2011

Time after Pentecost

Matthew 24:45-51
Parable of the unfaithful slave

"Who then is the faithful and wise slave, whom his master has put in charge of his household, to give the other slaves their allowance of food at the proper time? Blessed is that slave whom his master will find at work when he arrives. Truly I tell you, he will put that one in charge of all his possessions." (Matt. 24:45-47)

Psalm
Psalm 9:1-14
God's reward for the righteous

Additional Reading
Job 16:1-21
A lament about unjust punishment

Hymn: Lord Jesus, You Shall Be My Song, ELW 808

God our provider, you have blessed humankind with abundant food. Inspire us to share it freely so that when we meet you in the face of the hungry or as returning master we will be found to have been faithful and wise.

Thursday, November 17, 2011

Time after Pentecost

Elizabeth of Hungary, renewer of society, 1231

Psalm 95:1-7a
We are the people of God's pasture

O come, let us sing to the LORD;
    let us make a joyful noise to the rock of our salvation!
Let us come into his presence with thanksgiving;
    let us make a joyful noise to him with songs of praise!
For the LORD is a great God,
    and a great King above all gods.
In his hand are the depths of the earth;
    the heights of the mountains are his also.
The sea is his, for he made it,
    and the dry land, which his hands have formed. (Ps. 95:1-5)

Additional Readings
1 Kings 22:13-23
Israel like sheep without a shepherd

Revelation 14:1-11
Fear God and give God glory

Hymn: O Christ, What Can It Mean for Us, ELW 431

Cave and crag sing to you, O Rock of our salvation! Depth and height give sheep and goats their habitat. With earth and sea and all their creatures we join the everlasting song of praise.

Friday, November 18, 2011

Time after Pentecost

Revelation 22:1-9

Worship God alone

Then the angel showed me the river of the water of life, bright as crystal, flowing from the throne of God and of the Lamb through the middle of the street of the city. On either side of the river is the tree of life with its twelve kinds of fruit, producing its fruit each month; and the leaves of the tree are for the healing of the nations. Nothing accursed will be found there any more. But the throne of God and of the Lamb will be in it, and his servants will worship him; they will see his face, and his name will be on their foreheads. And there will be no more night; they need no light of lamp or sun, for the Lord God will be their light, and they will reign forever and ever. (Rev. 22:1-5)

Psalm

Psalm 95:1-7a
We are the people of God's pasture

Additional Reading

I Chronicles 17:1-15
David, shepherd and king of Israel

Hymn: Crown Him with Many Crowns, ELW 855

Lord God, you illuminate our hearts with visions of holiness and healing. Help us to return joyfully to the water of life where Christ, both shepherd and lamb, is enthroned with you forever.

Saturday, November 19, 2011

Time after Pentecost

Matthew 12:46-50
The true kindred of Jesus

While he was still speaking to the crowds, his mother and his brothers were standing outside, wanting to speak to him. Someone told him, "Look, your mother and your brothers are standing outside, wanting to speak to you." But to the one who had told him this, Jesus replied, "Who is my mother, and who are my brothers?" And pointing to his disciples, he said, "Here are my mother and my brothers! For whoever does the will of my Father in heaven is my brother and sister and mother." (Matt. 12:46-50)

Psalm
Psalm 95:1-7a
We are the people of God's pasture

Additional Reading
Isaiah 44:21-28
Cyrus, a shepherd for the Lord

Hymn: What God Ordains Is Good Indeed, ELW 776

Father in heaven, in Christ you enlarge our understanding of family beyond the ties of birth and blood. Assist us in recognizing all who seek to do your will as our sisters and brothers.

Sunday, November 20, 2011

Christ the King

Matthew 25:31-46
The separation of sheep and goats

"Then [the king] will say to those at his left hand, 'You that are accursed, depart from me into the eternal fire prepared for the devil and his angels; for I was hungry and you gave me no food, I was thirsty and you gave me nothing to drink, I was a stranger and you did not welcome me, naked and you did not give me clothing, sick and in prison and you did not visit me.' Then they also will answer, 'Lord, when was it that we saw you hungry or thirsty or a stranger or naked or sick or in prison, and did not take care of you?' Then he will answer them, 'Truly I tell you, just as you did not do it to one of the least of these, you did not do it to me.' " (Matt. 25:41-45)

Psalm
Psalm 95:1-7a
We are the people of God's pasture

Additional Readings
Ezekiel 34:11-16, 20-24
God will shepherd Israel

Ephesians 1:15-23
The reign of Christ

Hymn: Soon and Very Soon, ELW 439

O God of power and might, your Son shows us the way of service, and in him we inherit the riches of your grace. Give us the wisdom to know what is right and the strength to serve the world you have made, through Jesus Christ, our Savior and Lord, who lives and reigns with you and the Holy Spirit, one God, now and forever.

Monday, November 21, 2011

Time after Pentecost

Psalm 7
God the righteous judge

O let the evil of the wicked come to an end,
    but establish the righteous,
you who test the minds and hearts,
    O righteous God.
God is my shield,
    who saves the upright in heart.
God is a righteous judge,
    and a God who has indignation every day. (Ps. 7:9-11)

Additional Readings
Esther 2:1-18
Lowly Esther becomes queen

2 Timothy 2:8-13
Those who endure with Christ reign with him

Hymn: Rejoice, Ye Pure in Heart! ELW 873/874

O God, your indignation is kindled against those who harm the innocent. Give us discerning minds and hearts. Shield us from wickedness that we may neither suffer wrong nor cause scandal.

Tuesday, November 22, 2011

Time after Pentecost

Esther 8:3-17
Queen Esther saves her people

Then Esther spoke again to the king; she fell at his feet, weeping and pleading with him to avert the evil design of Haman the Agagite and the plot that he had devised against the Jews. The king held out the golden scepter to Esther, and Esther rose and stood before the king. She said, "If it pleases the king, and if I have won his favor, and if the thing seems right before the king, and I have his approval, let an order be written to revoke the letters devised by Haman son of Hammedatha the Agagite, which he wrote giving orders to destroy the Jews who are in all the provinces of the king. For how can I bear to see the calamity that is coming on my people? Or how can I bear to see the destruction of my kindred?" (Esther 8:3-6)

Psalm
Psalm 7
God the righteous judge

Additional Reading
Revelation 19:1-9
Praise of God's judgments

Hymn: The Trumpets Sound, the Angels Sing, ELW 531

God our deliverer, as Queen Esther risked death to plead for the life of her people, so King Jesus confronted the powers of evil for our sake. Where life is endangered, give us the courage and skill to speak and to act.

Wednesday, November 23, 2011

Time after Pentecost

Clement, Bishop of Rome, c. 100; Miguel Agustín Pro, martyr, 1927

John 5:19-40
The judgment of the Son

"Very truly, I tell you, the hour is coming, and is now here, when the dead will hear the voice of the Son of God, and those who hear will live. For just as the Father has life in himself, so he has granted the Son also to have life in himself; and he has given him authority to execute judgment, because he is the Son of Man. Do not be astonished at this; for the hour is coming when all who are in their graves will hear his voice and will come out—those who have done good, to the resurrection of life, and those who have done evil, to the resurrection of condemnation." (John 5:25-29)

Psalm
Psalm 7
God the righteous judge

Additional Reading
Ezekiel 33:7-20
The righteous will live

Hymn: You Are Mine, ELW 581

God of resurrection, we long to hear your voice. Call us to you now and at that final hour when the dead will rise. Summon us out of our graves and from everything that ensnares us in deadly ways.

Blessing of the Household for Thanksgiving Day

We gather this day to give thanks to God for the gifts of this land and its people, for God has been generous to us. As we ask God's blessing upon this food we share, may we be mindful of the lonely and the hungry.

As we prepare to offer thanks to God,
let us listen to the words of scripture:
I give thanks to my God always for you because of the grace of God that has been given you in Christ Jesus, for in every way you have been enriched in him, in speech and knowledge of every kind—just as the testimony of Christ has been strengthened among you—so that you are not lacking in any spiritual gift as you wait for the revealing of our Lord Jesus Christ. He will also strengthen you to the end, so that you may be blameless on the day of our Lord Jesus Christ. (1 Cor. 1:4-8)

Let us pray.
God most provident,
we join all creation in offering you praise through Jesus Christ.
For generations the people of this land have sung of your bounty.
With them, we offer you thanksgiving
for the rich harvest we have received at your hands.
Bless us and this food that we share with grateful hearts.
Continue to make our land fruitful
and let our love for you be seen in our pursuit of justice and peace
and in our generous response to those in need.
We ask this through Christ our Lord. Amen.

May Christ, the living bread, bring us to the feast of eternal life.
Amen.

Thursday, November 24, 2011

Day of Thanksgiving (U.S.A.)

**Justus Falckner, 1723; Jehu Jones, 1852,
William Passavant, 1894; pastors in North America**

Psalm 80:1-7, 17-19
We shall be saved

Give ear, O Shepherd of Israel,
  you who lead Joseph like a flock!
You who are enthroned upon the cherubim, shine forth
  before Ephraim and Benjamin and Manasseh.
Stir up your might,
  and come to save us!
Restore us, O God;
  let your face shine, that we may be saved. (Ps. 80:1-3)

Additional Readings
Zechariah 13:1-9
The coming day of God brings cleansing

Revelation 14:6-13
Hold fast to the faith

Hymn: Praise the Lord, Rise Up Rejoicing, ELW 544

Holy God, shepherd all who gather to feast around tables today. Bless those in solitude and those with company. Let our faces lighting up at those we love be a reflection of your own face shining on us.

Friday, November 25, 2011

Time after Pentecost

Isaac Watts, hymnwriter, 1748

I Thessalonians 4:1-18

A life pleasing God to the end

But we do not want you to be uninformed, brothers and sisters, about those who have died, so that you may not grieve as others do who have no hope. For since we believe that Jesus died and rose again, even so, through Jesus, God will bring with him those who have died. For this we declare to you by the word of the Lord, that we who are alive, who are left until the coming of the Lord, will by no means precede those who have died. For the Lord himself, with a cry of command, with the archangel's call and with the sound of God's trumpet, will descend from heaven, and the dead in Christ will rise first. Then we who are alive, who are left, will be caught up in the clouds together with them to meet the Lord in the air; and so we will be with the Lord forever. (1 Thess. 4:13-17)

Psalm
Psalm 80:1-7, 17-19
We shall be saved

Additional Reading
Zechariah 14:1-9
God will come to rule

Hymn: Lo! He Comes with Clouds Descending, ELW 435

God of the living and the dead, at the sound of the trumpet we will all be gathered together once again. Temper any anxieties that we have about the end times with faith in your eternal presence.

Saturday, November 26, 2011

Time after Pentecost

Micah 2:1-13
God will gather all

I will surely gather all of you, O Jacob,
   I will gather the survivors of Israel;
I will set them together
   like sheep in a fold,
like a flock in its pasture;
   it will resound with people.
The one who breaks out will go up before them;
   they will break through and pass the gate,
     going out by it.
Their king will pass on before them,
   the LORD at their head. (Micah 2:12-13)

Psalm
Psalm 80:1-7, 17-19
We shall be saved

Additional Reading
Matthew 24:15-31
Be ready for that day

Hymn: The King of Love My Shepherd Is, ELW 502

Shepherd of Jacob and Israel, you gather all peoples into your flock. May your kingdom come into our troubled world to create a common bond among those who have been scattered.

ADVENT

In the days of Advent, Christians prepare to celebrate the presence of God's Word among us in our own day. During these four weeks, we pray that the reign of God, which Jesus preached and lived, would come among us. We pray that God's justice would flourish in our land, that the people of the earth would live in peace, that the weak and the sick and the hungry would be strengthened, healed, and fed with God's merciful presence.

During the last days of Advent, Christians welcome Christ with names inspired by the prophets: wisdom, liberator of slaves, mighty power, radiant dawn and sun of justice, the keystone of the arch of humanity, and Emmanual—God with us.

Table Prayer for Advent

Blessed are you, O Lord our God,
the one who is, who was, and who is to come.
At this table you fill us with good things.
May these gifts strengthen us
to share with the hungry and all those in need,
as we wait and watch for your coming among us
in Jesus Christ our Lord. Amen.

The Advent Wreath

One of the best known customs for the season is the Advent wreath. The wreath and winter candle-lighting in the midst of growing darkness strengthen some of the Advent images found in the Bible. The unbroken circle of greens is clearly an image of everlasting life, a victory wreath, the crown of Christ, or the wheel of time itself. Christians use the wreath as a sign that Christ reaches into our time to lead us to the light of everlasting life. The four candles mark the progress of the four weeks of Advent and the growth of light. Sometimes the wreath is embellished with natural dried flowers or fruit. Its evergreen branches lead the household and the congregation to the evergreen Christmas tree. In many homes, the family gathers for prayer around the wreath.

Lighting the Advent Wreath
Use this blessing when lighting the first candle.

Blessed are you, O Lord our God, ruler of the universe.
You call all nations to walk in your light
and to seek your ways of justice and peace,
for the night is past, and the dawn of your coming is near.
Bless us as we light the first candle of this wreath.
Rouse us from sleep,
that we may be ready to greet our Lord when he comes
and welcome him into our hearts and homes,
for he is our light and our salvation.
Blessed be God forever.

Sunday, November 27, 2011

First Sunday of Advent

Mark 13:24-37

The coming of the Son of Man

"But about that day or hour no one knows, neither the angels in heaven, nor the Son, but only the Father. Beware, keep alert; for you do not know when the time will come. It is like a man going on a journey, when he leaves home and puts his slaves in charge, each with his work, and commands the doorkeeper to be on the watch. Therefore, keep awake—for you do not know when the master of the house will come, in the evening, or at midnight, or at cockcrow, or at dawn, or else he may find you asleep when he comes suddenly. And what I say to you I say to all: Keep awake." (Mark 13:32-37)

Psalm

Psalm 80:1-7, 17-19
We shall be saved

Additional Readings

Isaiah 64:1-9
God will come with power and compassion

I Corinthians 1:3-9
Gifts of grace sustain us

Hymn: Wake, Awake, for Night Is Flying, ELW 436

Stir up your power, Lord Christ, and come. By your merciful protection awaken us to the threatening dangers of our sins, and keep us blameless until the coming of your new day, for you live and reign with the Father and the Holy Spirit, one God, now and forever.

Monday, November 28, 2011

Week of Advent 1

Psalm 79

Prayer for deliverance

Do not remember against us the iniquities of our ancestors;
    let your compassion come speedily to meet us,
      for we are brought very low.
Help us, O God of our salvation,
    for the glory of your name;
deliver us, and forgive our sins,
    for your name's sake.
Why should the nations say,
    "Where is their God?"
Let the avenging of the outpoured blood of your servants
    be known among the nations before our eyes. (Ps. 79:8-10)

Additional Readings

Micah 4:1-5
A promise of peace

Revelation 15:1-8
A liturgy of glory

Hymn: Lord of Our Life, ELW 766

Merciful God, as nights grow longer we feel the shortness of our days and the depth of our need. Deliver us from all sins; those we have inherited, as well as those from our own generation.

Tuesday, November 29, 2011

Week of Advent 1

Revelation 18:1-10

Judgment upon human pride

After this I saw another angel coming down from heaven, having great authority; and the earth was made bright with his splendor. He called out with a mighty voice,

"Fallen, fallen is Babylon the great!
    It has become a dwelling place of demons,
a haunt of every foul spirit,
    a haunt of every foul bird,
    a haunt of every foul and hateful beast.
For all the nations have drunk
    of the wine of the wrath of her fornication,
and the kings of the earth have committed fornication with her,
    and the merchants of the earth have grown rich
        from the power of her luxury." (Rev. 18:1-3)

Psalm

Psalm 79

Prayer for deliverance

Additional Reading

Micah 4:6-13

A promise of restoration after exile

Hymn: Come, Thou Long-Expected Jesus, ELW 254

God, you are sovereign over city and nation, ruler and merchant. Guide our consumer habits to foster the common good, and enable our financial choices to honor Jesus of Nazareth, born among the poor he came to serve.

Wednesday, November 30, 2011

Andrew, Apostle

John 1:35-42
Jesus calls Andrew

One of the two who heard John speak and followed him was Andrew, Simon Peter's brother. He first found his brother Simon and said to him, "We have found the Messiah" (which is translated Anointed). He brought Simon to Jesus, who looked at him and said, "You are Simon son of John. You are to be called Cephas" (which is translated Peter). (John 1:40-42)

Psalm

Psalm 19:1-6
The heavens declare God's glory

Additional Readings

Ezekiel 3:16-21
A sentinel for the house of Israel

Romans 10:10-18
Faith comes from the word of Christ

Hymn: Jesus Calls Us; o'er the Tumult, ELW 696

Almighty God, you gave your apostle Andrew the grace to obey the call of your Son and to bring his brother to Jesus. Give us also, who are called by your holy word, grace to follow Jesus without delay and to bring into his presence those who are near to us, for he lives and reigns with you and the Holy Spirit, one God, now and forever.

_____

_____

_____

_____

_____

_____

_____

_____

_____

_____

Thursday, December 1, 2011

Week of Advent 1

Psalm 85:1-2, 8-13
Righteousness and peace

Let me hear what God the LORD will speak,
    for he will speak peace to his people,
    to his faithful, to those who turn to him in their hearts.
Surely his salvation is at hand for those who fear him,
    that his glory may dwell in our land.
Steadfast love and faithfulness will meet;
    righteousness and peace will kiss each other.
Faithfulness will spring up from the ground,
    and righteousness will look down from the sky.
The LORD will give what is good,
    and our land will yield its increase. (Ps. 85:8-12)

Additional Readings
Hosea 6:1-6
Return to the God of life and love

I Thessalonians 1:2-10
Paul thanks God for the Thessalonians

Hymn: People, Look East, ELW 248

God, guide us to be open to you in prayer. Help us to listen for your life-giving words of peace, love, and salvation. Speak to our longing and yearning hearts because we need you.

Friday, December 2, 2011

Week of Advent 1

Jeremiah 1:4-10
God appoints a prophet

Now the word of the LORD came to me saying,
  "Before I formed you in the womb I knew you,
  and before you were born I consecrated you;
  I appointed you a prophet to the nations."
Then I said, "Ah, Lord GOD! Truly I do not know how to speak, for I
am only a boy." But the LORD said to me,
  "Do not say, 'I am only a boy';
  for you shall go to all to whom I send you,
  and you shall speak whatever I command you,
  Do not be afraid of them,
  for I am with you to deliver you, says the LORD." (Jer. 1:4-8)

Psalm
Psalm 85:1-2, 8-13
Righteousness and peace

Additional Reading
Acts 11:19-26
The new community called "Christian"

Hymn: Here I Am, Lord, ELW 574

*Lord, as you called Jeremiah to be your prophet, help us to realize that
you are calling us to ministry. Through your knowledge and equipping
power, help us not to be afraid to share your good news with others.*

Saturday, December 3, 2011

Week of Advent I

Francis Xavier, missionary to Asia, 1552

Ezekiel 36:24-28
A new heart and a new spirit

I will take you from the nations, and gather you from all the countries, and bring you into your own land. I will sprinkle clean water upon you, and you shall be clean from all your uncleannesses, and from all your idols I will cleanse you. A new heart I will give you, and a new spirit I will put within you; and I will remove from your body the heart of stone and give you a heart of flesh. I will put my spirit within you, and make you follow my statutes and be careful to observe my ordinances. Then you shall live in the land that I gave to your ancestors; and you shall be my people, and I will be your God. (Ezek. 36:24-28)

Psalm
Psalm 85:1-2, 8-13
Righteousness and peace

Additional Reading
Mark 11:27-33
Jesus a prophet like John the Baptist

Hymn: God, My Lord, My Strength, ELW 795

Loving God, give us a new spirit. Soften our hearts of stone and fill them with your word. Strengthen us to follow you alone, rather than clinging to the false idols of this world.

Lighting the Advent Wreath

Use this blessing when lighting the first two candles.

Blessed are you, O Lord our God, ruler of the universe.
John the Baptist calls all people to prepare the Lord's way
for the kingdom of heaven is near.
Bless us as we light the candles on this wreath.
Baptize us with the fire of your Spirit,
that we may be a light shining in the darkness
welcoming others as Christ has welcomed us,
for he is our light and our salvation.
Blessed be God forever.

Sunday, December 4, 2011

Second Sunday of Advent

John of Damascus, theologian and hymnwriter, c. 749

Mark 1:1-8

John appears from the wilderness

John the baptizer appeared in the wilderness, proclaiming a baptism of repentance for the forgiveness of sins. And people from the whole Judean countryside and all the people of Jerusalem were going out to him, and were baptized by him in the river Jordan, confessing their sins. Now John was clothed with camel's hair, with a leather belt around his waist, and he ate locusts and wild honey. He proclaimed, "The one who is more powerful than I is coming after me; I am not worthy to stoop down and untie the thong of his sandals. I have baptized you with water; but he will baptize you with the Holy Spirit." (Mark 1:4-8)

Psalm

Psalm 85:1-2, 8-13
Righteousness and peace

Additional Readings

Isaiah 40:1-11
God's coming to the exiles

2 Peter 3:8-15a
Waiting for the day of God

Hymn: Hark! A Thrilling Voice Is Sounding! ELW 246

Stir up our hearts, Lord God, to prepare the way of your only Son. By his coming strengthen us to serve you with purified lives; through Jesus Christ, our Savior and Lord, who lives and reigns with you and the Holy Spirit, one God, now and forever.

Monday, December 5, 2011

Week of Advent 2

Psalm 27

God's level path

Teach me your way, O Lord,
 and lead me on a level path
 because of my enemies.
Do not give me up to the will of my adversaries,
 for false witnesses have risen against me,
 and they are breathing out violence.
I believe that I shall see the goodness of the Lord
 in the land of the living.
Wait for the Lord;
 be strong, and let your heart take courage;
 wait for the Lord! (Ps. 27:11-14)

Additional Readings

Isaiah 26:7-15
The way of the righteous is level

Acts 2:37-42
Baptism in the name of Jesus

Hymn: Lead Me, Guide Me, ELW 768

Faithful God, as you sent John the Baptist to prepare the way for Christ, lead and guide us in your ways. Give us strength to wait upon you, as you provide us with goodness, strength, and courage.

Tuesday, December 6, 2011

Week of Advent 2

Nicholas, Bishop of Myra, c. 342

Isaiah 4:2-6

God will wash Israel clean

On that day the branch of the LORD shall be beautiful and glorious, and the fruit of the land shall be the pride and glory of the survivors of Israel. Whoever is left in Zion and remains in Jerusalem will be called holy, everyone who has been recorded for life in Jerusalem, once the Lord has washed away the filth of the daughters of Zion and cleansed the bloodstains of Jerusalem from its midst by a spirit of judgment and by a spirit of burning. Then the LORD will create over the whole site of Mount Zion and over its places of assembly a cloud by day and smoke and the shining of a flaming fire by night. Indeed over all the glory there will be a canopy. It will serve as a pavilion, a shade by day from the heat, and a refuge and a shelter from the storm and rain. (Isa. 4:2-6)

Psalm

Psalm 27

God's level path

Additional Reading

Acts 11:1-18

John and Peter baptize

Hymn: Lost in the Night, ELW 243

Loving Lord, as you cleansed Israel and made it to be a holy people for your use, continue to restore our hearts for ministry. As you guided your chosen people by cloud and fire, continue to walk with us.

Wednesday, December 7, 2011

Week of Advent 2

Ambrose, Bishop of Milan, 397

Luke 1:5-17

The messenger in the temple

[T]he angel said to [Zechariah], "Do not be afraid, Zechariah, for your prayer has been heard. Your wife Elizabeth will bear you a son, and you will name him John. You will have joy and gladness, and many will rejoice at his birth, for he will be great in the sight of the Lord. He must never drink wine or strong drink; even before his birth he will be filled with the Holy Spirit. He will turn many of the people of Israel to the Lord their God. With the spirit and power of Elijah he will go before him, to turn the hearts of parents to their children, and the disobedient to the wisdom of the righteous, to make ready a people prepared for the Lord." (Luke 1:13-17)

Psalm
Psalm 27
God's level path

Additional Reading
Malachi 2:10—3:1
The coming messenger

Hymn: Comfort, Comfort Now My People, ELW 256

Promise-filled God, as your angel told Zechariah not to be afraid concerning the birth of his son John, help us also not to fear, because you promise to be with through all times.

Thursday, December 8, 2011

Week of Advent 2

Psalm 126
God does great things for us

When the LORD restored the fortunes of Zion,
    we were like those who dream.
Then our mouth was filled with laughter,
    and our tongue with shouts of joy;
then it was said among the nations,
    "The LORD has done great things for them."
The LORD has done great things for us,
    and we rejoiced. (Ps. 126:1-3)

Additional Readings
Habakkuk 2:1-5
A vision concerning the end

Philippians 3:7-11
The righteousness that comes through faith

Hymn: Hark, the Glad Sound! ELW 239

Saving God, as you restored the fortunes of Israel, help us to recognize the healing you bring to our own lives. Because of your love for us, we can rejoice in the great things you do.

Friday, December 9, 2011

Week of Advent 2

Philippians 3:12-16

The prize of God's call in Christ

Not that I have already obtained this or have already reached the goal; but I press on to make it my own, because Christ Jesus has made me his own. Beloved, I do not consider that I have made it my own; but this one thing I do: forgetting what lies behind and straining forward to what lies ahead, I press on toward the goal for the prize of the heavenly call of God in Christ Jesus. Let those of us then who are mature be of the same mind; and if you think differently about anything, this too God will reveal to you. Only let us hold fast to what we have attained. (Phil. 3:12-16)

Psalm

Psalm 126

God does great things for us

Additional Reading

Habakkuk 3:2-6

A prayer for God's glory and mercy

Hymn: My Faith Looks Up to Thee, ELW 759

Almighty God, you have guaranteed us the greatest prize ever known, eternal life with Jesus Christ. Help us to press on toward this goal, as we strive each day to cling to Christ our Savior.

Saturday, December 10, 2011

Week of Advent 2

Habakkuk 3:13-19
God's devastation, God's deliverance

Though the fig tree does not blossom,
  and no fruit is on the vines;
though the produce of the olive fails
  and the fields yield no food;
though the flock is cut off from the fold
  and there is no herd in the stalls,
yet I will rejoice in the LORD;
  I will exult in the God of my salvation.
GOD, the Lord, is my strength;
  he makes my feet like the feet of a deer,
  and makes me tread upon the heights. (Hab. 3:17-19)

Psalm
Psalm 126
God does great things for us

Additional Reading
Matthew 21:28-32
Resistance to God in the present generation

Hymn: Fling Wide the Door, ELW 259

God of deliverance, as you rescued your people during times of devastation, lift us when doubt, weakness, and tragedy overwhelm. Provide us with your strength as we praise you even in the midst of difficulties.

Lighting the Advent Wreath

Use this blessing when lighting three candles.

Blessed are you, O Lord our God, ruler of the universe.
Your prophets spoke of a day when the desert would blossom
and waters would break forth in the wilderness.
Bless us as we light the candles on this wreath.
Strengthen our hearts
as we prepare for the coming of the Lord.
May he give water to all who thirst,
for he is our light and our salvation.
Blessed be God forever.

Sunday, December 11, 2011

Third Sunday of Advent

John 1:6-8, 19-28

A witness to the light

This is the testimony given by John when the Jews sent priests and
Levites from Jerusalem to ask him, "Who are you?" He confessed
and did not deny it, but confessed, "I am not the Messiah." And they
asked him, "What then? Are you Elijah?" He said, "I am not." "Are
you the prophet?" He answered, "No." Then they said to him, "Who
are you? Let us have an answer for those who sent us. What do you
say about yourself?" He said,

"I am the voice of one crying out in the wilderness,
    'Make straight the way of the Lord,'"
as the prophet Isaiah said. (John 1:19-23)

Psalm

Psalm 126

*God does great things
for us*

Additional Readings

Isaiah 61:1-4, 8-11

*Righteousness and praise
flourish like a garden*

1 Thessalonians 5:16-24

*Kept in faith until the
coming of Christ*

Hymn: There's a Voice in the Wilderness, ELW 255

*Stir up the wills of your faithful people, Lord God, and open our ears to
the words of your prophets, that anointed by your Spirit, we may testify
to your light; through Jesus Christ, our Savior and Lord, who lives and
reigns with you and the Holy Spirit, one God, now and forever.*

Monday, December 12, 2011

Week of Advent 3

Psalm 125
Prayer for blessing

Those who trust in the LORD are like Mount Zion,
   which cannot be moved, but abides forever.
As the mountains surround Jerusalem,
   so the LORD surrounds his people,
   from this time on and forevermore.
For the scepter of wickedness shall not rest
   on the land allotted to the righteous,
so that the righteous might not stretch out
   their hands to do wrong.
Do good, O LORD, to those who are good,
   and to those who are upright in their hearts.
But those who turn aside to their own crooked ways
   the LORD will lead away with evildoers.
   Peace be upon Israel! (Ps. 125:1-5)

Additional Readings
1 Kings 18:1-18
Elijah condemns King Ahab

Ephesians 6:10-17
The armor of God against the powers

Hymn: Light One Candle to Watch for Messiah, ELW 240

Compassionate Lord, we seek your abundant blessings in our needy lives. Sustain us as evil and darkness continually attempt to disrupt our lives. Grant us inner peace and peace with others.

Tuesday, December 13, 2011

Week of Advent 3

Lucy, martyr, 304

Acts 3:17—4:4

Peter preaches about the prophets

While Peter and John were speaking to the people, the priests, the captain of the temple, and the Sadducees came to them, much annoyed because they were teaching the people and proclaiming that in Jesus there is the resurrection of the dead. So they arrested them and put them in custody until the next day, for it was already evening. But many of those who heard the word believed; and they numbered about five thousand. (Acts 4:1-4)

Psalm
Psalm 125
Prayer for blessing

Additional Reading
2 Kings 2:9-22
Elisha receives Elijah's spirit

Hymn: Gracious Spirit, Heed Our Pleading, ELW 401

Jesus, you are the resurrection and the life. As Peter and John proclaimed your good news, give us courage and protect us as we share your saving word with others.

Wednesday, December 14, 2011

Week of Advent 3

John of the Cross, renewer of the church, 1591

Mark 9:9-13

Questions about Elijah

As they were coming down the mountain, he ordered them to tell no one about what they had seen, until after the Son of Man had risen from the dead. So they kept the matter to themselves, questioning what this rising from the dead could mean. Then they asked him, "Why do the scribes say that Elijah must come first?" He said to them, "Elijah is indeed coming first to restore all things. How then is it written about the Son of Man, that he is to go through many sufferings and be treated with contempt? But I tell you that Elijah has come, and they did to him whatever they pleased, as it is written about him." (Mark 9:9-13)

Psalm

Psalm 125

Prayer for blessing

Additional Reading

Malachi 3:16—4:6

Elijah and the coming one

Hymn: Tree of Life and Awesome Mystery, ELW 334

God of life, as the disciples gazed upon Christ's transfigured body, may we know with certainty that you are alive in our midst, and may our own hearts be turned to serve you.

Thursday, December 15, 2011

Week of Advent 3

Psalm 89:1-4, 19-26

I sing of your love

I will sing of your steadfast love, O LORD, forever;
  with my mouth I will proclaim your faithfulness to all generations.
I declare that your steadfast love is established forever;
  your faithfulness is as firm as the heavens.
You said, "I have made a covenant with my chosen one,
  I have sworn to my servant David:
'I will establish your descendants forever,
  and build your throne for all generations.'" (Ps. 89:1-4)

Additional Readings

2 Samuel 6:1-11
The advent of the ark of the Lord

Hebrews 1:1-4
In the last days God speaks by a son

Hymn: Great Is Thy Faithfulness, ELW 733

We will sing of your love forever, gracious God. We will proclaim your faithfulness to the generations. Thanks be to you for choosing us as your very own, and using us to share your never-ending hope with others.

Friday, December 16, 2011

Week of Advent 3

Hebrews 1:5-14

The advent of one higher than angels

For to which of the angels did God ever say,
  "You are my Son;
    today I have begotten you"?
Or again,
  "I will be his Father,
    and he will be my Son"?
And again, when he brings the firstborn into the world, he says,
  "Let all God's angels worship him."
Of the angels he says,
  "He makes his angels winds,
    and his servants flames of fire."
But of the Son he says,
  "Your throne, O God, is forever and ever,
    and the righteous scepter is the scepter of your kingdom.
  You have loved righteousness and hated wickedness;
  therefore God, your God, has anointed you
    with the oil of gladness beyond your companions." (Heb. 1:5-9)

Psalm
Psalm 89:1-4, 19-26
I sing of your love

Additional Reading
2 Samuel 6:12-19
The ark of God enters Jerusalem

Hymn: As the Dark Awaits the Dawn, ELW 261

Prepare us for your coming among us, O God. Help us to praise your only-begotten Son who was worshiped and announced by angels, and who sits on your heavenly throne forever.

Saturday, December 17, 2011

Week of Advent 3

O Wisdom,
proceeding from the mouth of the Most High,
pervading and permeating all creation,
mightily ordering all things:
Come and teach us the way of prudence.

John 7:40-52
The Messiah, David, and Bethlehem

When they heard these words, some in the crowd said, "This is really the prophet." Others said, "This is the Messiah." But some asked, "Surely the Messiah does not come from Galilee, does he? Has not the scripture said that the Messiah is descended from David and comes from Bethlehem, the village where David lived?" So there was a division in the crowd because of him. Some of them wanted to arrest him, but no one laid hands on him. (John 7:40-44)

Psalm
Psalm 89:1-4, 19-26
I sing of your love

Additional Reading
Judges 13:2-24
The birth of Samson

Hymn: O Come, O Come, Emmanuel, ELW 257

Saving God, we praise you for sending Jesus to be the Savior of the world. As you brought fulfillment to ancient dreams and hopes through Christ's birth in Bethlehem, may he bring peace into our world today.

Lighting the Advent Wreath
Use this blessing when lighting all four candles.

Blessed are you, O Lord our God, ruler of the universe.
In your Son, Emmanuel,
you have shown us your light
and saved us from the power of sin.
Bless us as we light the candles on this wreath.
Increase our longing for your presence,
that at the celebration of your Son's birth
his Spirit might dwell anew in our midst,
for he is our light and our salvation.
Blessed be God forever.

Sunday, December 18, 2011

Fourth Sunday of Advent

O Adonai and ruler of the house of Israel,
who appeared to Moses in the burning bush
and gave him the Law on Sinai:
Come with an outstretched arm and redeem us.

Luke 1:26-38
The angel appears to Mary

In the sixth month the angel Gabriel was sent by God to a town in Galilee called Nazareth, to a virgin engaged to a man whose name was Joseph, of the house of David. The virgin's name was Mary. And he came to her and said, "Greetings, favored one! The Lord is with you." But she was much perplexed by his words and pondered what sort of greeting this might be. The angel said to her, "Do not be afraid, Mary, for you have found favor with God. And now, you will conceive in your womb and bear a son, and you will name him Jesus." (Luke 1:26-31)

Psalm
Luke 1:46b-55
The Mighty One raises the lowly

Additional Readings
2 Samuel 7:1-11, 16
God's promise to David

Romans 16:25-27
The mystery revealed in Jesus Christ

Hymn: The Angel Gabriel from Heaven Came, ELW 265

Stir up your power, Lord Christ, and come. With your abundant grace and might, free us from the sin that would obstruct your mercy, that willingly we may bear your redeeming love to all the world, for you live and reign with the Father and the Holy Spirit, one God, now and forever.

Monday, December 19, 2011

Week of Advent 4

O Root of Jesse,
standing as an ensign before the peoples,
before whom all kings are mute,
to whom the nations will do homage:
Come quickly to deliver us.

Luke 1:46b-55

The Lord lifts up the lowly

"My soul magnifies the Lord,
  and my spirit rejoices in God my Savior,
for he has looked with favor on the lowliness of his servant.
  Surely, from now on all generations will call me blessed;
for the Mighty One has done great things for me,
  and holy is his name.
His mercy is for those who fear him
  from generation to generation." (Luke 1:46b-50)

Additional Readings

1 Samuel 1:1-18
Hannah is promised a child

Hebrews 9:1-14
Christ comes as high priest

Hymn: Canticle of the Turning, ELW 723

God of heaven and earth, as Mary praised you for choosing her to be the mother of the Lord, help us to praise you as well. You alone are mighty and holy, full of goodness and mercy.

Tuesday, December 20, 2011

Week of Advent 4

Katharina von Bora Luther, renewer of the church, 1552

O Key of David and scepter of the house of Israel,
you open and no one can close,
you close and no one can open:
Come and rescue the prisoners
who are in darkness and the shadow of death.

Hebrews 8:1-13
The mediator replaces the sanctuary

But Jesus has now obtained a more excellent ministry, and to that degree he is the mediator of a better covenant, which has been enacted through better promises. (Heb. 8:6)

Additional Readings

1 Samuel 1:19-28
Hannah presents Samuel to God

Luke 1:46b-55
The Lord lifts up the lowly

Hymn: Savior of the Nations, Come, ELW 263

Jesus our high priest, we give thanks that by your life you made the greatest sacrifice for us, and as our mediator at the throne of heaven you have made us heirs of a new covenant that is everlasting.

Wednesday, December 21, 2011

Week of Advent 4

O Dayspring,
splendor of light everlasting:
Come and enlighten those who sit in darkness
and in the shadow of death.

1 Samuel 2:1-10
Hannah's song

Hannah prayed and said,
"My heart exults in the LORD;
  my strength is exalted in my God.
My mouth derides my enemies,
  because I rejoice in my victory.
"There is no Holy One like the LORD,
  no one besides you;
  there is no Rock like our God.
Talk no more so very proudly,
  let not arrogance come from your mouth;
for the LORD is a God of knowledge,
  and by him actions are weighed." (1 Sam. 2:1-3)

Additional Readings
Mark 11:1-11
Jesus enters Jerusalem

Luke 1:46b-55
The Lord lifts up the lowly

Hymn: My Soul Does Magnify the Lord, ELW 882

Purpose-filled God, as Hannah gave you thanks and praise for blessing
her with a child, may we always praise you with our hearts and souls,
for no one else is holy like you.

Thursday, December 22, 2011

Week of Advent 4

O King of the nations, the ruler they long for,
the cornerstone uniting all people:
Come and save us all,
whom you formed out of clay.

Psalm 96
Let the earth be glad

Say among the nations, "The LORD is king!
  The world is firmly established; it shall never be moved.
  He will judge the peoples with equity."
Let the heavens be glad, and let the earth rejoice;
  let the sea roar, and all that fills it;
  let the field exult, and everything in it.
Then shall all the trees of the forest sing for joy
  before the LORD; for he is coming,
  for he is coming to judge the earth.
He will judge the world with righteousness,
  and the peoples with his truth. (Ps. 96:10-13)

Additional Readings
Zephaniah 3:8-13
A people humble and lowly

Romans 10:5-13
The word is near you

Hymn: All Earth Is Hopeful, ELW 266

We rejoice in you, O God of creation, who comes to judge the earth with
righteousness and truth. As even the trees sing with joy, enable us to
worship you without end.

Friday, December 23, 2011

Week of Advent 4

O Emmanuel, our king and our lawgiver,
the anointed of the nations and their Savior:
Come and save us, Lord our God.

Romans 13:11-14
Salvation is near

Besides this, you know what time it is, how it is now the moment for you to wake from sleep. For salvation is nearer to us now than when we became believers; the night is far gone, the day is near. Let us then lay aside the works of darkness and put on the armor of light; let us live honorably as in the day, not in reveling and drunkenness, not in debauchery and licentiousness, not in quarreling and jealousy. Instead, put on the Lord Jesus Christ, and make no provision for the flesh, to gratify its desires. (Rom. 13:11-14)

Psalm
Psalm 96
Let the earth be glad

Additional Reading
Zephaniah 3:14-20
God is in your midst

Hymn: Each Winter As the Year Grows Older, ELW 252

God of light, the time of salvation is near! Help us to lay aside the works of darkness and put on your armor of light. Enable us to live honorably as we await the return of our Savior Jesus Christ.

Over the centuries, various customs have developed which focus the household on welcoming the light of Christ: the daily or weekly lighting of the Advent wreath, the blessing of the lighted Christmas tree, the candle-lit procession of Las Posadas, the flickering lights of the luminaria, the Christ candle at Christmas.

The Christian household not only welcomes the light of Christ at Christmas, but celebrates the presence of that light throughout the Twelve Days, from Christmas until the Epiphany, January 6. In the Christmas season, Christians welcome the light of Christ that is already with us through faith. In word and gesture, prayer and song, in the many customs of diverse cultures, Christians celebrate this life-giving Word and ask that it dwell more deeply in the rhythm of daily life.

Table Prayer for the Twelve Days of Christmas

With joy and gladness we feast upon your love, O God.
You have come among us in Jesus, your Son,
and your presence now graces this table.
May Christ dwell in us that we might bear his love to all the world,
for he is Lord forever and ever. Amen.

Blessing of the Christmas Tree

Let the heavens rejoice, and let the earth be glad;
let the sea thunder and all that is in it;
let the field be joyful and all that is therein.
Then shall all the trees of the wood shout for joy
at your coming, O LORD,
for you come to judge the earth.
You will judge the world with righteousness
and the peoples with your truth. (Ps. 96:11-13)

Be praised, O God, for the blessings around us that point to you.
Be praised, O God, for the signs of this holy season
that awaken in us wonder.
Praise for the steadfast green of this tree,
like your love, enduring all seasons.
Praise for the light that illumines our darkness,
like Christ, who brings light to the world.
Join our voices with those of the tree and of all creation,
who sing at your coming:
Glory to God in the highest, and peace to God's people on earth.
Amen.

Blessing of the Nativity Scene

*This blessing may be used when figures are added to the nativity scene
throughout the days of Christmas.*

Bless us, O God, bless us who gather around this stable.
As we celebrate Christ's birth into the world,
may we receive the Christ child into our hearts
with gratitude and song. Amen.

Saturday, December 24, 2011

Nativity of Our Lord
Christmas Eve

Luke 2:1-14 [15-20]
God with us

In that region there were shepherds living in the fields, keeping watch over their flock by night. Then an angel of the Lord stood before them, and the glory of the Lord shone around them, and they were terrified. But the angel said to them, "Do not be afraid; for see—I am bringing you good news of great joy for all the people: to you is born this day in the city of David a Savior, who is the Messiah, the Lord. This will be a sign for you: you will find a child wrapped in bands of cloth and lying in a manger." (Luke 2:8-12)

Psalm	**Additional Readings**	
Psalm 96	Isaiah 9:2-7	Titus 2:11-14
Let the earth be glad	*A child is born for us*	*The grace of God has appeared*

Hymn: Angels We Have Heard on High, ELW 289

Almighty God, you made this holy night shine with the brightness of the true Light. Grant that here on earth we may walk in the light of Jesus' presence and in the last day wake to the brightness of his glory; through your Son, Jesus Christ our Lord, who lives and reigns with you and the Holy Spirit, one God, now and forever.

Sunday, December 25, 2011

Nativity of Our Lord
Christmas Day

John 1:1-14
The Word became flesh

In the beginning was the Word, and the Word was with God, and the Word was God. He was in the beginning with God. All things came into being through him, and without him not one thing came into being. What has come into being in him was life, and the life was the light of all people. The light shines in the darkness, and the darkness did not overcome it. (John 1:1-5)

Psalm
Psalm 98
The victory of our God

Additional Readings
Isaiah 52:7-10
Heralds announce God's salvation

Hebrews 1:1-4 [5-12]
God has spoken by a son

Hymn: O Come, All Ye Faithful, ELW 283

Almighty God, you gave us your only Son to take on our human nature and to illumine the world with your light. By your grace adopt us as your children and enlighten us with your Spirit, through Jesus Christ, our Redeemer and Lord, who lives and reigns with you and the Holy Spirit, one God, now and forever.

Monday, December 26, 2011

Stephen, Deacon and Martyr

Acts 6:8—7:2a, 51-60

Stephen is stoned to death

Now during those days, when the disciples were increasing in number, the Hellenists complained against the Hebrews because their widows were being neglected in the daily distribution of food. And the twelve called together the whole community of the disciples and said, "It is not right that we should neglect the word of God in order to wait on tables. Therefore, friends, select from among yourselves seven men of good standing, full of the Spirit and of wisdom, whom we may appoint to this task, while we, for our part, will devote ourselves to prayer and to serving the word." What they said pleased the whole community, and they chose Stephen, a man full of faith and the Holy Spirit, together with Philip, Prochorus, Nicanor, Timon, Parmenas, and Nicolaus, a proselyte of Antioch. (Acts 6:1-5)

Psalm
Psalm 17:1-9, 15
I call upon you, O God

Additional Readings
2 Chronicles 24:17-22
Zechariah is stoned to death

Matthew 23:34-39
Jesus laments that Jerusalem kills her prophets

Hymn: What Child Is This, ELW 296

We give you thanks, O Lord of glory, for the example of Stephen the first martyr, who looked to heaven and prayed for his persecutors. Grant that we also may pray for our enemies and seek the forgiveness of those who hurt us, through Jesus Christ, our Savior and Lord, who lives and reigns with you and the Holy Spirit, one God, now and forever.

Tuesday, December 27, 2011

John, Apostle and Evangelist

John 21:20-25

The beloved disciple remains with Jesus

Peter turned and saw the disciple whom Jesus loved following them; he was the one who had reclined next to Jesus at the supper and had said, "Lord, who is it that is going to betray you?" When Peter saw him, he said to Jesus, "Lord, what about him?" Jesus said to him, "If it is my will that he remain until I come, what is that to you? Follow me!" So the rumor spread in the community that this disciple would not die. Yet Jesus did not say to him that he would not die, but, "If it is my will that he remain until I come, what is that to you?"

This is the disciple who is testifying to these things and has written them, and we know that his testimony is true. But there are also many other things that Jesus did; if every one of them were written down, I suppose that the world itself could not contain the books that would be written. (John 21:20-25)

Psalm

Psalm 116:12-19
The death of faithful servants

Additional Readings

Genesis 1:1-5, 26-31
Humankind is created by God

1 John 1:1—2:2
Jesus, the word of life

Hymn: The Bells of Christmas, ELW 298

Merciful God, you have revealed the mysteries of your Word made flesh through John the apostle and evangelist. Let the brightness of your light shine on your church, so that all your people, instructed in the holy gospel, may walk in the light of your truth and attain eternal life, through Jesus Christ, our Savior and Lord, who lives and reigns with you and the Holy Spirit, one God, now and forever.

Wednesday, December 28, 2011

The Holy Innocents, Martyrs

Matthew 2:13-18
Herod kills innocent children

Now after [the wise men] had left, an angel of the Lord appeared to Joseph in a dream and said, "Get up, take the child and his mother, and flee to Egypt, and remain there until I tell you; for Herod is about to search for the child, to destroy him." Then Joseph got up, took the child and his mother by night, and went to Egypt, and remained there until the death of Herod. This was to fulfill what had been spoken by the Lord through the prophet, "Out of Egypt I have called my son." When Herod saw that he had been tricked by the wise men, he was infuriated, and he sent and killed all the children in and around Bethlehem who were two years old or under, according to the time that he had learned from the wise men. (Matt. 2:13-16)

Psalm
Psalm 124
We have escaped like a bird

Additional Readings
Jeremiah 31:15-17
Rachel weeps for her children

1 Peter 4:12-19
Continue to do good while suffering

Hymn: How Long, O God, ELW 698

We remember today, O God, the slaughter of the innocent children of Bethlehem by order of King Herod. Receive into the arms of your mercy all innocent victims. By your great might frustrate the designs of evil tyrants and establish your rule of justice, love, and peace, through Jesus Christ, our Savior and Lord, who lives and reigns with you and the Holy Spirit, one God, now and forever.

Thursday, December 29, 2011

Fifth Day of Christmas

Psalm 148
God's splendor is over earth and heaven

Praise the LORD!
Praise the LORD from the heavens;
   praise him in the heights!
Praise him, all his angels;
   praise him, all his host!
Praise him, sun and moon;
   praise him, all you shining stars!
Praise him, you highest heavens,
   and you waters above the heavens! (Ps. 148:1-4)

Additional Readings
Isaiah 49:5-15
God like a nursing mother

Matthew 12:46-50
Jesus' true family

Hymn: Joy to the World, ELW 267

O God, we praise you for all creation, for the heights of the heavens, and for your holy angels that serve you night and day. We praise you most of all for giving us Jesus Christ, the Savior of the world.

Friday, December 30, 2011

Sixth Day of Christmas

2 Peter 3:8-13

A thousand years as one day

But do not ignore this one fact, beloved, that with the Lord one day is like a thousand years, and a thousand years are like one day. The Lord is not slow about his promise, as some think of slowness, but is patient with you, not wanting any to perish, but all to come to repentance. But the day of the Lord will come like a thief, and then the heavens will pass away with a loud noise, and the elements will be dissolved with fire, and the earth and everything that is done on it will be disclosed. (2 Peter 3:8-10)

Psalm
Psalm 148
God's splendor is over earth and heaven

Additional Reading
Proverbs 9:1-12
Your days will be multiplied

Hymn: When Long before Time, ELW 861

Gracious Lord, at the culmination of a year we are grateful for your faithfulness and for your patience with us. As we anticipate a new year, help us to order our lives to your guidance.

Saturday, December 31, 2011

Seventh Day of Christmas

John 8:12-19
I am the light

Again Jesus spoke to them, saying, "I am the light of the world. Whoever follows me will never walk in darkness but will have the light of life." Then the Pharisees said to him, "You are testifying on your own behalf; your testimony is not valid." Jesus answered, "Even if I testify on my own behalf, my testimony is valid because I know where I have come from and where I am going, but you do not know where I come from or where I am going. You judge by human standards; I judge no one. Yet even if I do judge, my judgment is valid; for it is not I alone who judge, but I and the Father who sent me." (John 8:12-16)

Psalm
Psalm 148
God's splendor is over earth and heaven

Additional Reading
1 Kings 3:5-14
God grants a discerning mind

Hymn: Love Has Come, ELW 292

God, you are the light of the world. Shine your eternal light into the darkness of our lives so we can see your love and mercy. May our lives reflect your brilliance to others around us.

Lesser Festivals and Commemorations

January 1 – Name of Jesus Every Jewish boy was circumcised and formally named on the eighth day of his life. Already in his infancy, Jesus bore the mark of a covenant that he made new through the shedding of his blood on the cross.

January 2 – Johann Konrad Wilhelm Loehe Wilhelm Loehe was a pastor in nineteenth-century Germany. From the small town of Neuendettelsau he sent pastors to North America, Australia, New Guinea, Brazil, and the Ukraine.

January 15 – Martin Luther King Jr. Martin Luther King Jr. is remembered as an American prophet of justice among races and nations. Many churches hold commemorations near Dr. King's birth date of January 15, in conjunction with the American civil holiday honoring him.

January 17 – Antony of Egypt Antony was one of the earliest Egyptian desert fathers. He became the head of a group of monks that lived in a cluster of huts and devoted themselves to communal prayer, worship, and manual labor.

January 17 – Pachomius Another of the desert fathers, Pachomius was born in Egypt about 290. He organized hermits into a religious community in which the members prayed together and held their goods in common.

January 18 – Confession of Peter; Beginning of the Week of Prayer for Christian Unity The Week of Prayer for Christian Unity is framed by two commemorations, the Confession of Peter and the Conversion of Paul. On this day the church remembers that Peter was led by God's grace to acknowledge Jesus as "the Christ, the Son of the living God" (Matt. 16:16).

January 19 – Henry When Erik, King of Sweden, determined to invade Finland for the purpose of converting the people there to Christianity, Henry went with him. Henry is recognized as the patron saint of Finland.

January 21 – Agnes Agnes was a girl of about thirteen living in Rome, who had chosen a life of service to Christ as a virgin, despite the Roman emperor Diocletian's ruling that had outlawed all Christian activity. She gave witness to her faith and was put to death as a result.

January 25 – Conversion of Paul; End of the Week of Prayer for Christian Unity As the Week of Prayer for Christian Unity comes to an end, the church remembers how a man of Tarsus named Saul, a former persecutor of the early Christian church, was led to become one of its chief preachers.

January 26 – Timothy, Titus, Silas On the two days following the celebration of the Conversion of Paul, his companions are remembered. Timothy, Titus, and Silas were missionary coworkers with Paul.

January 27 – Lydia, Dorcas, Phoebe On this day the church remembers three women who were companions in Paul's ministry.

January 28 – Thomas Aquinas Thomas Aquinas was a brilliant and creative theologian who immersed himself in the thought of Aristotle and worked to explain Christian beliefs in the philosophical culture of the day.

February 2 – Presentation of Our Lord Forty days after the birth of Christ the church marks the day Mary and Joseph presented him in the temple in accordance with Jewish law. Simeon greeted Mary and Joseph, responding with the canticle that begins "Now, Lord, you let your servant go in peace."

February 3 – Ansgar Ansgar was a monk who led a mission to Denmark and later to Sweden. His work ran into difficulties with the rulers of the day, and he was forced to withdraw into Germany, where he served as a bishop in Hamburg.

February 5 – The Martyrs of Japan In the sixteenth century, Jesuit missionaries, followed by Franciscans, introduced the Christian faith in Japan. By 1630, Christianity was driven underground. This day commemorates the first martyrs of Japan, twenty-six missionaries and converts, who were killed by crucifixion.

February 14 – Cyril, Methodius These brothers from a noble family in Thessalonika in northeastern Greece were priests who are regarded as the founders of Slavic literature. Their work in preaching and worshiping in the language of the people is honored by Christians in both East and West.

February 18 – Martin Luther On this day Luther died at the age of sixty-two. For a time, he was an Augustinian monk, but it is primarily for his work as a biblical scholar, translator of the Bible, reformer of the liturgy, theologian, educator, and father of German vernacular literature that he is remembered.

February 23 – Polycarp Polycarp was bishop of Smyrna and a link between the apostolic age and the church at the end of the second century. At the age of eighty-six he was martyred for his faith.

February 25 – Elizabeth Fedde Fedde was born in Norway and trained as a deaconess. Among her notable achievements were the establishment of the Deaconess House in Brooklyn and the Deaconess House and Hospital of the Lutheran Free Church in Minneapolis.

March 1 – George Herbert Herbert was ordained a priest in 1630 and served the little parish of St. Andrew Bremerton until his death. He is best remembered, however, as a writer of poems and hymns such as "Come, my way, my truth, my life" and "The King of love my shepherd is."

March 2 – John Wesley, Charles Wesley The Wesleys were leaders of a revival in the Church of England. Their spiritual methods of frequent communion, fasting, and advocacy for the poor earned them the name "Methodists."

March 7 – Perpetua, Felicity In the year 202 the emperor Septimius Severus forbade conversions to Christianity. Perpetua, a noblewoman, Felicity, a slave, and other companions were all catechumens at Carthage in North Africa, where they were imprisoned and sentenced to death.

March 10 – Harriet Tubman, Sojourner Truth Harriet Tubman helped about 300 slaves to escape via the Underground Railroad until slavery was abolished in the United States. After slavery was abolished in New York in 1827, Sojourner Truth became deeply involved in Christianity, and in later life she was a popular speaker against slavery and for women's rights.

March 12 – Gregory the Great Gregory held political office and at another time lived as a monk, all before he was elected to the papacy. Having also established a school to train church musicians, Gregorian chant is named in his honor.

March 17 – Patrick Patrick went to Ireland from Britain to serve as a bishop and missionary. He made his base in the north of Ireland and from there made many missionary journeys, with much success.

March 19 – Joseph The Gospel of Luke shows Joseph acting in accordance with both civil and religious law by returning to Bethlehem for the census and by presenting the child Jesus in the temple on the fortieth day after his birth.

March 21 – Thomas Cranmer Cranmer's lasting achievement is contributing to and overseeing the creation of the Book of Common Prayer, which remains (in revised form) the worship book of the Anglican Communion. He was burned at the stake under Queen Mary for his support of the Protestant Reformation.

March 22 – Jonathan Edwards Edwards was a minister in Connecticut and has been described as the greatest of the New England Puritan preachers. Edwards carried out mission work among the Housatonic Indians of Massachusetts, and became president of the College of New Jersey, later to be known as Princeton University.

March 24 – Oscar Arnulfo Romero Romero is remembered for his advocacy on behalf of the poor in El Salvador, though it was not a characteristic of his early priesthood. After several years of threats to his life, Romero was assassinated while presiding at the eucharist.

March 25 – Annunciation of Our Lord Nine months before Christmas the church celebrates the annunciation. In Luke the angel Gabriel announces to Mary that she will give birth to the Son of God, and she responds, "Here am I, the servant of the Lord."

March 29 – Hans Nielsen Hauge Hans Nielsen Hauge was a layperson who began preaching in Norway and Denmark after a mystical experience that he believed called him to share the assurance of salvation with others. At the time itinerant preaching and religious gatherings held without the supervision of a pastor were illegal, and Hauge was arrested several times.

March 31 – John Donne This priest of the Church of England is commemorated for his poetry and spiritual writing. Most of his poetry was written before his ordination and is sacred and secular, intellectual and sensuous.

April 4 – Benedict the African Although Benedict was illiterate, his fame as a confessor brought many visitors to him, and he was eventually named superior of a Franciscan community. A patron saint of African Americans, Benedict is remembered for his patience and understanding when confronted with racial prejudice and taunts.

April 6 – Albrecht Dürer, Matthias Grünewald, Lucas Cranach These great artists revealed through their work the mystery of salvation and the wonder of creation. Though having remained a Roman Catholic, at Dürer's death Martin Luther wrote to a friend, "Affection bids us mourn for one who was the best." Several religious works are included in Grünwald's small surviving corpus, the most famous being the Isenheim Altarpiece. Lucas Cranach was widely known for his woodcuts, some of which illustrated the first German printing of the New Testament.

April 9 – Dietrich Bonhoeffer In 1933, and with Hitler's rise to power, Bonhoeffer became a leading spokesman for the Confessing Church, a resistance movement against the Nazis. After leading a worship service on April 8, 1945, at Schönberg prison, he was taken away to be hanged the next day.

April 10 – Mikael Agricola Agricola began a reform of the Finnish church along Lutheran lines. He translated the New Testament, the prayerbook, hymns, and the mass into Finnish and through this work set the rules of orthography that are the basis of modern Finnish spelling.

April 19 – Olavus Petri, Laurentius Petri These two brothers are commemorated for their introduction of the Lutheran movement to the Church of Sweden after studying at the University of Wittenberg. Together the brothers published a complete Bible in Swedish and a revised liturgy in 1541.

April 21 – Anselm This eleventh-century Benedictine monk stands out as one of the greatest theologians between Augustine and Thomas Aquinas. He is perhaps best known for his "satisfaction" theory of atonement, where God takes on human nature in Jesus Christ in order to make the perfect payment for sin.

April 23 – Toyohiko Kagawa Toyohiko Kagawa's vocation to help the poor led him to live among them. He was arrested for his efforts to reconcile Japan and China after the Japanese attack of 1940.

April 25 – Mark Though Mark himself was not an apostle, it is likely that he was a member of one of the early Christian communities. The gospel attributed to him is brief and direct and is considered by many to be the earliest gospel.

April 29 – Catherine of Siena Catherine of Siena was a member of the Order of Preachers (Dominicans), and among Roman Catholics she was the first woman to receive the title Doctor of the Church. She also advised popes and any uncertain persons who told her their problems.

May 1 – Philip, James Philip and James are commemorated together because the remains of these two saints were placed in the Church of the Apostles in Rome on this day in 561.

May 2 – Athanasius At the Council of Nicea in 325 and when he himself served as bishop of Alexandria, Athanasius defended the full divinity of Christ against the Arian position held by emperors, magistrates, and theologians.

May 4 – Monica Almost everything known about Monica comes from Augustine's *Confessions*, his autobiography. Her dying wish was that her son remember her at the altar of the Lord, wherever he was.

May 8 – Julian of Norwich Julian was most likely a Benedictine nun living in an isolated cell attached to the Carrow Priory in Norwich, England. When she was about thirty years old, she reported visions that she later compiled into a book, *Sixteen Revelations* *of Divine Love*, which is a classic of medieval mysticism.

May 9 – Nicolaus Ludwig von Zinzendorf Drawn from an overly intellectual Lutheran faith to Pietism, at the age of twenty-two Count Zinzendorf permitted a group of Moravians to live on his lands. Zinzendorf participated in worldwide missions emanating from this community and is also remembered for writing hymns characteristic of his Pietistic faith.

May 14 – Matthias After Christ's ascension, the apostles met in Jerusalem to choose a replacement for Judas. Though little is known about him, Matthias had traveled among the disciples from the time of Jesus' baptism until his ascension.

May 18 – Erik Erik, long considered the patron saint of Sweden, ruled there from 1150 387 to 1160. He is honored for efforts to bring peace to the nearby pagan kingdoms and for his crusades to spread the Christian faith in Scandinavia.

May 21 – Helena Helena was the mother of Constantine, a man who later became the Roman emperor. Helena is remembered for traveling through Palestine and building churches on the sites she believed to be where Jesus was born, where he was buried, and from which he ascended.

May 24 – Nicolaus Copernicus, Leonhard Euler Copernicus formally studied astronomy, mathematics, Greek, Plato, law, medicine, and canon law and is chiefly remembered for his work as an astronomer and his idea that the sun, not the earth, is the center of the solar system. Euler is regarded as one of the founders of the science of pure mathematics and made important contributions to mechanics, hydrodynamics, astronomy, optics, and acoustics.

May 27 – John Calvin Having embraced the views of the Reformation by his mid-twenties, John Calvin was a preacher in Geneva, was banished once, and later returned to reform the city with a rigid, theocratic discipline. Calvin is considered the father of the Reformed churches.

May 29 – Jiří Tranovský Jiří Tranovský is considered the "Luther of the Slavs" and the father of Slovak hymnody. He produced a translation of the Augsburg Confession and published his hymn collection *Cithara Sanctorum* (Lyre of the Saints), also known as the Tranoscius, which is the foundation of Slovak Lutheran hymnody.

May 31 – Visit of Mary to Elizabeth Sometime after the Annunciation, Mary visited her cousin Elizabeth, who greeted Mary with the words, "Blessed are you among women," and Mary responded with her famous song, the Magnificat.

June 1 – Justin Justin was a teacher of philosophy and engaged in debates about the truth of Christian faith. Having been arrested and jailed for practicing an unauthorized religion, he refused to renounce his faith and he and six of his students were beheaded.

June 3 – The Martyrs of Uganda King Mwanga of Uganda was angered by Christian members of the court whose first allegiance was not to him but to Christ. On this date in 1886, thirty-two young men were burned to death for refusing to renounce Christianity. Their persecution led to a much stronger Christian presence in the country.

June 3 – John XXIII Despite the expectation upon his election that the seventy-seven year old John XXIII would be a transitional pope, he had great energy and spirit. He convened the Second Vatican Council in order to open the windows of the church. The council brought about great changes in Roman Catholic worship and ecumenical relationships.

June 5 – Boniface Boniface led large numbers of Benedictine monks and nuns in establishing churches, schools, and seminaries. Boniface was preparing a group for confirmation on the eve of Pentecost when he and others were killed by a band of pagans.

June 7 – Seattle The city of Seattle was named after Noah Seattle against his wishes. After Chief Seattle became a Roman Catholic, he began the practice of morning and evening prayer in the tribe, a practice that continued after his death.

June 9 – Columba, Aidan, Bede These three monks from the British Isles were pillars among those who kept alive the light of learning and devotion during the Middle Ages. Columba founded three monasteries, including one on the island of Iona, off the coast of Scotland. Aidan, who helped bring Christianity to the Northumbria area of England, was known for his pastoral style and ability to stir people to charity and good works. Bede was a Bible translator and scripture scholar who wrote a history of the English church and was the first historian to date events *anno Domini* (A.D.), the "year of our Lord."

June 11 – Barnabas Though he was not among the Twelve mentioned in the gospels, the book of Acts gives Barnabas the title of apostle. When Paul came to Jerusalem after his conversion, Barnabas took him in over the fears of the other apostles who doubted Paul's discipleship.

June 14 – Basil the Great, Gregory of Nyssa, Gregory of Nazianzus, Macrina The three men in this group are known as the Cappadocian fathers; all three explored the mystery of the Holy Trinity. Basil's Longer Rule and Shorter Rule for monastic life are the basis for Eastern monasticism to this day, and express a preference for communal monastic life over that of hermits. Gregory of Nazianzus defended Orthodox trinitarian and Christological doctrine, and his preaching won over the city of Constantinople. Gregory of Nyssa is remembered as a writer on spiritual life and the contemplation of God in worship and sacraments. Macrina was the older sister of Basil and Gregory of Nyssa, and her teaching was influential within the early church.

June 21 – Onesimos Nesib Onesimos, an Ethiopian, was captured by slave traders and taken from his homeland to Eritrea, where he was bought, freed, and educated by Swedish missionaries. He translated the Bible into Oromo and returned to his homeland to preach the gospel there.

June 24 – John the Baptist The birth of John the Baptist is celebrated exactly six months before Christmas Eve. For Christians in the Northern Hemisphere, these two dates are deeply symbolic, since John said that he must decrease as Jesus increased. John was born as the days are longest and then steadily decrease, while Jesus was born as the days are shortest and then steadily increase.

June 25 – Presentation of the Augsburg Confession On this day in 1530 the German and Latin editions of the Augsburg Confession were presented to Emperor Charles of the Holy Roman Empire. The Augsburg Confession was written by Philipp Melanchthon and endorsed by Martin Luther and consists of a brief summary of points in which the reformers saw their teaching as either agreeing with or differing from that of the Roman Catholic Church of the time.

June 25 – Philipp Melanchthon Though he died on April 19, Philipp Melanchthon is commemorated today because of his connection with the Augsburg Confession. Colleague and co-reformer with Martin Luther, Melanchthon was a brilliant scholar, known as "the teacher of Germany."

June 27 – Cyril Remembered as an outstanding theologian, Cyril defended the orthodox teachings about the person of Christ against Nestorius, who was at that time bishop of Constantinople. Eventually it was decided that Cyril's interpretation, that Christ's person included both divine and human natures, was correct.

June 28 – Irenaeus Irenaeus believed that only Matthew, Mark, Luke, and John were trustworthy gospels. As a result of his battles with the gnostics he was one of the first to speak of the church as "catholic," meaning that congregations did not exist by themselves, but were linked to one another throughout the whole church.

June 29 – Peter, Paul One of the things that unites Peter and Paul is the tradition that says they were martyred together on this date in A.D. 67 or 68. What unites them even more closely is their common confession of Jesus Christ.

July 1 – Catherine Winkworth, John Mason Neale Many of the most beloved hymns in the English language are the work of these gifted poets. Catherine Winkworth devoted herself to the translation of German hymns into English, while John Mason Neale specialized in translating many ancient Latin and Greek hymns.

July 3 – Thomas Alongside the doubt for which Thomas is famous, the gospel according to John shows Thomas moving from doubt to deep faith. Thomas makes one of the strongest confessions of faith in the New Testament, "My Lord and my God!" (John 20:28).

July 6 – Jan Hus Jan Hus was a Bohemian priest who spoke against abuses in the church of his day in many of the same ways Luther would a century later. The followers of Jan Hus became known as the Czech Brethren and later became the Moravian Church.

July 11 – Benedict of Nursia Benedict is known as the father of Western monasticism. Benedict encourages a generous spirit of hospitality. Visitors to Benedictine communities are to be welcomed as Christ himself.

July 12 – Nathan Söderblom In 1930, this Swedish theologian, ecumenist, and social activist received the Nobel Prize for peace. Söderblom organized the Universal Christian Council on Life and Work, which was one of the organizations that in 1948 came together to form the World Council of Churches.

July 17 – Bartolomé de Las Casas Bartolomé de Las Casas was a Spanish priest and a missionary in the Western Hemisphere. Throughout the Caribbean and Central America he worked to stop the enslavement of native people, to halt the brutal treatment of women by military forces, and to promote laws that humanized the process of colonization.

July 22 – Mary Magdalene The gospels report Mary Magdalene was one of the women of Galilee who followed Jesus. As the first person to whom the risen Lord appeared, she returned to the disciples with the news and has been called "the apostle to the apostles" for her proclamation of the resurrection.

July 23 – Birgitta of Sweden Birgitta's devotional commitments led her to give to the poor and needy all that she owned while she began to live a more ascetic life. She founded an order of monks and nuns, the Order of the Holy Savior (Birgittines), whose superior was a woman.

July 25 – James James was one of the sons of Zebedee and is counted as one of the twelve disciples. James was the first of the Twelve to suffer martyrdom and is the only apostle whose martyrdom is recorded in scripture.

July 28 – Johann Sebastian Bach, Heinrich Schütz, George Frederick Handel These three composers did much to enrich the worship life of the church. Johann Sebastian Bach drew on the Lutheran tradition of hymnody and wrote about two hundred cantatas, including at least two for each Sunday and festival day in the Lutheran calendar of his day. George Frederick Handel was not primarily a church musician, but his great work *Messiah* is a musical proclamation of the scriptures. Heinrich Schütz wrote choral settings of biblical texts and paid special attention to ways his composition would underscore the meaning of the words.

July 29 – Mary, Martha, Lazarus of Bethany Mary and Martha are remembered for the hospitality and refreshment they offered Jesus in their home. Following the characterization drawn by Luke, Martha represents the active life, and Mary, the contemplative.

July 29 – Olaf Olaf is considered the patron saint of Norway. While at war in the Baltic and in Normandy, he became a Christian, then returned to Norway, declared himself king, and from then on Christianity was the dominant religion of the realm.

August 8 – Dominic Dominic believed that a stumbling block to restoring heretics to the church was the wealth of clergy, so he formed an itinerant religious order, the Order of Preachers (Dominicans), who lived in poverty, studied philosophy and theology, and preached against heresy.

August 10 – Lawrence Lawrence was one of seven deacons of the congregation at Rome and, like the deacons appointed in Acts, was responsible for financial matters in the church and for the care of the poor.

August 11 – Clare At age 18, Clare of Assisi heard Francis preach a sermon. With Francis's help she and a growing number of companions established a women's Franciscan community, called the Order of Poor Ladies, or Poor Clares.

August 13 – Florence Nightingale, Clara Maass Nightingale led a group of thirtyeight nurses to serve in the Crimean War, where they worked in appalling conditions. She returned to London as a hero and there resumed her work for hospital reform. Clara Maass was born in New Jersey and served as a nurse in the Spanish-American War, where she encountered the horrors of yellow fever. Later responding to a call for subjects in research on yellow fever, Maass contracted the disease and died.

August 14 – Maximilian Kolbe, Kaj Munk Confined in Auschwitz, Father Kolbe was a Franciscan priest who gave generously of his meager resources, and finally volunteered to be starved to death in place of another man who was a husband and father. Kaj Munk, a Danish Lutheran pastor and playwright, was an outspoken critic of the Nazis. His plays frequently highlighted the eventual victory of the Christian faith despite the church's weak and ineffective witness.

August 15 – Mary, Mother of Our Lord The honor paid to Mary as mother of our Lord goes back to biblical times, when Mary herself sang "from now on all generations will call me blessed" (Luke 1:48). Mary's song speaks of reversals in the reign of God: the mighty are cast down, the lowly are lifted up, the hungry are fed, and the rich are sent away empty-handed.

August 20 – Bernard of Clairvaux Bernard was a Cistercian monk who became an abbot of great spiritual depth. Through translation his several devotional writings and hymns are still read and sung today.

August 24 – Bartholomew Bartholomew is mentioned as one of Jesus' disciples in Matthew, Mark, and Luke. Except for his name on these lists of the twelve, little is known.

August 28 – Augustine As an adult Augustine came to see Christianity as a religion appropriate for a philosopher. Augustine was baptized by Ambrose at the Easter Vigil in , was made bishop of Hippo in 396, and was one of the greatest theologians of the Western church.

August 28 – Moses the Black A man of great strength and rough character, Moses the Black was converted to Christian faith toward the close of the fourth century. The change in his heart and life had a profound impact on his native Ethiopia.

September 2 – Nikolai Fredrik Severin Grundtvig Grundtvig was a prominent Danish theologian of the nineteenth century. From his university days he was convinced that poetry spoke to the human spirit better than prose, and he wrote more than a thousand hymns.

September 9 – Peter Claver Peter Claver was born into Spanish nobility and was persuaded to become a Jesuit missionary. He served in Cartagena (in what is now Colombia) by teaching and caring for the slaves.

September 13 – John Chrysostom John was a priest in Antioch and an outstanding preacher. His eloquence earned him the nickname "Chrysostom" ("golden mouth"), but he also preached against corruption among the royal court, whereupon the empress sent him into exile.

September 14 – Holy Cross Day The celebration of Holy Cross Day commemorates the dedication of the Church of the Resurrection in 335 on the location believed to have been where Christ was buried.

September 16 – Cyprian During Cyprian's time as bishop many people had denied the faith under duress. In contrast to some who held the belief that the church should not receive these people back, Cyprian believed they ought to be welcomed into full communion after a period of penance.

September 17 – Hildegard of Bingen Hildegard lived virtually her entire life in convents, yet was widely influential. She advised and reproved kings and popes, wrote poems and hymns, and produced treatises in medicine, theology, and natural history.

September 18 – Dag Hammarskjöld Dag Hammarskjöld was a Swedish diplomat and humanitarian who served as secretary general of the United Nations. The depth of Hammarskjöld's Christian faith was unknown until his private journal *Markings* was published following his death.

September 21 – Matthew Matthew was a tax collector, an occupation that was distrusted, since tax collectors were frequently dishonest and worked as agents for the Roman occupying government; yet it was these outcasts to whom Jesus showed his love. Since the second century, tradition has attributed the first gospel to him.

September 29 – Michael and All Angels The scriptures speak of angels who worship God in heaven, and in both testaments angels are God's messengers on earth. Michael is an angel whose name appears in Daniel as the heavenly being who leads the faithful dead to God's throne on the day of resurrection, while in the book of Revelation, Michael fights in a cosmic battle against Satan.

September 30 – Jerome Jerome translated the scriptures into the Latin that was spoken and written by the majority of people in his day. His translation is known as the Vulgate, which comes from the Latin word for "common."

October 4 – Francis of Assisi Francis renounced wealth and future inheritance and devoted himself to serving the poor. Since Francis had a spirit of gratitude for all of God's creation, this commemoration has been a traditional time to bless pets and animals, creatures Francis called his brothers and sisters.

October 4 – Theodor Fliedner Fliedner's work was instrumental in the revival of the ministry of deaconesses among Lutherans. Fliedner's deaconess motherhouse in Kaiserswerth, Germany, inspired Lutherans all over the world to commission deaconesses to serve in parishes, schools, prisons, and hospitals.

October 6 – William Tyndale Tyndale's plan to translate the scriptures into English met opposition from Henry VIII. Though Tyndale completed work on the New Testament in 1525 and worked on a portion of the Old Testament, he was tried for heresy and burned at the stake.

October 7 – Henry Melchior Muhlenberg Muhlenberg was prominent in setting the course for Lutheranism in the United States by helping Lutheran churches make the transition from the state churches of Europe to independent churches of America. Among other things, he established the first Lutheran synod in America and developed an American Lutheran liturgy.

October 15 – Teresa of Ávila Teresa of Ávila (also known as Teresa de Jesús) chose the life of a Carmelite nun after reading the letters of Jerome. Teresa's writings on devotional life are widely read by members of various denominations.

October 17 – Ignatius Ignatius was the second bishop of Antioch in Syria. When his own martyrdom approached, he wrote in one of his letters, "I prefer death in Christ Jesus to power over the farthest limits of the earth . . . . Do not stand in the way of my birth to real life."

October 18 – Luke Luke, as author of both Luke and Acts, was careful to place the events of Jesus' life in both their social and religious contexts. Some of the most loved parables and canticles are found only in this gospel.

October 23 – James of Jerusalem James is described in the New Testament as the brother of Jesus, and the secular historian Josephus called James the brother of Jesus, "the so-called Christ." Little is known about James, but Josephus reported that the Pharisees respected James for his piety and observance of the law.

October 26 – Philipp Nicolai, Johann Heermann, Paul Gerhardt These three outstanding hymnwriters all worked in Germany in the seventeenth century during times of war and plague. Philipp Nicolai's hymns "Wake, awake, for night is flying" and "O Morning Star, how fair and bright!" were included in a series of meditations he wrote to comfort his parishioners during the plague. The style of Johann Heermann's hymns (including "Ah, holy Jesus") moved away from the more objective style of Reformation hymnody toward expressing the emotions of faith. Paul Gerhardt, whom some have called the greatest of Lutheran hymnwriters, lost a preaching position at St. Nicholas's Church in Berlin because he refused to sign a document stating he would not make theological arguments in his sermons.

October 28 – Simon, Jude Little is known about Simon and Jude. In New Testament lists of the apostles, Simon the "zealot" or Cananaean is mentioned, but he is never mentioned apart from these lists. Jude, sometimes called Thaddeus, is also mentioned in lists of the twelve.

October 31 – Reformation Day By the end of the seventeenth century, many Lutheran churches celebrated a festival commemorating Martin Luther's posting of the Ninety-five Theses, a summary of abuses in the church of his time. At the heart of the reform movement was the gospel, the good news that it is by grace through faith that we are justified and set free.

November 1 – All Saints Day The custom of commemorating all of the saints of the church on a single day goes back at least to the third century. All Saints Day celebrates the baptized people of God, living and dead, who make up the body of Christ.

November 3 – Martín de Porres Martín was a lay brother in the Order of Preachers (Dominicans) and engaged in many charitable works. He is recognized as an advocate for Christian charity and interracial justice.

November 7 – John Christian Frederick Heyer, Bartholomaeus Ziegenbalg, Ludwig Nommensen Heyer was the first missionary sent out by American Lutherans, and he became a missionary in the Andhra region of India. Ziegenbalg was a missionary to the Tamils of Tranquebar on the southeast coast of India. Nommensen worked among the Batak people, who had previously not seen Christian missionaries.

November 11 – Martin of Tours In 371 Martin was elected bishop of Tours. As bishop he developed a reputation for intervening on behalf of prisoners and heretics who had been sentenced to death.

November 11 – Søren Aabye Kierkegaard Kierkegaard, a nineteenth-century Danish theologian whose writings reflect his Lutheran heritage, was the founder of modern existentialism. Kierkegaard's work attacked the established church of his day— its complacency, its tendency to intellectualize faith, and its desire to be accepted by polite society.

November 17 – Elizabeth of Hungary This Hungarian princess gave away large sums of money, including her dowry, for relief of the poor and sick. She founded hospitals, cared for 392 orphans, and used the royal food supplies to feed the hungry.

November 23 – Clement Clement is best remembered for a letter he wrote to the Corinthian congregation still having difficulty with divisions in spite of Paul's canonical letters. Clement's letter is also a witness to early understandings of church government and the way each office in the church works for the good of the whole.

November 23 – Miguel Agustín Pro Miguel Agustín Pro grew up among oppression in Mexico and he worked on behalf of the poor and homeless. Miguel and his two brothers were arrested, falsely accused of throwing a bomb at the car of a government official, and executed by a firing squad.

November 24 – Justus Falckner, Jehu Jones, William Passavant Not only was Falckner the first Lutheran pastor to be ordained in North America, but he published a catechism that was the first Lutheran book published on the continent. Jones was the Lutheran church's first African American pastor and carried out missionary work in Philadelphia, which led to the formation there of the first African American Lutheran congregation (St. Paul's). William Passavant helped to establish hospitals and orphanages in a number of cities and was the first to introduce deaconesses to the work of hospitals in the United States.

November 25 – Isaac Watts Watts wrote about six hundred hymns, many of them in a two-year period beginning when he was twenty years old. When criticized for writing hymns not taken from scripture, he responded that if we can pray prayers that are not from scripture but written by us, then surely we can sing hymns that we have made up ourselves.

November 30 – Andrew Andrew was the first of the Twelve. As a part of his calling, he brought other people, including Simon Peter, to meet Jesus.

December 3 – Francis Xavier Francis Xavier became a missionary to India, Southeast Asia, Japan, and the Philippines. Together with Ignatius Loyola and five others, Francis formed the Society of Jesus (Jesuits).

December 4 – John of Damascus John left a career in finance and government to become a monk in an abbey near Jerusalem.

He wrote many hymns as well as theological works, including *The Fount of Wisdom*, a work that touches on philosophy, heresy, and the orthodox faith.

December 6 – Nicholas Nicholas was a bishop in what is now Turkey. Legends that surround Nicholas tell of his love for God and neighbor, especially the poor.

December 7 – Ambrose Ambrose was baptized, ordained, and consecrated a bishop all on the same day. While bishop he gave away his wealth and lived in simplicity.

December 13 – Lucy Lucy was a young Christian of Sicily who was martyred during the persecutions under Emperor Diocletian. Her celebration became particularly important in Sweden and Norway, perhaps because the feast of Lucia (whose name means "light") originally fell on the shortest day of the year.

December 14 – John of the Cross John was a monk of the Carmelite religious order who met Teresa of Ávila when she was working to reform the Carmelite Order and return it to a stricter observance of its rules. His writings, like Teresa's, reflect a deep interest in mystical thought and meditation.

December 20 – Katharina von Bora Luther Katharina took vows as a nun, but around age twenty-four she and several other nuns who were influenced by the writings of Martin Luther left the convent. When she later became Luther's wife, she proved herself a gifted household manager and became a trusted partner.

December 26 – Stephen Stephen, a deacon and the first martyr of the church, was one of those seven upon whom the apostles laid hands after they had been chosen to serve widows and others in need. Later, Stephen's preaching angered the temple authorities, and they ordered him to be put to death by stoning.

December 27 – John John, the son of Zebedee, was a fisherman and one of the Twelve. Tradition has attributed authorship of the gospel and the three epistles bearing his name to the apostle John.

December 28 – The Holy Innocents The infant martyrs commemorated on this day were the children of Bethlehem, two years old and younger, who were killed by Herod, who worried that his reign was threatened by the birth of a new king named Jesus.

Waking Prayers

We give thanks to you, heavenly Father,
through Jesus Christ your dear Son,
that you have protected us through the night
from all harm and danger.
We ask that you would also protect us today
from sin and all evil,
so that our life and actions may please you.
Into your hands we commend ourselves:
our bodies, our souls, and all that is ours.
Let your holy angels be with us,
so that the wicked foe may have no power over us.
Amen.

Luther's morning prayer

Jesus, bright morning star,
show us your mercy.
See Revelation 22:16

Upon waking, one may make the sign of the cross and say:

In the name of the Father,
and of the Son,
and of the Holy Spirit. Amen.

or

The Sacred Three be over me,
the blessing of the Trinity.

A Simplified Form for Morning Prayer

OPENING

O Lord, open my lips,
and my mouth shall proclaim your praise.
Glory to the Father, and to the Son,
and to the Holy Spirit:
as it was in the beginning, is now,
and will be forever. Amen.
The alleluia is omitted during Lent.
[Alleluia.]

PSALMODY

*The psalmody may begin with Psalm 63, Psalm 67, Psalm 95, Psalm 100, or an-
other psalm appropriate for morning. Psalms provided in this book for each week
may be used instead of or in addition to the psalms mentioned.*

A time of silence follows.

A hymn may follow (see the suggested hymn for each day).

READINGS

*One or more readings for each day may be selected from those provided in this
book. The reading of scripture may be followed by silence for reflection.*

The reflection may conclude with these or similar words.

Long ago God spoke to our ancestors
in many and various ways by the prophets,
but in these last days God has spoken to us by the Son.

GOSPEL CANTICLE

The song of Zechariah may be sung or said.

Blessed are you, Lord, the God of Israel,
you have come to your people and set them free.
You have raised up for us a mighty Savior,
born of the house of your servant David.
Through your holy prophets, you promised of old
to save us from our enemies,
from the hands of all who hate us,
to show mercy to our forebears,
and to remember your holy covenant.
This was the oath you swore to our father Abraham:
to set us free from the hands of our enemies,
free to worship you without fear,
holy and righteous before you, all the days of our life.

And you, child, shall be called the prophet of the Most High,
for you will go before the Lord to prepare the way,
to give God's people knowledge of salvation
by the forgiveness of their sins.
In the tender compassion of our God
the dawn from on high shall break upon us,
to shine on those who dwell in darkness and the shadow of death,
and to guide our feet into the way of peace.

PRAYERS

Various intercessions may be spoken at this time. The prayer provided in this book for each day may also be used.

The following prayer is especially appropriate for morning.

Almighty and everlasting God,
you have brought us in safety to this new day.
Preserve us with your mighty power,
that we may not fall into sin
nor be overcome in adversity.

In all we do, direct us to the fulfilling of your purpose;
through Jesus Christ our Lord.
Amen.

THE LORD'S PRAYER

Our Father in heaven,
  hallowed be your name,
  your kingdom come,
  your will be done, on earth as in heaven.
Give us today our daily bread.
Forgive us our sins
  as we forgive those who sin against us.
Save us from the time of trial
  and deliver us from evil.
For the kingdom, the power, and the glory are yours,
  now and forever. Amen.

BLESSING

Let us bless the Lord.
Thanks be to God.
Almighty God,
the Father, ☩ the Son, and the Holy Spirit,
bless and preserve us.
Amen.

Additional materials for daily prayer are available in Evangelical Lutheran
Worship *(pp. 295-331) and may supplement this simple order.*

A Simplified Form for Evening Prayer

OPENING

Jesus Christ is the light of the world,
the light no darkness can overcome.
Stay with us, Lord, for it is evening,
and the day is almost over.
Let your light scatter the darkness
and illumine your church.

PSALMODY

*The psalmody may begin with Psalm 141, Psalm 121, or another psalm
appropriate for evening. Psalms provided in this book for each week may be
used instead of or in addition to the psalms mentioned.*

A time of silence follows.

A hymn may follow (see the suggested hymn for each day).

READINGS

*One or more readings for each day may be selected from those provided in this
book. The reading of scripture may be followed by silence for reflection.*

The reflection may conclude with these or similar words.

Jesus said, I am the light of the world.
Whoever follows me will never walk in darkness.

GOSPEL CANTICLE

The song of Mary may be sung or said.

My soul proclaims the greatness of the Lord,
my spirit rejoices in God my Savior,
for you, Lord, have looked with favor on your lowly servant.
From this day all generations will call me blessed:
you, the Almighty, have done great things for me,
and holy is your name.
You have mercy on those who fear you,
from generation to generation.
You have shown strength with your arm
and scattered the proud in their conceit,
casting down the mighty from their thrones
and lifting up the lowly.
You have filled the hungry with good things
and sent the rich away empty.
You have come to the aid of your servant Israel,
to remember the promise of mercy,
the promise made to our forebears,
to Abraham and his children forever.

PRAYERS

*Various intercessions may be spoken at this time. The prayer provided in this
book for each day may also be used.*

The following prayer is especially appropriate for evening.

We give thanks to you, heavenly Father,
through Jesus Christ your dear Son,
that you have graciously protected us today.
We ask you to forgive us all our sins, where we have done wrong,
and graciously to protect us tonight.
For into your hands we commend ourselves:
our bodies, our souls, and all that is ours.

Let your holy angels be with us,
so that the wicked foe may have no power over us.
Amen.

THE LORD'S PRAYER

**Our Father in heaven,
hallowed be your name,
your kingdom come,
your will be done, on earth as in heaven.
Give us today our daily bread.
Forgive us our sins
as we forgive those who sin against us.
Save us from the time of trial
and deliver us from evil.
For the kingdom, the power, and the glory are yours,
now and forever. Amen.**

BLESSING

Let us bless the Lord.
Thanks be to God.
The peace of God,
which surpasses all understanding,
keep our hearts and our minds in Christ Jesus.
Amen.

Additional materials for daily prayer are available in Evangelical Lutheran Worship *(pp. 295-331) and may supplement this simple order.*

At Bedtime

We give thanks to you, heavenly Father,
through Jesus Christ your dear Son,
that you have graciously protected us today.
We ask you to forgive us all our sins,
where we have done wrong,
and graciously to protect us tonight.
For into your hands we commend ourselves:
our bodies, our souls, and all that is ours.
Let your holy angels be with us,
so that the wicked foe may have no power over us.
Amen.

Luther's evening prayer

Keep watch, dear Lord, with those who work or watch or weep this night, and give your angels charge over those who sleep. Tend the sick, give rest to the weary, bless the dying, soothe the suffering, comfort the afflicted, shield the joyous; and all for your love's sake. Amen.

Gracious God, we give you thanks for the day, especially for the good we were permitted to give and to receive; the day is now past and we commit it to you. We entrust to you the night; we rest securely, for you are our help, and you neither slumber nor sleep; through Jesus Christ our Lord. Amen.

Night Prayers with Children

Dear Jesus,
as a hen covers her chicks with her wings to keep them safe,
protect us this night under your golden wings;
for your mercy's sake. Amen.

Now I lay me down to sleep,
I pray the Lord my soul to keep.
God's love stay with me through the night
and keep me safe till morning light.

Lord, keep us safe this night,
secure from all our fears.
May angels guard us while we sleep,
till morning light appears.

A parent or caregiver may trace the cross on the child's forehead or heart and say one of these blessings:

God the Father, Son, and Holy Spirit watch over you.

May God protect you through the night.

May the Lord Jesus keep you in his love.

May the light of Christ be with us.